Tinker, Evers, and Chance

Tinker, Evers, and Chance

A Triple Biography

GIL BOGEN

McFarland & Company, Inc., Publishers
Jefferson, North Carolina, and London

LIBRARY OF CONGRESS CATALOGUING-IN-PUBLICATION DATA

Bogen, Gil, 1925–
    Tinker, Evers, and Chance : a triple biography / Gil Bogen.
        p.   cm.
    Includes bibliographical references and index.

    ISBN 0-7864-1681-5 (softcover : 50# alkaline paper) ∞

    1. Tinker, Joe, 1880–1948.   2. Evers, Johnny[, 1881–1947].
3. Chance, Frank L. (Frank Leroy), 1877–1924.   4. Baseball
players—United States—Biography.   I. Title.
GV865.A1B59   2003
796.357'092'2—dc22   2003019551

British Library cataloguing data are available

On the cover: Johnny Evers, Frank Chance and Joe
Tinker at West Side Grounds, 1911 (*Chicago Daily
News negatives collection, Chicago Historical Society*)

Manufactured in the United States of America

*McFarland & Company, Inc., Publishers
    Box 611, Jefferson, North Carolina 28640
        www.mcfarlandpub.com*

To my wife Rosalyn with hugs and kisses for helping to shape the story. She patiently listened to my ideas, difficulties and frustrations as she read and edited the manuscript, then polished it until it shone.

Acknowledgments

A marvelous and most wonderful group of people helped me put this book together: John and Tom Evers (great-grandnephews of Johnny Evers), the Tinker family (Jaque, Gloria, Tom and Jay) and the Chance family (Jeri, Bert and Frank). They provided intimate details, photographs, stacks of old newspaper clippings and treasured memories. The characters then became alive. Without these three families, there would be no well-rounded, exciting, fully developed story.

A very special thank you to Peter Golenbock, author and co-author of at least 21 books, including *Wrigleyville*. When I asked for permission to quote from this book, he replied, "Dear Gil: You have my permission to use anything and everything you see fit to use. Have at it. All the very best, Peter Golenbock." Peter's generosity and friendship touched me in a very special way. It was an extraordinary gesture and will be with me always.

I also tip my hat to 17 people who searched, searched and searched until they found what I was looking for. They were invaluable in providing essential information and photographs. Thanks to the staff at the Chicago Historical Society; the National Baseball Hall of Fame; Orange County Historical Museum and County Courthouse in Orlando; Archive Center at Rollins College in Florida; Hesburgh Library at the University of Notre Dame; Office of the UIC Historian at the University of Illinois in Chicago; Troy Public Library; Fresno Public Library and Historical Society in California; University of Florida Library; University of California at Berkely; University of California at San Francisco; and the Los Angeles County Record Center.

A hearty thanks to a great bunch of guys who love baseball and helped bring this book to fruition. They dug for information and gave it freely. They are members of the Society for American Baseball Research (SABR): Dave Anderson, Lawrence Baldassaro, Jim Binswanger, Cliff Blau, Ralph Caola, Jim Charlton, Rory Costello, Tom Davis, Bill Deane, Chuck Brodsky, Larry Epke, Cappy Gagnon, Bill Hickman, Roger Hawks, Jerry Jackson, Kerry Keene, Sean Lahman, R. J. Lesch, Len Levin, Frederic London, John Matthew IV, Skip McAfee, Wayne McElreavy, Marc Okkonen, Charlie O'Reilly, Clifford Otto, Bobby Plapinger, Mark Rucker, Steve Steinberg, Trey Strecker, Dick Thompson, Bob Timmermann, Max Weder, Mark Wernick and Russell Wolinsky.

The townspeople in Muscotah, Kansas, also helped me immensely. They take pride in talking about Joe Tinker. They've kept Joe's memory alive and have built a lasting memorial. Thanks to Terry and Janiece Huntley, Murray McGee, Judy Smith (postmaster), Kevin Smith (Judy's son), and Tom Wilson. We've communicated so much, they are like family.

Thank you, thank you, thank you, to a group of people who dived right in and contributed in a variety of ways: Ellen Patton Anderson, special collections librarian at the University of Central Florida; Bill Becker, director of Centroplex (the city department that manages Tinker Field for the City of Orlando); Tom Bowersox III, manager of the Sanford-Orlando Kennel Club; Philip Holmes, retired archivist in Fremont, California; Ruth Kursman, Supervisor, Greenwood Cemetery in Orlando; Scott Lloyd, groundskeeper at Tinker Field; Stan Peschel of Daimler Chrysler in Stuttgart, Germany; Robert and Judy Rosencranz of Highland Park, Illinois; George Rugg, curator of the Joyce Sports Research Collection at the University of Notre Dame; Greg Thompson, manager of Tinker Field; Rev. Bruce Urich, Winter Park, Florida; Sandra Gale Watrous, a distant relative of Edythe (Pancake) Chance; Bob Welch, Orlando photographer and Geraldine Zambri, city clerk, Longwood, Florida.

How could I have completed the manuscript without ongoing help from Steve Strella, friend and neighbor? His knowledge of computers and all of their intricacies enabled me to finger the keys once again after confounding problems had shut me down.

I am, and always will be, indebted to all of you.

Contents

Introduction

Three men, three lives, joined together by everlasting memories in baseball history. On September 14, 1902, in Chicago, where the Cubs were playing the Cincinnati Reds, a long-forgotten scorer put down on a scorecard in front of him: "Double play, Tinker, Evers and Chance." On the following day, September 15, in another game with the Reds, the scorecard read: "Double play, Tinker to Evers to Chance."

The scorer didn't know it, but he had put down something for the history books. He had linked on paper, for the first and second times, a double-play combination that became one of the greatest, one of the most colorful and certainly one of the most memorable of all time.

Joe Tinker, Johnny Evers and Frank Chance were men of iron breed, rugged of body and spirit. They were hard men in a clutch. By slowing down or shutting off traffic on the basepaths when it looked as though a ball game might get away, they helped win four pennants for the Chicago Cubs in five seasons (1906–1910). They were at the core of the Cubs' striking force that dominated the National League.

They were symbols of ferocity. They fought with John McGraw and his Giants, with Fred Clarke and his Pirates, with all other rivals they faced, and in so doing helped win back-to-back World Series championships for Chicago.

1

What was it that molded and shaped them, made them sparkle with split-second timing and excellence? What made them gel into a "Trio of Bear Cubs" that helped the team dominate the world of baseball for record setting years? No one can answer these questions with certainty.

Some argue it was due to the strategy and skill they had developed in getting on base, moving runners, stealing bases, getting the run home and winning by one run. The great majority of games in the low-scoring deadball era were often decided by one run.

Others claim that most important of all was the quality of mind that gave the trio the reputation of being brainy in contrast to those players who were merely good mechanical workers. They argue that no feature of natural ease or aptitude or genuine native talent for playing the game can ever successfully compete with brains. Just look at the difficulty other teams had in trying to outmaneuver the quick-thinking Frank Chance. The average fan couldn't see it, but on every pitch, the minds of the Cub players were working hard. They were a team, individual players working as a unit. And the heart of that unit was Tinker, Evers and Chance.

There are a great many that do not agree with this point of view. They point to the record books. Other than Chance, who had respectable but not great stats, those of Tinker and Evers were nothing more than average. The detractors show that the trio never led the league in double plays, that it was a myth, created by the renowned and widely read columnist of his day, Franklin P. Adams, who wrote the eight-line poem "Baseball's Sad Lexicon." If not for Adams, the detractors say, those three guys would be no different than Whitney, Foster and Wood, long forgotten names, stored away in dusty, files.

The Tinker, Evers and Chance bashers take it one step further. They talk about their selection into the Hall of Fame and claim they don't belong there. They point to other players with better numbers who are not in the Hall. They point to the fact that the trio was not elected by the Baseball Writers Association of America but was selected by the Committee for Old-Timers in 1946, decades after they retired from baseball. If they were so great, they say, why weren't they voted in earlier? They also say it was cronyism and Adams's poem that got them into the hallowed Hall.

Bill James supported these remarks in his 1995 book, *Whatever Happened to the Hall of Fame?* James compared Chance, Evers and Tinker to Perez, McPhee and Davis, players not yet in the Hall. He compared their numbers and went on to say "The 1946 group induction of Tinker, Evers and Chance is the Hall of Fame's most ridiculed selection." He concluded, "the three were as bad as people say."

All of these arguments except for one are legitimate. The one that does not seem reasonable is the claim that if they were so great, they should have been elected earlier.

The first Hall of Fame election was in 1936, but actual induction was delayed until formal opening of the Hall on June 12, 1939. One player was elected in 1942 and none in 1945. Based on this, it seems fair to say that Tinker, Evers and Chance were inducted early on into the Hall.

In regard to the legitimate arguments, when the last page of this book has been turned, a case will have been made, based on fact and additional numbers, that Tinker, Evers and Chance deserved entry into the Hall of Fame—that they were indeed, three of the greatest players ever to don a uniform, ever to step onto a baseball diamond, ever to play the national game.

Baseball's Sad Lexicon

These are the saddest of possible words:
"Tinker to Evers to Chance."
Trio of bear cubs, and fleeter than birds,
Tinker and Evers and Chance.
Ruthlessly pricking our gonfalon bubble,
Making a Giant hit into a double—
Words that are heavy with nothing but trouble:
"Tinker to Evers to Chance."

—Franklin P. Adams*

*Adams, known to his readers as F.P.A., was among the most well-known newspaper columnists of his day. Born in Chicago, he was a die-hard Cubs fan. At age 22 he moved to New York City. Here he worked for the New York Evening Mail and had his own column, Always in Good Humor. He was syndicated in six newspapers and read by everyone.

In summer, he would journey to the Polo Grounds with friends Grantland Rice, Damon Runyon and, when in town, Ring Lardner. Often, he bet gleefully against the Giants. F.P.A. would often win his bet and left the Polo Grounds feeling good about his favorite team.

On July 18, 1910, the New York Evening Mail composition room called, telling him his column was eight lines short. He scrawled out this poem and it was published that day.

CHAPTER 1

The Early Years

Frank Chance, 1877–1897

Frank LeRoy Chance was born on September 9, 1877. Many sources say he was born in Fresno, California. Others say Modesto. Still others claim it was Salida and that his family moved to Fresno a year later.[1] A December 11, 1937, article in the *Fresno Bee*, however, reported Frank's parents moving to Fresno in 1877, the year of Frank's birth. It therefore seems reasonable to say that Frank may have been a native Fresnan. He came from English-Scotch extraction, but his parents were American born.[2]

William Harvey Chance, Frank's father, a native of Andrew County, Missouri, was six years old when, in 1846, the family crossed the plains by wagon on their way to California.[3] They had joined other California-bound settlers in search of a better way of life. His father died in 1852 and William, from age twelve on, had to support the family. He was a wage earner until 1862, then began farming on his own, renting land near Stockton. He remained six years, before moving to Stanislaus County, where he purchased property and continued his farming operations. In 1877, he came to Fresno County and engaged in farming on a larger scale, later expanding his efforts to include ranching, thus adding much to the wealth he had already acquired. He built a home at 837 O Street and in 1880 entered mercantile life in Fresno. Being a smart businessman, he made wise investments in real estate, but his health began to decline. He gradually withdrew from active business life. Nevertheless, he was a large stockholder in, director and vice president of, the First National Bank of Fresno. He died in 1892.[4]

Mary Russell, Frank's mother, was born in Green County, Missouri. At age five, the family started west in a covered wagon drawn by an ox-team. They settled in Eugene, Oregon, later moved to Red Bluff, California, and still later to Stanislaus County, California. It was here she met William Harvey Chance. They married on September 25, 1870.[5] The 1880 census reported seven children. By 1900 only six were alive: William Arthur, Alonzo Dennis, Sarah Estella, Charles Claude, Albert Russell and Frank LeRoy.

Frank is said to have started school in Fresno, played hooky with the rest of the gang, fought when the occasion arose and early on showed a fondness for baseball.[6] It was the first sport established in Fresno and by 1888, eleven-year-old Frank was a member of the first organized "kid" team in Fresno.

That "kid" nine was the *Fresno Evening Expositor* team managed by Andrew Duncan.[7] They started out playing on city lots, but they wanted to be a real team. They wanted to look professional. So they bravely approached W.H. Daniels, the man in charge of circulation for a local newspaper.

One of the kids is reported to have said, "Say, Mister Daniels, don't yer believe Mister Ferguson will give us a uniform if we organize a baseball club and call it the Expositor. You know he gave the band those nobby suits."

Mr. Daniels said he thought the boys could get the suits. On being approached, the publisher of the paper said he wanted to encourage all harmless and beneficial sports among the young and to go ahead.

The eleven youths were hurried to the tailoring establishment of L.F. Winchell where they were measured. Suits arrived on a Friday. On Saturday, the boys in uniform paid the *Expositor's* editorial room a call. The caps, shirts and breeches were maroon colored trimmed with white braid. There were two rows of braid around the caps and a stripe down each trouser leg. There was a broad belt at the waist. Across the front of the shirt, in a semicircle, was the word Expositor in large white letters. The stockings were black. The suits were indeed attractive, having been manufactured by Kutner, Goldstein & Co.

After admiration and praise from the editorial staff, the proud members of the team strutted off to a nearby empty lot and played nine local boys their own age. They suddenly melded together with a new kind of chemistry. Whether the easy victory had something to do with the new uniforms, or just excellent playing, is difficult to say. At any rate, even though they won 13–3, the boys claimed the decisions made by the umpire were "rocky and way off too."[8]

After this victory, the team announced they would take on all challenges from any team in the county under sixteen years of age. The boys made a name for themselves. They dominated every team they faced when they played valley competition from Visalia, Madera, Merced and Tulare. *The Evening Expositor* editor offered to hire any member of the team who wanted a job as a carrier. Most of the boys hired on.[9]

When the team posed for a picture in 1888, Frank Chance was so small he was told to lie down in front of the group. He stretched himself out on the floor, a catcher's mask in front of him even though he wasn't the catcher.[10] A November 27, 1889, article in *The Fresno Evening Expositor* had Frank Chance playing first and Frank Homan catching. Homan was to be Chance's future brother-in-law.

In addition to excellence in baseball, Frank Chance was said to have done well in his studies. Extensive and in depth research reveal nothing regarding his education.

There is a consensus in the literature about Frank Chance that he graduated from Fresno High School in 1892. Prior to his graduation he is said to have had romantic inclinations toward one of his classmates, Edythe Pancake, a fair-haired, blue-eyed beauty born in Fresno. Frank reportedly carried Edythe's books to school, and in the long winter evenings they pored over their dreary tasks together. This allowed sufficient time for school matters to finally sink in.[11] But did this really happen?

Ray Silvia, of the Fresno Public Library, uncovered convincing information showing that Frank Chance and Edythe Pancake never graduated from Fresno High. The information came from the *Fresno High School's Centennial, 1889 to 1989.*

The first student body in 1889 numbered fifty. Forty-seven of those names had photographs. The first graduating class was in 1891. Names and photos can again be seen. This visibility was followed for every graduating class including 1899, one year after Frank Chance entered professional baseball. Frank and Edythe's name do not appear in any of the graduating classes. Nor do any of Frank's siblings. This also applies to Edythe's eleven siblings. If any of them went to Fresno High, they did not graduate.[12]

As to Edythe's birthplace, records show she was born on January 19,

1882 in Illinois.[13] Additional research shows Edythe's father Stewart, in McDonough County, Illinois, [14] from 1871 to 1884, in Salt Lake City from 1884 through 1886 and then in California.

Going back to the Fresno high school records, an interesting aspect of these records are the names of Expositor baseball team members who posed with Frank in 1888. Manager A.F. Duncan and Montgomery Thomas are listed in the first student body in 1889, but their names do not appear in any of the graduating classes. Three members of the team graduated in 1893: W.R. Monroe, F.H. Freeman and F.A. Homan.

There is also information about Frank Chance going to college. The *New York Evening World* had him going to Washington College at Irvington, California from 1893 to 1895, and playing ball as catcher for the college nine. Instead of finishing school, the *World* had him in Sullivan, Illinois, playing ball for a semipro club for $40 a month. In 1897, the *World* had him back in college and catching for the Fresno Republican Tigers, a team of semi-professional quality managed by James A. Ward.[15]

Volume 3 of *Los Angeles from the Mountains to the Sea* also had Frank going to Washington College for three years, then hurrying off to Sullivan, Illinois, in 1896 to play semipro ball. It claimed that because of his mother's objections, he returned to California in 1897, began working in the office of Dr. Doyle and playing ball in the *Fresno Examiner* tournament.[16]

The November 3, 1906, issue of *Sporting Life* saw it differently. It had Frank going to college from 1892 to 1896, then getting a DDS after attending Washington College and the Dental College of San Francisco. Other sources had him going to the UC at Berkeley. All of this information does not hold up when looking at recent replies from various institutions.

David Kessler, at the Bancroft Reference Library at UC Berkeley, had records going back to the 1890s. There was no record of Frank Chance.

Valerie Wheat, Reference Archivist at UC San Francisco, found no reference to Frank Chance in any of their records going back to 1882. Old baseball rosters at UCSF did not include Frank Chance as a member of the team.

Philip Holmes, a retired archivist in Fremont, California, came up with a great deal of information about Washington College. It opened in 1872. It was a non-sectarian college until 1883. After that, it became a sectarian college under the auspices of the Christian Church. It had classical, scientific, Biblical, commercial and artistic departments. There is no evidence they taught dental or medical courses. The school prepared students for other colleges. Washington College closed its doors in 1894 and reopened them in 1896 as the Curtner Seminary.[17]

One source of information claiming that Frank Chance went to Washington College was found in a November 18, 1910, Irvington newspaper. It said, "Frank Chance, the celebrated baseball manager of Chicago accompanied by his wife and his brother, Alonzo Chance and his wife, of Fresno, were the guests of Rev. J. Durham and family Thursday. Frank was once a student at the old Washington College of Irvington and has ever had a warm spot in his heart for the old town and the old friends he had there years ago before his phenomenal success in the realm of baseball." This linked Frank Chance to the Rev. Durham and possibly to Washington College.

According to Philip Holmes, J. Durham was a Professor of Natural Sciences and Rhetoric at Washington College. He became vice president and then president in 1887. He was also a minister in the Christian Church. He is seen in a photo with the graduating class of 1891 sitting on the college steps. Also seen in this photo is W.A. Chance, Frank's brother. Another brother, A.D. Chance, is recorded as being in the 1892 class at Washington College. This also linked Washington College to the Chance family.

Frank's mother Mary, was a charter member of the First Christian Church of Fresno. She was active in church work until a few years before her death.[18] It seems reasonable to assume that Mary's church activities linked her and the family to the Rev. J. Durham, who was a minister in the Church.

Philip Holmes, the retired archivist, reported that Washington College admitted high school students and had a curriculum for them. He said this was a common practice in those days. It is therefore possible that Frank's mother wanted her children to attend a Christian high school and Frank may have gone there, but there is no record of this.

The Washington College catalogue lists William Arthur Chance in the Commercial Class of 1888 and in the Academic Class of 1891. It lists Alonzo Dennis Chance in the Commercial Class of 1889. Holmes reported on March 12, 2002, "I still have no evidence that Frank attended here as his brothers did." Holmes also checked the Rev. Durham documents.

In regard to baseball, the archivist found no evidence of a baseball team at Washington College. Nevertheless, Philip Holmes may be wrong. On March 11, 1991, he responded to questions put to him by Fred Ryor who reportedly was writing about baseball in California and Frank Chance's early years. One of the questions asked, "Did Washington College have a team?" The answer, "Yes, some years."[19]

When this was brought to the attention of Holmes, he had no recollection of it. He could only say that based on his current search, he found nothing to prove that baseball was played at the college.

This was pursued further. Fred Ryor was found in Martinez, California. He replied via e-mail on March 20, 2002, saying he was the one who had contacted Holmes. He did not reply to questions about Frank Chance playing baseball at Washington College.

Other avenues were explored. Russell Cappy Gagnon, former president of the Society of American Baseball Research (SABR) and former chairman of the Collegiate Baseball Committee, was the recognized specialist on the early history of college baseball. He reported: "I have never been able to track down Frank Chance's college affiliation." He also said, "Many colleges enrolled students all the way down to kindergarten and permitted high school age kids to play on the school team."

Roger Hawks, a SABR, member agreed. He said, "I can add to the information you got from Cappy about high school students playing on college teams. In my own research on college football circa 1900–1905, I found several instances of students from the local high school playing football at the college but not taking classes at the college. I also found hints that some college students occasionally played on the high school football team. I have seen several instances of people playing football for a college without ever setting foot in a classroom, and I am sure that Cappy has similar examples for baseball."

The website, www.fresnogrizzlies.com/history.htm, said nothing about Frank's schooling. It told how the fledgling California League led by Frank Chance and Manager Russ Walberg in 1898, began playing in Barton's and Walker's Belmont Stadium. Fans called the team the Tigers because of the bright red stripes on their uniforms.

The website was in error. It was not 1898. This is supported by a photograph of Frank Chance as a member of the Fresno Republicans (Tigers) taken in 1897. Another photo shows Frank as a member of the 1897 Fresno football team.[20]

The Fresno Republicans quickly folded because of its 5–14 record.[21] Frank Chance however, was a constant topic of conversation because of his hitting, throwing and speed around the bases.

One thing seems fairly certain. We will probably never know just how it all happened, but based on everything that's been said, and everything that's been written, there are conclusions to be made.

Frank Chance drew attention to his hitting, throwing and all-around backstop work, gaining a reputation as a catcher. He may have gone to Washington College. He may have played semi-pro ball in Sullivan,

The Fresno Expositor team, Frank Chance sprawled front left, 1888 (Fresno Historical Society).

Illinois. There may have been objections on the part of his mother and she may have kept clamoring for Frank to return and take up something sensible, but as of now, we can't prove any of this.

What we know with absolute certainty is that nothing could keep Frank away from baseball. He did not like and would not have been happy with the sedentary life of any other occupation. Playing baseball was the only thing he wanted to do.[22]

In 1897 he began playing with the Fresno Republican Tigers, hitting a whopping .479 in the Examiners State League tournament. This fantastic BA attracted the attention of major league scouts. A bidding frenzy started, Baltimore outbidding Chicago by $300 dollars. Frank liked Chicago because he heard that Tim Donohue, the only catcher on the team, was going to be laid up with a sore thumb. It wasn't long before the Chicago National League club signed him to a contract.[23]

Poster ad: The Fresno Tigers, Frank Chance lower left, 1897 (Fresno Historical Society).

Who should be given credit for discovering Frank Chance? Bill Lange, an outfielder of Cap Anson's old White Stockings, has often been credited with finding him. Here too, the truth will probably never be known. James A. Hart, who was president of the Chicago club when Chance arrived, said years later:

> It was in the fall of 1897 that he first reported to the club. Baseball on the Pacific coast was demoralized in those days. That fall, an amateur tournament for a trophy cup was arranged by a San Francisco newspaper in an effort to revive the sport. One of the teams contesting in that tourney was the Fresno Tigers. Henry Harris, former owner of the San Francisco club, saw the Tigers play and immediately wrote me of its catcher, a big, husky chap, over six feet tall and weighing about 190 pounds, who looked good. His name was Frank Chance. I opened correspondence with him, soon came to terms and signed him for the season of 1898. After I had signed him, I learned that he had given Danny Long, a for-

mer player for Oakland and Baltimore, a promise of a commission to place him with some eastern team. Long wrote me of a promising catcher he had in view, but refused to give his name until I agreed to pay the commission. I was convinced that he meant Frank Chance and after I had signed him, I notified Long that I could not use his player, as I had just signed Frank Chance. Later, Long threatened to sue Frank for that commission, but Frank settled rather than fight it out in court.

About the time Frank signed, Fred Carroll, formerly catcher for Pittsburgh, and who lived in California, wrote me about Frank Chance. He saw Frank at the same time Harris did, in the tourney.

The fourth "tip" on Frank Chance to the Chicago club came from Cal McVey, who wrote Anson, but not until after Frank had signed. Bill Lange had nothing to do with finding Frank, and never heard of him until I asked Bill to look the youngster over when he went back to the coast that fall.[24]

Although Henry Harris reportedly gave James Hart the first tip that led to the discovery, Frank himself gave the credit to McVey, once a National League star for the Cincinnati Red Stockings.

The credit for the discovery of Frank Chance becomes less transparent when one considers a report by Bill Lange, who saw him play in a college game. Lange reportedly said, "There's the most promising young player I ever saw. Some day he'll be a wonder." Lange said he notified Anson, who offered Frank Chance a try-out in the spring of 1897 but refused to pay his railroad fare to Chicago.[25]

Frank, with a determination that became so characteristic of him in his mature years, reportedly refused the offer. Frank then played with the Fresno amateur team that summer and made a still more brilliant record. Anson saw the light and signed him. When spring came, Anson was gone and Tom Burns became manager of the Chicago National League team.

One thing is for certain. Regardless of the correct version, when Frank went east to join the Chicago team, he proved he could throw, run and hit. He was without minor league experience and is one of the few stars who broke into the big league straight from the amateurs, at a salary of $1,200 a year.[26]

Joe Tinker, 1880–1901

Joseph Bert Tinker was born on July 27, 1880, in Muscotah, Kansas, a small town not known for much of anything. His parents were Samuel and Elizabeth (Williams) Tinker, but there has been and continues to be a lot of speculation about the identity of his biological father.

Muscotah resident Terry Huntley, a walking encyclopedia on the town's history, holds to the belief that Tinker was born out of wedlock and didn't have a father around the house to shape the early years of his life.[27]

Muscotah resident Tom Wilson, a whiz on Tinker, has information from his grandmother Iva Cooper telling him the same thing. "She and I had talks about Joe Tinker in 1951 when I was laid up in bed recovering from an accident. I can still see my grandma's face. I can still hear her telling me, 'A lot of people gave Joe's mother a bad time because she had Joe out of wedlock, and that was the reason she moved away. His real father was a railroad worker who was out of town much of the time.'"

When John Angelo wrote the editor of *The Sporting News* in 1940, he raised a tantalizing question and stoked the fire under the out of wedlock issue. "When stories run in your paper about Italian players," he said, "why don't you include Joe Tinker? I've been reading baseball for twenty years and never have I seen the fact mentioned that Tinker is of Italian extraction. And where do you think I found out that he was of that nationality? In an Italian paper and later in the *American Magazine*. Tinker's original name slips my mind."

The editor didn't buy it. He replied, "Sorry, but we'll have to register an error against you on this one, Brother Angelo. Tinker was born July 27, 1880, at Muscotah, Kansas, of Irish and German parentage."[28]

Kevin Smith, son of the postmaster in Muscotah, was in full agreement. He was absolutely convinced Tinker's father could not have been an Italian. "Impossible," the young man said in an October 26, 2001, communication, "no Italians lived here."

R.J. Lesch, of Iowa didn't agree. He hurried off an e-mail on November 1, 2001, that said: "Many Italians, including two of my great-great-grandfathers worked on the railroad construction crews in the 1880s. It was common in the West and it wouldn't surprise me if the father of Joe Tinker turned out to be a laborer on one of those crews."

When Kevin learned of this, he took off for a nearby town and went straight to the library. He scrolled down rolls of microfilm and read old Muscotah newspapers.

When Kevin arrived home, he said: "I stand corrected. I read about four Italians injured in an accident on a handcar. But the thing that really caught my eye was an article definitely proving me wrong. It said, 'One would have thought they were in Italy if they had passed through the railway station this Thursday. A group of forty Italians were chattering in their native tongue.' Maybe none lived here," Kevin concluded, "but they sure were around."

The idea that Joe Tinker was born out of wedlock continues to be a touchy topic for some Tinkers while other members of the family view it with no concern. This can be readily seen by what they do, what they say and how they say it.

Tom Tinker, a grandson, calmly tells the story about his grandfather being born out of wedlock. It doesn't bother him or his wife, Gloria. In fact, it is clearly evident that they are truly proud of their famous grandfather. They talk about and display a vast collection of Tinker photographs and memorabilia, found and bought over the years.[29]

Jay Tinker, another grandson, vigorously denies the "tall tale" as he calls it. "This rumor has been dragging on as long as I can remember," he said. "It used to drive my father ballistics and I know it isn't so. My mom said so. She should know. She knew Joe Tinker. Joe told her it was a rumor that someone started. Joe Tinker's name was really Tinker and Samuel Tinker was his real father. If there is even a shred of truth in that tall tale of Joe being a bastard child, it would only mean that Samuel married Elizabeth Williams after Joe was born."[30]

To prove his point, Jay pulled out a photo of a watch and said, "This is Joe Tinker's good luck watch, given to him by his father around the time he started playing big league baseball. This huge pocket watch was a low cost timepiece that was commonly called a $3 watch. It lacks all the rare gems and metals that those good timepieces had, but Joe had it on the field of play throughout most of his time in the major leagues.

"Joe gave this lucky watch to John B. Dane in the 1920s. He was traveling the vaudeville circuit as a magician and introduced my mother, Ruth Dane, to William Tinker, Joe's youngest son, and they later married. My grandfather Dane, kept the watch with his personal effects until he died in January 1968. The watch went to my father and then to me. I don't think Joe Tinker really thought this watch a token of good luck. I think he carried it out of respect for his father."

Jay has strong feelings for his famous grandfather. In addition to the watch, he has another piece of baseball history that was handed down to his father and then to him. It's a beautiful silver trophy cup given to Joe Tinker by the Royal Arch Masons after he joined the Federal League in 1914.[31]

It is difficult if not impossible to prove the out of wedlock story. Putting this question to the most fanatical Cub fan would only draw a blank stare. Even the incredibly well stocked library at the Baseball Hall of Fame in Cooperstown sheds little light on the subject of Tinker's parents, or on his early life. Almost nothing has been written or recorded about it. To make matters worse, sources that provide some information commonly offer varying accounts of incidents and often contradict each other.[32]

Who is to be believed? What is to be believed? How should one proceed in trying to uncover the truth? The townspeople of Muscotah have pondered these questions. Murray McGee, a long time resident of Muscotah, wanted to trace Tinker's footsteps in the town to show visitors where he was born and where he lived. He started digging. He soon learned how impossible it was. There were no records of Joe Tinker's existence or that of any other Tinker in Muscotah during the late 1870s and early 1880s. Not even in the federal census records.[33]

What was Murray to rely on? You may have guessed. It was from hand-me-down stories by townspeople. Piecing it all together, Murray seemed pretty certain that Joe Tinker was born in a house on Main Street, a block away from the post office. The house was demolished about twenty-five years ago. Only a tall tree now occupies the 20-by-150 foot lot that fronts Highway K9, US 159.[34] Terry Huntley took a photo of this now famous piece of sod and distributes it with a great deal of pride.[35]

When did the Tinkers move away? Where did they go? How many members of the family were there? These questions are not easily answered.

Taking the last question first, all of the Tinker clan agreed on a family anecdote that Joe Tinker had a twin brother. *Baseball Magazine* didn't agree. In an article titled, "Joseph Tinker the Shortstop Manager and His Remarkable Career," it said, "...Tinker was one of twins and his sister died leaving him with no other brothers or sisters...."[36]

We don't know if it was a brother or sister, but if we accept one or the other, there were four members in the Tinker family. *Baseball Magazine* had the family moving away when Tinker was two, while other sources say he was five. It therefore seems fair to say that the Tinkers left town and planted roots elsewhere between 1882 and 1885.

Dan Johnson, of the *Kansas City Kansan*, took to following Tinker's trail. He reported that after leaving Muscotah, the family went by horse and buggy to Grasshopper Falls (now called Valley Falls), made their way to Topeka and ended up in Kansas City, Kansas (KCK). Lists of residents in the greater KCK area at the time show a Samuel V. Tinker living at 1015 E. 10th Street from 1896 to 1900.

Johnson went on to say that Samuel V. Tinker worked as a laborer in 1896, as an apprentice to Lawrence Brothers Company in 1897, a machinist in 1898, a paperhanger in 1899 and a "kalsominer" in 1900. A kalsominer mines calcimine, a white or tinted wash for walls and ceilings. After 1900 there is no listing for Samuel V. Tinker in KCK. The Tinker clan just vanished. Was this Joe Tinker's father?[37]

Going back to *Baseball Magazine*, it said nothing about Joe Tinker's father working for the railroad as had been rumored. It did say, "Tinker's father was a contractor by preference and the town of Muscotah offered scant opportunity for the larger operation. A small town in the midst of a fertile farming district is not the best possible scene for talents of this nature. Consequently, Tinker senior, sought the greater resources of the growing City of Kansas...."

Joe Tinker added credence to Samuel V. Tinker being his father in an August 27, 1913, *New York Evening Telegram* newspaper article, "How I Became A Ball Player." Talking about his playing ball in Kansas City, he said, "I was just about fourteen years of age at that time and was working as an apprentice for a paperhanger. I used to put the paste on the paper and played ball on Saturday and Sunday...."

It seems reasonable to speculate that Joe started out by following in his father's footsteps as a paperhanger. He changed his mind quickly, according to the article.

Paperhanging did not appeal to me. I wanted to be a ball player. During the summer, whenever the Kansas City team was playing at home, I used to slip away from work and sneak over the fence, carry bats or do any odd job I could inside the ballpark for the sake of seeing the games.

It was in 1899 that my first chance came. I was nineteen years when an opportunity allowed me to play with the Parsons (Kansas) semi-professional club.

I played there for about two months and in July of the same year joined the Coffeyville (Kansas) team, receiving $35 a month for playing third base. While there, the Kansas City Western League club played us a series of three exhibition games. We lost, but I made an impression by my playing and was recommended to "Billy" Hulen, the famous left-handed shortstop who was then managing the Pueblo club. I was given a trial.

The following year I joined the Denver team and was played at second base. I had always been a third baseman from the very beginning of my career and I could not accustom myself to second. I made a botch of it and was released in June to the Great Falls (Montana) team of the Pacific Northwest League. John McCloskey, one-time manager of the St. Louis Cardinals, was then at the head of the Great Falls club and he was in need of a second baseman, so I was played there again.

Again I failed and was turned over to the Helena club of the same league. I managed to finish the season there. The next year, the league transferred several of its franchises and Portland was included in the circuit. I was sent to Portland and played at my old position, third base.

Just as soon as I got on third I started to play ball. I hit well and fielded well and Frank Selee's attention was called to my work. He signed me and I was ordered to join the Chicago team at their spring training camp the following spring, 1902, at Champaign, Illinois.

There were ten infielders trying out that spring, and when I learned that, I was prepared to return to Portland at any moment. I never dreamed that I had a chance, and my hopes were blasted into nothingness when Selee asked me what position I liked most, and after learning that I considered myself nothing but a third baseman, announced that he wanted me to play shortstop.[38]

What Tinker failed to mention was that during the early years, when he was fourteen, he pitched, caught, played the outfield and the infield indiscriminately. Gradually however, he began to settle down to the left of the infield. His pitching was confined to days when no one else could be found to fill the box. His outfielding was meager, because it was apparent from the outset that he was a natural born infielder. His catching dreams were dissipated by being hit in the neck by a foul tip that caused all his hopes behind the plate to disappear in a cloud of twinkling stars and meteors. He confined himself to second, third and short, since first was supposed to be forbidden territory, owing to his lack of height. Third base was Tinker's choice. He played it with skill but was now being asked to move over, to play the shortstop position.

Tinker also failed to mention how he really got started prior to his playing semi-professional ball. He said nothing about joining his school team called the Footpads. Tinker was the star of the team and distinguished himself in many hard fought contests. Once out of school, he began playing in the Kansas City League with the John Taylors, named for a prominent businessman in Kansas City who was their patron saint and financial backer. Tinker distinguished himself even though his club did not.

A year later, his first real start was made when the John Taylors sold him for $3 to Hagen's Tailors, his first experience of being traded. With Tinker on the field, they won the Kansas City championship. The happy nine was presented with $50. Tinker's share was $2.50, the first money he ever earned playing ball.

Tinker then started at a manual training school where he played football as well as baseball. He held down a right end position with a good deal of energy, but he never liked the game and never stood out as a star as he did in baseball.

When Tinker said he played for Parsons and then went to Coffeyville, he left out some fascinating details. He did go to Parsons, Kansas, and played on a semi-professional team. The players on this historic club were troubled by disputes over salary. They solved this difficult problem by eliminating salaries altogether and shared the proceeds of the games according to a cooperative plan. From the proceeds of the assembled farmers who came to witness these games, the ambitious athletes frequently divided an "immense" sum. Tinker's share sometimes approached $1 on a particularly lucrative Sunday afternoon.

During these strenuous times, the town of Ellsworth, Kansas sought a game with Parsons's Paragons and forwarded $11.50 to cover transportation charges. When this sum arrived, they were astonished. It was the largest amount they had ever received from the game. When they regained their composure, they decided by unanimous vote that no such fortune should ever be expended on transportation. They talked it over, put the money away and left Parsons on a "friendly" freight train. All went well for the first six miles of their journey but a brakeman discovered the team ensconced in the rear of a vacant boxcar, and booted them off the train.

The team landed in the dust of a Kansas prairie with no money in their pocket, so they all trudged back to their various homes. Thus did the obtuse sensibilities of one ignorant train hand shatter the hopes of an entire club. It was a "cruel blow" to the national game but brighter days were in store for Tinker.

It was in that same season that he received an offer of $35 a month and room and board to come and play with the Coffeyville team. No such salary had ever crossed Tinker's mind. He accepted the offer and waited in suspense for fear the contract would be rescinded before his acceptance reached its destination. His fear, however, was unfounded and to Coffeyville he went. Once there, he lived up to the height of his expectations. In 1898, the Coffeyville team played several exhibition games. Tinker's play was an exciting topic of conversation. This came to the attention of Bill Hulen who, after seeing Tinker play, recommended him to the Denver Tigers of the Western League.

They signed him for $75 a month, but Tebeau, the manager of the team, was not impressed with Tinker's ability at the keystone sack (his laurels had all been at third). Tinker would have to play second base or get off the team.

Tinker did both. He played that bag, or tried to, for 32 games. In June 1900, he was released. Undismayed, he sought other worlds to conquer.

He went to Great Falls, Montana, a team lower down on the totem pole. Again he did not do well at second. So he was turned over to the Helena club and finished the 1900 season there. As Joe stated earlier, he spent the following year with the Portland Webfoots of the Pacific Northwest League. He spent the entire season at third base. He batted .290 and his fielding was brilliant. His work for pennant-winning Portland in 1901 attracted the attention of several scouts.

Chicago was more energetic than other teams in the bidding war. That fall, Tinker signed his name to a new contract on a look-see basis. He put on a Colts uniform in the spring of 1902, but the Colts had the option of sending him back to Portland if they didn't like him.[39]

Johnny Evers, 1881–1902

Johnny Evers was born on July 22, 1881, in South Troy, New York, to John Joseph Evers, Sr., a governmental clerk, and Ellen Keating Evers, an Irish immigrant. He was the fourth of nine children (six boys and three girls). Johnny, as he was called, was born into a real baseball family. His brothers, father and several uncles were all ball players.

His uncle, Thomas Francis Evers, was the first among them to play at the professional level. Thomas left Troy to play for the Baltimore franchise in the old American Association in 1882, then moved to Washington of the short-lived Union Association in 1884. His career statistics were below average: a .230 lifetime batting average, 110 games and 99 hits. All of his games were played at second base and he led the Union Association in errors with 92 in 1884. It is therefore easy to understand why he chose to become a clerk for the government in Washington, D.C., leaving future baseball fame to his nephew Johnny.[40]

Almost as soon as Johnny was able to walk he was exposed to the world of politics, hard work and, of course, athletics. This characterized the predominantly Irish Catholic neighborhood in which he lived. With so many members of his family and his friends playing baseball, Johnny grew up on the sandlots of Troy where he developed and honed his skills to razor sharp perfection.

After graduating from Saint Joseph's Elementary School, Johnny attended St. Joseph's Christian Brothers Teacher's School to learn the sign writers trade. Painting signs on windows and fences was what he had in mind for the rest of his life. He was getting on nicely when he suddenly came down with painter's colic, a disease contracted from the poisons in paint. He stopped painting and for a while worked in a Troy collar factory. Johnny graduated from Christian Brothers in 1898. Although it can be said that he received a good formal education, he got his baseball schooling on the lots of South Troy. He never played with kids of his own age and was always the "child wonder" of the sandlots. That he was an apt pupil there can be no doubt.[41]

He continued to work in the collar factory and played ball with several teams. In 1900 and 1901 he began playing with his own team. The Cheer-ups scrimmaged several local squads, paid by Johnny from his weekly salary of four $1 bills. He wanted to keep his team together because he knew they were capable of drawing a crowd and keeping it. The team won the championship of a small Troy league in 1901. Johnny was discovered that fall when his team played a group of local professional players returning to Troy at the end of their season.

Troy was one of eight upstate New York teams in the compact New York State League. The class B league was about to start its sixth consecutive season. It was an established minor league with a remarkable degree of stability under the strong leadership of its original president, John H. Farrell.

The Troy franchise, managed by Lou Bacon, offered Johnny a contract for the 1902 season after seeing him play third base. Bacon was impressed. Surprisingly, Evers turned down the contract because he feared he wouldn't make it in baseball. A twist of fate however, brought Bacon and Evers together in the spring of 1902.[42]

In an interview he gave to Robert Ripley of the *Globe*, Evers said:

> Well, one day, I happened to attend a ball game. The Troy team was playing the Cuban Giants. I was settin' in the grand stand near the players' bench watching them practice when I heard the manager of the Troy team moaning the loss of his shortstop, someone named Pugh. It seemed that this player had been taken suddenly ill, which left the team in a bad hole at the last moment. Well sir, I heard them grumbling and swearing at the state of affairs until something happened to me. I could never describe it. I only know that I left my seat without a word to anyone and vaulted over the rail to the players bench, walked up to the manager and told him I was a ballplayer and to put me in the game as substitute for the sick shortstop. That was instinct, I guess. I don't know what else. I had never even hoped to be a ball player before.
>
> "Well, the manager looked me over in a surprised sort of way and I felt myself getting smaller than I already was, and then said, 'Get in a suit, kid. I guess you will have to do.' I did! And I did pretty well too, for the sick player was never able to get his regular job back. I played regularly from the first game.[43]

When Johnny played his first game, his uniform and cap were too big. The shirt looked like a balloon just before being inflated and his ears were the only things that interfered with the cap fitting over his head like a bag. In regard to the hat, one fan, when he saw the youngster coming on the field shouted, "Yes, he's under there. I saw him go under."[44]

When the new Troy third baseman appeared in his ludicrous getup, there was a howl of protest from the fans. The impression spread around that some comedy stunt was going to be perpetrated. No one believed that the slender representative within the large uniform could really play ball. "Take the child out!" yelled some of the jesters.

The howls died down once the game started. The first eight or so balls went straight to Evers or to his immediate neighborhood. He speared balls one handed, he dug 'em out of the dirt and he went out into left field for them. In short, he took everything around the lot but tickets. The Evers contingent from Troy, comfortably situated in the bleachers, went wild. Johnny just grinned out of the corner of his mouth and continued to pluck 'em out of the dirt. The fans joshed him and he joshed back as he pulled down a liner.

The crowd ceased to laugh at the funny little figure in the big suit. They groaned when he doubled with three men on the bases. The rest of the Troy team caught the aggressive spirit, perked up and won the game. It was the first victory in three weeks. The Albany fans were so irritated over the outcome that they blamed it on the umpire.

Evers proved he wasn't a "flash in the pan" by continuing his work. Troy took the series from Albany and went back home on Sunday a winner. Troy rooters came out in force the following Sunday and Evers celebrated the occasion by getting a uniform to fit him. He kept right on going, always fighting, always joshing the crowd, always aggressive. The Troy club began to win now and then.[45]

Due to Johnny's good play (much of it in the outfield), the nineteen-year-old, 110-pound Johnny Evers was given a spot on the roster. In a May 7 exhibition game, Johnny played shortstop for the first time. Two days later, on May 9, Troy opened its regular season playing visiting Ilion on the local Laureate grounds. Appearing in the box score as leadoff batter was Johnny Evers.

A local newspaper reported, "Evers and the crowd were disappointed." Evers's team lost that opening game before a meager crowd of 300 which "braved the chilly atmosphere."[46]

Evers got his first hit as a professional player in his second game. Troy won its third game over Utica, 4–3, when Evers doubled between two other hits during an eighth-inning rally. "The ball struck the top of the fence," the sportswriter said, "and bounded back into the field, knocking the Trojan out of a home run."

Continuous praiseworthy comments appeared concerning the play of Troy's shortstop. Most of it referred to his defensive ability. During the first week of the season the *Amsterdam Evening Recorder* said: "Evers, who

Troy	AB	R	H	O	A	E
Evers, ss	3	0	0	3	3	0
Smith, cf	4	0	1	1	0	0
Mahar, rf	4	1	1	0	0	1
Rafter, c	3	1	1	6	4	1
Hilley, 3b	3	1	0	0	2	0
Shortell, 2b	3	0	1	3	1	2
Marshall, 1f	3	0	1	2	0	0
Raub, 1b	3	0	0	9	1	2
Robertaille, p	4	0	0	0	3	1
*Pugh	0	0	0	0	0	0
Totals	30	3	5	24	14	7

Batted for Raub in ninth

Ilion	AB	R	H	O	A	E
Raidy, ss	2	1	0	2	4	0
Eagan, cf	3	0	0	0	0	1
Hanley, rf	4	0	1	2	0	0
McAdams, c	4	1	1	9	0	0
Earl, 1b	3	2	1	9	0	0
Siegel, cf	4	1	1	0	0	0
Hinchman, 2b	3	0	0	2	0	0
Arlington, 3b	3	1	2	1	1	0
Thatcher, p	3	0	0	2	1	0
Totals	29	6	6	27	6	1

Troy—020 001 000–3
Ilion—100 410 00x–6

Two Base Hits–Smith, Rafter, Shortell. Stolen Bases–Mahar, Earl. Bases on Balls–Off Robertaille 2, off Thatcher 3. Struck out–By Robertaille 3, By Thatcher 9. Hit by Pitched Balls–Rafter, Eagan. Wild Pitch–Thatcher. Umpire Hunt. Time–1.30

plays shortstop for Troy, is a beardless youth who is said to be nineteen years old. He bids fair to develop into a promising professional. Evers had eight chances yesterday and he accepted every one of them." A week later, the *Evening Recorder* said, "Evers took everything in a graceful way." A week after that, *The Sporting News* said, "Johnny Evers, who is playing short, is considered by the baseball writers in every city where he has appeared, to be the find of the season. He has more than made good...."

In early June, Troy beat Binghamton, 12–6. The Schenectady press wrote, "Evers's work at short, accepting 12 chances, was the feature. Little Evers grabbed up a number of difficult ones and planked them over to first in fine style."

The Evening Recorder, in mid-June, reported, "Young Evers still keeps up his grand work at short for the Troy club, and his brilliant performances are conclusive proof that the kid is a natural ballplayer, and not an accident." The same paper later said, "For Troy, there is always one player who is always to be found in the game no matter how the contest is going. Evers. He can hit and field and his appearance calls for a generous reception from the spectators."[47]

In late June, even though he injured his foot, he hit a home run over the right field fence as Troy lost, 8–1. Early July found the team struggling. They won one game in fifteen days when little Johnny Evers hit a home run in the twelfth inning to beat Utica, 4–3. He erred once in 15 chances that day. Reports of his defensive ability continued.

But on August 16, the local press reported that he made three errors in a 4–2 loss to Binghamton. It was soon learned after the game that "his father was near death's door." It was the first time all season that he played poorly. He then missed about a week of play after his father died on August 21st in his home at 385 Third St. The funeral, on August 24th, was one of the largest ever witnessed in the city. Nearby St Joseph's Church thronged with mourners.

Then it was back to work for Johnny Evers. Troy won 2–1 in a game replete with sensational fielding, Evers excelling for Troy. Despite the presence of four future major leaguers (Edward Hilley, Alex Hardy, Chick Robertaille and George "Hooks" Wiltse) on the team, Troy lost many more games, finishing in seventh place.

Yet Evers, that skinny infielder, hit amazingly well in his first year of organized baseball. He managed a respectable .285 average during the 1902 season in 84 games. Lou Bacon, team owner and manager, was impressed. He signed the youth to a $60 a month contract. This was more than young Evers ever earned in a variety of unskilled jobs. Besides the extra income, it was a chance to play professional baseball.[48]

That chance came along rather quickly when the Chicago Colts' second baseman, Bobby Lowe, suffered a leg injury late in the 1902 season. A Chicago scout in the Collar City, watching one of Troy's pitchers, received news of Lowe's mishap. The Colts' manager Frank Selee informed him that an infielder was needed. So at the age of twenty-one, the spotlight fell on Johnny Evers.

Johnny was leading the New York State League in homers at the time with 10. Despite the fact that Johnny, a left-handed batter, attributed many of his roundtrippers to Troy's shallow right-field wall, he was considered a "demon slugger" and was signed to a $100 a month contract by the Chicago club. Troy Manager Bacon was unhappy losing Evers, so he wired Selee asking him for either a $200 purchase price or the return of the fiery Evers. Chicago sent the check.[49]

In early September, *The Sporting News* simply reported: "SS Evers of Troy has been sold to the Chicago N.L. team. He has the goods, all right." It was "the goods," otherwise known as an indomitable spirit that enabled skinny little Johnny Evers to launch a professional baseball career.[50]

CHAPTER 2

Getting Started

Frank Chance, 1898

When Frank Chance joined the Chicago Colts at West Baden Springs, Indiana on March 8,1898, long-time manager Cap Anson, also called "Pop", who had signed Chance, was gone. Since "Pop" had abandoned the team, some sportswriters took to calling them Orphans.[51] Frank and the other teammates knew that by losing their leader they had lost their one and only superstar, the one man who could guide and advise them. It didn't make anyone feel better when Tom Burns, the team's former third baseman, took over as the new manager.

Frank Chance, a twenty-one year old with a 6-foot, 2-inch frame, soon impressed the new manager. He liked the rookie's ruggedness, his smarts, his confidence, his coolness, his strength and the remarkable gnarled, twisted fingers on his hands, battered out of shape by hundreds of foul tips showing plenty of catching experience.[52] The other players on the team, including old timers, must have taken notice of Frank, who had the shoulders of a train fireman, the waist of a chorus girl and the legs of a weight lifter.

Frank Chance caught the attention of baseball writer Harvey T.

Woodruff, who wrote, "Chance is of prepossessing appearance and decidedly of athletic build, of more than medium height with square shoulders, and weighs 188 pounds. In manner he is unassuming but speaks with a quiet confidence of his own ability to keep up with the fast company in the National league. There is no braggadocio.

"In speaking of his ability this morning he said: 'What I don't know about baseball would fill several large volumes, but I am willing to learn. I pick up things rather quickly. I hope there is someone who will put me on the right track. This is my first experience among good players.'

"Chance has a good position at the bat. The indication is that he will be able to hit well even against the league pitchers."[53]

Another writer wrote: "When he was given the opportunity to work behind the bat, he stopped the pitched balls with the ends of his fingers, the foul tips with his knees, and the wild pitches with the top of his head. But the young man could take the punishment and come back for more."[54]

These accolades were particularly noteworthy in an era when baseball was a much harder game, when tolerance for pain was part of a résumé for a rookie.

As practice sessions progressed, it soon became evident to Frank that he was wrong in thinking that Tim Donahue was going to be laid up with a sore thumb. Tim played well and kept his job as first string catcher.

On April 29, 1898, the baseball season started at the West Side Grounds in Chicago at Polk Street and Lincoln Avenue (now Wolcott Street). The place was packed. The opening of the home season was like a great public reception. It would be fair to say that Frank Chance was a bit nervous.

The crowd poured out in perfect weather to greet Manager Tom Burns and his Chicago team. Nearly 8,000 fans were out, to see Louisville play Chicago. The crowd included the old fans as well as the new. As Burns's men displayed the ginger and snap during practice that bespoke of real winners, there were city officials seated nearby who were heard to say, "This looks like old times."

Ex-Mayor John P. Hopkins was there as was ex-State Treasurer Henry Wulff, President Daniel Healy of the County Board of Commissioners, County Commissioners Erickson and Irwin, as well as judges, aldermen, ex-aldermen and dozens of other city and state politicians. Baseball bigwigs, such as A.G. Spalding, ex-president of the Chicago baseball club, P.L. Auten, president of the Pittsburg club and Harry Pulliam, president of the Louisville club, sat beside these elected officials. They were all out to enjoy the opening of the baseball season.[55]

Here was Frank Chance, eager to show his stuff. At 2 P.M. the game began but Frank was in the dugout watching Tim Donahue crouching low behind the plate, Louisville batting. A walk and a hit made Louisville look dangerous in the opening inning, but Clark Griffith struck the next two out to silence the threat.

The Orphans, still trying to emulate the greatness of their former leader, did not disappoint the crowd as they began to bombard Fraser, the Louisville pitcher. Smith's error and a walk to Lange started the trouble. Bill Dahlen hit safely and went around to third on Stafford's fumble. Everitt, Ryan and Connor ganged up on the Louisville pitcher and before the inning was over, the Orphans had four runs. The bombardment continued until it was obvious that the game had turned into a rout.

Chicago played brilliantly and it was the beginning of the ninth. Griffith lobbed the ball and Fraser lined to Conner. With two outs to go, Manager Burns decided to take Donahue out and put Chance in. The game was momentarily interrupted.

Crouching low with his glove held in the strike zone, Frank watched Griffith throw a fast one and Stafford hit safely. Ritchey hit one high to right and Kilroy misjudged and lost it. Hoy's drive went straight to Conner. Two out and Wagner at bat. He swung and foul-tipped the ball. Frank threw off his mask knowing he could end the game by catching the high foul tip but he didn't reach the ball in time.

Wagner then hit the ball to Dahlen at short who scooped it up and fired to Everitt at first. But Griffith, the pitcher, had a queer superstition. He believed it was bad luck to win a game by a shutout so he yelled to "Wild Bill" to drop the ball. The order was obeyed and Stafford scored. Kilroy lost Nance's fly near the fence and Ritchey tallied. A moment later Smith's hot bounder struck Nance as he tried to advance ending the game. Final tally, 16–2.

The following day, April 30, 1898, *The Chicago Tribune* reported:

> Season begins well. The Chicago ball team was enthusiastically greeted at home and cheered by a big crowd. They responded by a dashing game and a victory. But for Griffith's pet superstition, that it is unlucky to shut out a club, not a Colonels' name would have been engraved upon the scoreboard.
>
> In the eighth, with the Colonels blanked, Griffith lobbed the ball. Even then Louisville could not score until "Griff" called to Everitt to drop the throw. The one intentional error let in a run and marred Chicago's fielding score. With the score 16–1, Nance's fly fell back of Kilroy and destroyed the 'heaven-sent ratio,' for Ritchey tallied with the Colonels' second run.
>
> Chance caught the last two outs yesterday. Manager Burns wanted the

crowd to have a glimpse of his coast wonder. Chance was overanxious
and he let a foul fly go down, losing his only chance.

Frank later declared he could have caught that foul tip but Clark
Griffith, the Chicago pitcher, had called to him to let the ball drop. "Griff,"
Frank said, "thought it was unlucky to win by a shutout."[56]
After his first game, Frank continued sitting in the dugout with not
much to do. Finally, on May 11, he replaced Donahue and got into a game.
It was Chicago against the Cleveland Spiders. It was the first time Frank
had a chance to bat as he came to the plate with Denton (Cy) Young on
the mound. Frank had heard of this Eastern Ohio farm-boy, nicknamed,
"Cy" because of his cyclone-like, blinding fastball. Of all pitchers to face
his first time up! He did not get a hit in his two times at bat. It didn't
make him feel any better about himself when most of his teammates also
failed to hit the demon fast or killer drop ball.
Frank had better luck the next day when he singled against Frank
Wilson but he didn't get many at bats because he came into the game in
late innings. Nevertheless, the Chicago correspondent for *Sporting News*,
Bill Phelon, was keenly aware of the rookie, and on May 21, ran the following story: "Chance got a show in the Cleveland games and did fair
work. The big elephant, so the boys say, can hit and throw like a shot,
while his speed on the bases is past all admiration. He can't catch so good
and must learn all the points in this regard. One thing that hurts his back-
stopping is the shape of his hands, which look like Silver Flint's after a
generation of hard battling."
The way it was going, Frank figured he wasn't going to catch in more
than 30, perhaps 35 games for the season. So he jumped at the chance to
play outfield when the opportunity arose. His chance came on July 1 when
he was put in late in the game. Eyeing the batter and watching the pitch,
Chance heard the crack of the bat and saw the ball in the air heading his
way. His speed and instinct carried him to where he needed to be to haul
the ball down. In the next inning, with a man on third, another crack of
the bat and off he went. As the ball landed in his glove, Chance whirled
and threw it home for a close play at the plate.
On the following day, *The Chicago Tribune* reported, "Frank Chance
made two pretty catches yesterday and showed himself a useful utility
man. His throw to the plate was a beauty, and a shadow of a second more
would have given him an assist."
Frank soon proved he could hit not only singles, but extra-base hits
as well. On July 3, he hit his first double off Chick Fraser. On July 13, he
powered his first homer off Roy Evans of Washington. July 20 saw him

slam his first triple off Wiley Piatt of the Phils. And his speed around the bases was nothing short of phenomenal.

Nevertheless, Frank had a problem. He had the damnedest habit of getting hurt when behind the plate. This was something he had become accustomed to when playing in Fresno and he shrugged it away as he had always done.[57]

Thus it went for the season. The Orphans finished with an 85–65 win-loss record, coming in fourth in a field of a dozen, 17 games behind Boston, the league leader; not too bad a job by Tom Burns in his first year as manager.

Frank finished the season having played in 53 games out of 152 (33 as catcher, 17 in the outfield and 3 times at first). With 147 at bats, he got 41 hits for an average of .279, pretty good for a rookie sitting on the bench most of the time.

Frank's return home was greeted with jubilation. A party was held at the Cosmopolitan Restaurant where Frank was a guest at the reunion of the old Fresno Republican team. He was big and husky and had the appearance of a professional athlete.

One person asked, "how do you like eastern baseball?"

"It's way up," Frank replied. "Baseball in the east is very different from California baseball. The players back there have snap about their work that is seldom met with on a California field. Besides, they are tricky and understand a thousand little turns that only puzzle a player who has not trained with them. The Californians practice the science of baseball, while eastern players take for granted a general knowledge of the game and devote their time to the finer points involved.

"All the California players did extremely well. There wasn't one who didn't do first class work and finished the season well up toward the front rank. Besides myself there were Van Haltren, Reitz, Lange, Hughes and Mertes."[58]

Besides seeing old friends, Frank was courting his favorite gal, Edythe.

Frank Chance, 1899

This courtship came to fruition in the spring of 1899. Frank proposed to Edythe and she said "yes." They planned to keep it secret but the story suddenly broke in *The Fresno Chronicle*.

The headline said, "Catcher Chance to Wed a Fresno Girl." It went on to say

On the heels of the news that Bill Lange is engaged comes the announcement that Frank Chance has plighted his troth to a pretty Fresno girl and will make her his wife at the close of the present baseball season. Chance's fiancée is Miss Edythe Pancake who is now living in Chicago. He is at present at Hudson Hot Springs, N. M., training with the rest of the Chicago team. Chance is somewhat different from most players. He is the son of a rich man who does not object to his son playing the national sport professionally. Chance's fiancée was surprised when the secret of her engagement became known.

"No, Frank never told it outright," she declared positively. "It was that rascal, Mr. Lange. Mr. Lange and Frank, you know, are great friends. I suppose he kept talking and bragging about his girl out in San Francisco until Frank couldn't stand it any longer and just let the cat out of the bag. Then, of course, Mr. Lange went right to a reporter and told him all about it, just for a joke, I presume."[59]

The idea of getting married at the close of the baseball season had been talked about but no definite decision had been reached. Frank wanted to be certain he would remain in Chicago. If so, he wanted a house for his bride, not the small, make-do apartment at 1762 Lexington, a few blocks away from the West Side Grounds.[60] Be that as it may, he was happy that his sweetheart was in Chicago even for a little while.

The season started where it had left off the year before. Frank was again second string catcher and soon found that he wasn't being put in to play the outfield. So he sat in the dugout watching every player and every play. He was able to observe and think about the way the team was being managed and, possibly mismanaged. In doing so, Frank began to plan and create a style of management that would become unique and so characteristic of him in future years.

The season ended with the Orphans having a 75–73 win-loss record, worse than the previous year, placing eighth in a field of twelve, 25 games behind the league leader Brooklyn. Frank however, must have been personally satisfied. He had done better in his 64 games and 192 at bats with an average of .286, seven points higher than the year before. Yet he was troubled about his getting hurt behind the plate.

He also wasn't happy, nor was Edythe, about postponing their wedding. Frank thought it best they wait a while. He had heard rumors that Manager Burns was out because of the team's downhill slide. A new chief would be on board in spring and Frank wasn't sure about his future. He wasn't making it as a catcher but he felt good about his batting average. He continued to show everyone he could hit. That was encouraging. Time would tell.

Frank hurried back to Fresno to attend his sister Stella's wedding.

He was giving away the bride to Frank Homan, his former teammate on the Fresno Expositor club. The wedding was to take place at his mother's home at 837 O Street and he had volunteered to help with the wedding invitations.[61]

In addition to being helpful, Frank conjured up a romantic vision. He and his two brothers conspired to make the presence of the newlyweds known to the world after they boarded a train to San Francisco. A placard was to be placed outside the window of their seat reading "My wife and I."[62]

Mrs. Mary Chance

announces the marriage of her daughter

Estelle,

to

Mr. Frank A. Homan,

Wednesday, January the third,

nineteen hundred.

Fresno, California.

Frank Chance's sister marries his 1888 teammate (Fresno Historical Society).

Frank Chance, 1900

Frank had enjoyed his stay at home as well as a few side trips. When spring training got underway in 1900, he found his teammates calling him "Husk." He didn't object to the name, in fact he liked it. He was proud of the brawl he had started in Corbett's Broadway cafe where he had accused Jim Corbett of fixing a fight with Kid McCoy. He was even prouder of slugging it out with the champ before being dragged away by others.[63] After that, because of his pounding fists and his husky appearance, he had been dubbed, "Husk." The name stuck.[64]

When Tom Loftus came on as the new manager, he too called Frank by his new name without giving it a second thought. Frank felt special. He had high hopes of becoming the first string catcher but continued to have injuries in handling foul tips. Tim Donahue, on the other hand, was doing just fine. So as second string catcher Frank found himself warming the bench much of the time, became discouraged and was on the verge of quitting. However, he continued to watch and think.[65]

On September 11, Frank Chance was jarred to the bone when Johnny Kling, a new catcher, joined the team. Why did the club need a third catcher? Was Frank on his way out? Was management tired of his injuries behind the plate?

He watched the new man start a game and saw that Kling was a one-of-a-kind catcher. He didn't have to stand, stride and throw before letting go of the ball. Kling threw from a crouch. All he had to do was snap his wrist and off it would go, cutting off a runner in a crucial play. Best of all, Kling wasn't getting hurt behind the plate as he worked the ball to the corners to fool the umpires into calling the pitch a strike. To top it all off, this new guy took a damn good swing at the ball, getting hits on line drives to the outfield.

Frank knew the team didn't need three catchers. One of the three had to be let go. Since he wasn't being used in the outfield as in the past he was afraid his future with the team would soon be over. With the season coming to an end he hated the idea of going back to Fresno a failure.

He was batting .295, but he knew there was no future sitting in the dugout most of the time waiting for a chance to play. Yet it was better than going home to Fresno where he would either go into banking or earn a livelihood from some other business venture. Then again, if he went home there would be no uncertainties. He would know his place, his future. He could put down roots and marry Edythe, who was now back in Fresno.

As the season closed, with eight teams in the league (four teams had been dropped), Chicago's hopes for a better year had gone downhill. The team finished with a 65–75 win-loss record, tied for fifth with St. Louis, 19 games behind first place Brooklyn.

Frank saw that Kling had done pretty good for himself. Playing in 15 games with 51 at bats, he totaled 15 hits, 3 of them doubles, 1 triple, batting in 7 runs and scoring 8 with a batting average of .294, a fine start for a rookie.

Frank saw that his ability as a catcher didn't come close to the new kid on the block. He packed his things and headed back to Fresno not knowing if he would be back next year.

Frank Chance, 1901

The 1901 season started with a minor explosion of sorts. Ban Johnson, president of the Western League, was no longer happy with his minor league status. Waving a committee report put together by Charles

Comiskey, Connie Mack and John McGraw, he upgraded his circuit to major league status by eliminating the despicable reserve clause and "stealing" talent away from the National League by paying bigger bucks.

The National League had been behaving like any other monopoly, having imposed a $2,400 cap on salaries. National League players had had enough. They packed their gloves, bats, spikes and other paraphernalia and headed for other ballparks. Hardest hit by these defections was the Chicago team. When the dust had settled, many Chicago players were gone. Sarcastic sportswriters began calling the team "Remnants." But *The Chicago Tribune* continued calling them Colts.

When Frank Chance arrived for spring training, he learned that Tim Donahue had not been one of the defectors. He had been let go. Frank was delighted that he was still a member of the team. He soon came to realize however, that Tom Loftus was going to stick with Kling as first string catcher. While Frank continued to display good skill as a batsman, with excellent speed on the base paths, his glove work had not improved.

With his fourth year in the majors, Frank seemed doomed to remain a back-up catcher. At times he felt like quitting, but he kept his mouth shut and his eyes open, using his time in the dugout as he always had done, watching every batter, every play, every strategy used by both managers. When a play had not gone well, he quickly understood why. Instinctively, he came to know how it should have been handled. Frank thereby absorbed a great deal of knowledge during his long occupancy on the bench.[66]

As the season progressed, Frank found himself getting into more games. He loved working behind the batter, but continued to experience injuries. When hurt, he would merely spit tobacco juice onto the wound and go on with the game.[67]

A more serious injury occurred when a wild pitch was thrown at his head while he was batting. While other batters would step away or fall to the ground, Frank refused to be brushed away from the plate. He took the blow. His teammates would carry him to Cook County Hospital across the street from the West Side Grounds. Some of his mates would jokingly ask him why he didn't sign up for the Spanish army and get it over with quicker.[68]

Frank took the punishment. Nearly all members of the team were firmly convinced that "Husk" would never make it as a catcher, that he would be crippled or dead following one of those beanballs.

In spite of his propensity for injuries, the club carried him on its payroll and used him to advantage, for he could hit the ball and run like the wind. Yet Frank began to see a slow decline in his batting average.

He was playing more and getting more hits than previous years and batting in more runs, but he had far more times at bat. That just didn't sit well with his overall average. When the season ended, Frank's batting average had dipped to .278. The injuries behind the plate with occasional trips to Cook County Hospital continued to plague him and the team.

The team finished a miserable sixth, escaping the cellar by only 1 game with a 52–86, 37 games behind first place Pittsburgh. The Chicago fans displayed their feelings by staying home. Attendance plummeted from 424,352 in 1898, to 352,130 in 1899, to 248,577 in 1900 and 205,071 in 1901. The loss in revenues was most disturbing. James A. Hart, owner of the team, had to fix the problem. Something had to be done. And it had to be done now!

CHAPTER 3

Turnaround

1902

James A. Hart desperately wanted a winner. He paid close attention to the twelve-year, successful managerial career of Frank Selee, a former haberdasher and long time skipper of the Boston Braves who had never played in a major league game. Hart was impressed by the five pennants this man had won in the 1890s while finishing only once below .500.

Hart knew that Selee's contract was due to expire at the end of the 1901 season. As soon as the season ended, Hart signed him for 1902. Hart knew that his new manager had tuberculosis, but Selee seemed to be on the mend. He seemed to be doing well.

When the 1902 spring training camp opened, the players found a slender man with a thick, shaggy, walrus type mustache bidding them welcome. When they had suited up and were out on the field tossing and batting the ball around, Selee decided that the only way to build the team was to focus on the young. He wanted his youngsters to be aggressive and high-spirited so that's exactly what he looked for. He knew each player's background and potential.

In talking with sportswriters who visited the camp, he emphasized youth in rebuilding the team. One newspaper liked the idea of youngsters playing the game and began referring to the team as Cubs. Selee didn't want that name. He liked Colts as in the days of Anson and was happy that *The Chicago Tribune* continued using it.[69]

Selee knew talent. He had a keen sense of knowing what position a player should play and why. To play for Selee, a player not only needed to be aggressive and high spirited, but he had to be bold and smart as well.

As Selee watched the team practice, he began to size up each man. He was determined to whip the team into shape, starting immediately. Selee knew about Joe Tinker, a 5-foot, 10-inch, 175-pound third baseman who helped Portland win the pennant in the Pacific Northwest League. He knew about his brilliant fielding. He knew about his solid .290 batting average. Watching Tinker at third, he noted his ability to cover a wide expanse of ground, his sure hands, his quickness and his strong arm as he fired the ball to first. Selee considered how effective Tinker might be at short. The manager talked to the rookie about playing a new position.

Joe refused. He insisted he was a third baseman and fiercely protested becoming a shortstop. He remembered how badly he had played when shifted to another position, but Selee wouldn't give in. With great difficulty, Selee finally persuaded Joe to at least give it a try, promising to put Joe back at third if he didn't do well at short. Selee instinctively knew what that final outcome would be. He knew that Joe Tinker would be a great shortstop.[70]

Selee turned his attention to Kling. He became keenly aware of his ability to throw with accuracy and speed from a crouched position. Behind the plate he had hustle. Kling was smart. He knew how to handle pitchers. He handled foul tips without injury and was a terrific hitter. Selee decided that Kling was his starting catcher.

What about Frank Chance? He heard about his whopping .479 batting average when playing with the Fresno Tigers. He knew it was Chance more than anyone who helped that team win games. Watching him now behind the plate, it was obvious he'd never make the grade. The foul tips did him in. But boy could he hit! And his speed around the bases alone could help win games. It would be a waste for him to remain a backup catcher. Frank Chance had to be in the starting lineup, so Selee decided to put him at first. Frank wouldn't hear of it. He refused, saying he was a catcher not a first baseman. True to his nature, Frank held his ground with determination. He could always return home and go into banking where real money was made.[71]

Selee knew about this man's independence and his wealthy background and took a softer tone. He praised his hitting, his ability to steal bases, the need for the team to have him in every starting lineup, the contribution he would make to the winning of games. As a last offering, Selee offered to pay him more money to show he was really needed.

It worked in part. Frank Chance finally agreed to play first if he could also catch. His gut had always told him he was a catcher and that's what he wanted to be. Selee agreed, knowing it would be best for now to let both men catch. The manager also knew that Frank would ultimately change his mind once he saw what a peach of a first baseman he would be.

Shifting his thoughts to other positions: Bobby Lowe had second sewed up, Dexter was okay at third, Jimmy Slagle, who had just been brought up from Boston, was solid in center as was Miller in left. Congalton or Jones could be used in right until a better man was found. As far as pitching: Jack Taylor was turning into a good starter, Jocko Menefee and Pop Williams would do for now, and the new pitcher, Carl Lundgren, plucked straight from the University of Illinois campus, was a godsend. He had led his school to the intercollegiate championship and great things were expected of him.

The club was beginning to shape up but it still had many frayed edges. He had work to do. He would ask George Huff, his friend and athletic director at the University of Illinois, to find star players to shore up the weak spots. Huff was one of the best baseball scouts around and Selee knew the job would get done.[72]

The season opened in Cincinnati on April 17. Selee sat in the dugout knowing that for now he had been wise to put Chance in as starting catcher. A promise was a promise. For the future however, Selee knew Chance would handle first. Although it was 1902, Frank Selee was already gearing up for 1903.

As he watched his men play ball, he studied them: Joe Tinker was fast. Playing short, he instinctively knew where the ball was headed the moment it struck the bat. His reach with the glove to the right or left was on the mark and slick. He was a fighter, no longer the genial and good-natured guy when off the field. The transformation was remarkable. At the plate he was a light hitter but with time and experience he would improve.

Chance continued to have problems behind the plate but was good with the lumber. He expressed confidence. He could slam it out of the infield and run like the wind. When at bat, he crowded the plate and the look on his face changed dramatically. His normally handsome features took on a defiant scowl as if daring the pitcher to throw one down the middle. He suddenly became a ruthless fighter.

Selee knew that if the pitcher threw one at his head, Frank Chance was ready to endure the pain. Was he deliberately allowing himself to be hit so he could get on base? It was a good possibility. Did winning a game mean so much to him? Or was he willing to take the punishment as a way of making up for his ineptness behind the plate? Selee had no answers. He'd wait until next year when Chance would be at first full time.

The game was going well. Jack Taylor was doing a superb job against Cincinnati, not only with his pitching but also with his hitting. He would be an excellent starter. The game ended with Chicago beating Cincinnati 6–1, a nice way to start the season. Selee knew he had put together the nucleus of a formidable team.

CHICAGO	*AB*	*R*	*H*	*O*	*A*	*E*
Slagle, cf	3	0	0	4	0	0
Miller, lf	4	1	1	5	0	0
Dexter, 3b	5	0	0	1	1	1
Congalton, rf	3	2	1	2	0	0
Chance, c	3	1	1	2	0	0
Lowe, 2b	4	0	3	2	3	0
O'Hagan, 1b	4	0	1	9	0	1
Tinker, ss	4	1	1	2	2	0
Taylor, p	3	1	3	0	5	0
Totals	33	6	11	27	11	2

CINCINNATI	*AB*	*R*	*H*	*O*	*A*	*E*
Hoy, cf	4	1	0	1	0	0
Dobbs, lf	3	0	1	4	1	0
Beckley, 1b	4	0	2	8	1	0
Crawford, rf	3	0	0	2	1	0
Beck, 2b	4	0	2	5	2	0
Corcoran, ss	4	0	0	1	2	2
Steinfeldt, 3b	3	0	0	2	5	1
Bergen, c	4	0	1	3	3	0
Swormstedt, p	3	0	1	1	2	0
*Peitz	1	0	0	0	0	0
Totals	33	1	7	27	17	3

*Batted for Swormstedt in ninth

```
              Chicago      010 200 201—6
              Cincinnati   100 000 000—1
```

Two base hits: Tinker, Beckley, Beck, Lowe, Taylor; three base hits: Miller, Taylor; stolen base: O'Hagan; double plays: Tinker, Lowe and O'Hagan; Dobbs and

Steinfeldt; bases on balls: off Taylor 2, off Swormstedt 4; struck out: by Taylor 2, by Swormstedt 2; umpire: Emalie; Time: 1.50.

The season moved forward. The team was doing better than the year before. Carl Lundgren, the new pitcher, split his first two decisions in spite of a low ERA. Jack Taylor as usual was the workhorse, doing much better than 1901 when he was 13–19 for the year with an ERA of 3.36. If he kept up his current pace he would have a great year.

As for the infielders, Chance was solid at the plate, hitting doubles, a few triples and one home run. He showed his speed by leading the team in stolen bases. Best of all, he didn't object when Selee started putting him at first on a more frequent basis, allowing Kling to take over behind the plate full time.

Tinker was something else! Although his batting average was not that great, he did much better in a clutch, always getting a hit with men on base. Late in the season, he and Kling were neck and neck with 46 RBIs, far ahead of the rest of the team.

Bobby Lowe, the captain and second baseman, continued his excellent glove work at second. He also showed some power with his 11 doubles, 1 triple and 3 homers. In the final weeks of the season, Lowe sustained an injury but still could play. Selee demanded another infielder just in case. At this time, a number of big league clubs were trying to appraise the value of Troy's star pitcher and a Chicago scout received Selee's urgent request on August 31.

Johnny Evers had just finished a game, eager to help his Troy team beat Albany and win it all in the New York State League. Evers had whaled a triple off Jimmy Pastorious, but his thoughts were not completely on baseball. He had buried his father on August 24 and had been feeling down. Nevertheless, when he was offered the opportunity of reporting to the Chicago team, he said goodbye to his teammates and left Troy with only a handbag and a pocketful of black cigars.

He had never heard of a sleeping coach so he dozed in the uncomfortable "smoker" all the way to New York. As soon as the train came to a stop in the Forty-Second Street station, Johnny leaped out and after a little difficulty found his way to the Pennsylvania terminal to Jersey City. There he boarded a train for Philadelphia still chewing on a black cigar to forget how hungry he was.

The Chicago team was concluding a series in Philadelphia. When Johnny was dropped off at Germantown Junction, renamed North Philadelphia, he was met by an emissary from Manager Frank Selee.

Without a moment for rest or food, he was hurried to the Junction Hotel at Broad and Lehigh Avenue and hurriedly put on an oversized uniform. On September 1, he boarded a bus to join the team.

Some of the Chicago players did not take kindly to the fresh, skinny kid and looked upon the acquisition of Evers as more or less of a joke. When they saw that Selee was intent on playing the frail lad, the players almost went on strike. "This kid will be killed and we'll all be accessories," they told Selee.

Frank Selee paid them no mind. He wanted to get a look at this nineteen-year-old shortstop who threw right-handed and batted left, this scrappy little kid from Troy weighing a little over 100 pounds with a wet towel around his waist. This frail wonder boy, skinny as a rail, had powered a triple only yesterday. Yes. Selee wanted to get a look at him.

As Johnny's name was put down on the roster, some of the older players wondered if Selee had gone wacky, putting in a kid destined to be carried off the field on a stretcher. They made the mistake of underestimating the toughness and character of this little guy.

Selee saw it differently. He was impressed by what he had heard about little Johnny Evers, and he needed another infielder. So he juggled his lineup. Johnny was to play short, Tinker moved to third, Lowe remained at second to see if he was still fit to play and Jocko Menefee took over first. Chance was out with an injury.

Played out from loss of sleep and ravenous from hunger, Evers did his best to show the mettle that was in him. Always peppery, he tried to be even more so now but his efforts were hollow. No one in the world could have done his best under those circumstances. He bobbled three balls, and on one of them made a wild throw. Even though deep down in his heart he saw himself boarding the train for home, he never quit trying. Yet he had to admit that he made a miserable failure of it all. The game was over. The little fellow donned his clothes and waited for his teammates, rather uncertain as to what his reception would be.

His teammates were not angry with him for botching matters that afternoon. Their camaraderie helped him settle in. He went to dinner with them and tried to forget that his dessert would probably be spiced with "Notice of Release." It wasn't. Instead, Selee told him what time to report the next afternoon. He advised him to go to bed and make up some of the sleep he had missed.

"Then you're not going to 'can' me after the fizzle I made?" asked Johnny, amazed.

"We don't do things that way in the big leagues," answered Selee, who always maintained a full understanding of the game and the people who played it. "I heard of you riding down from Troy in the smoker, without eating anything for twelve hours except a sandwich. No wonder you had a bad afternoon. I'll bet a bat that you will have a better day tomorrow."

The manager was right. The following day, September 2, the same infield line-up took the field and Evers played without a mishap. Frank Selee had been studying this mighty mite. Using his keen sense of vision, sprinkled with a bit of Selee magic, the manager concluded that he would move Evers to second, Tinker back to short and give Bobby Lowe a much needed rest that afternoon in Brooklyn.[73]

Evers played flawlessly. For the day he had no putouts, four assists and no errors. Best of all, Frank Selee liked what he saw and decided to keep Evers at that position, at least for the time being.

The end of the season was fast approaching. Selee was pleased at his team's progress. It looked as if they might end the season slightly above a .500 average, far better than the year before. All they needed was a little luck.

By September 13, Selee saw the team holding its own even though Frank Chance had not yet returned to combat. He also saw a kind of chemistry between Tinker and Evers, something he could not yet define, a kind of smoothness in the way they handled plays together. He became aware of it during the game when they executed a double play from Tinker to Evers to Menefee. Tinker scooped up the ball on the run and without any hesitation tossed it to Evers who was ready with his pivot, and with a flashy hard throw had the runner out in plenty of time. Not a bad combination.

On the following day, September 14, against Cincinnati. Chance was back in the line-up playing first. Tinker was at short. Evers at second. Alex Hardy was dueling it out with Bill Phillips, the opposing pitcher. Selee was in the dugout studying his players, pleased at the way they were hitting and handling the ball. Chance, as usual, was connecting. He had gotten his second hit, not bad after a long layoff. Tinker and Evers still had that chemistry but suddenly Chance was drawn into the mix. A hot grounder easily scooped up by Tinker, a flip to Evers who fired it to first. Smooth as silk. Be that as it may, the Reds beat the Colts, 8–6.

An unnamed scorer missed a golden opportunity to establish himself in the annals of baseball history that day. This was the first double play by the trio. He had put it down in the box score as, "Double plays— Tinker, Evers and Chance." The *Chicago Tribune* printed the box score.

On the following day, September 15, 1902, in a game against the Reds with Carl Lundgren pitching, another unnamed scorer recorded another double play. He put it down as, "Tinker to Evers to Chance." An immortal line of baseball poetry had unwittingly been written.

Tinker, Evers and Chance Broke the Ice on September 14, 1902

The first Tinker-to-Evers-to-Chance double play ever recorded in a box score took place on September 14, 1902, at Chicago. The box score of the game:

Chicago	*AB*	*H*	*PO*	*A*	*E*
Slagle, lf	5	1	3	0	1
Dobbs, cf	5	2	1	1	0
Chance, 1b	4	2	8	0	2
Kling, c	4	0	7	1	0
Tinker, ss	5	1	2	3	0
Schaefer, 3b	4	2	1	3	0
Evers, 2b	4	1	2	6	0
Menefee, rf	3	0	2	0	0
Hardy, p	4	1	1	0	0
Totals	38	10	27	14	3

Cincinnati	*AB*	*H*	*PO*	*A*	*E*
Donlin, lf	5	0	1	0	1
Beckley, 1b	5	0	9	0	0
Crawford, rf	5	2	3	0	0
Seymour, cf	4	2	5	0	0
Peitz, 2b	2	1	4	5	1
Corcoran, ss	3	1	0	6	1
Steinfeldt, 3b	3	1	2	0	0
Bergen, c	4	2	3	0	0
Phillips, p	4	1	0	0	0
Totals	35	10	27	11	3

Chicago	000 000 204—6
Cincinnati	023 010 101—8

Two-base hits: Peitz; three-base hits: Crawford, Phillips; struck out (by Hardy): Crawford, Phillips, Peitz; by Phillips: Slagle, Tinker (2); double plays: Tinker, Evers and Chance; Dobbs and Tinker; Schaefer, Evers and Chance; Corcoran, Pietz and Beckley, 2; left on bases: Chicago 7, Cincinnati 4; time of game: 1.40; umpire: Brown; attendance: 8,500.

The season was over. Chicago finished with 68–69, coming in fifth, close to beating out Cincinnati, who was fourth with 70–70. Had the Colts taken the double-header on September 15th, they would have been in fourth place. Still, Selee was pleased. His team had far surpassed the miserable 1901 record of 53–86, when they finished sixth.

Selee was also pleased with Chance, who covered first in 38 games and caught 29, finishing the season with a .284 batting average, getting 8 doubles, 4 triples and 1 homer. He also stole 28 bases, surpassed only by Jimmy Slagle, who led the team with 40. In spite of these good numbers, Selee was troubled. Chance continued crowding the plate with a scowl on his face. It was as if he were at war with the hurler, almost asking to have the ball thrown at various parts of his anatomy, including his head.

Selee saw Tinker as one great rookie. He had played the new position at short full time and seemingly enjoyed his new spot. There were no complaints. He had a batting average of .273 with 17 doubles, 5 triples and 2 homers plus 28 stolen bases. Best of all, he turned out to be a fantastic clutch hitter, driving in 54 runs, winning ball games that were needed to carry the team to the top. Tinker's RBI total was second only to Johnny Kling who had 57.

As for Johnny Evers, Selee smiled as he thought about the slim little fellow who was fast on his feet, a mere bundle of nerves and bones, with a big stubborn jaw that stood out as the most prominent part of his anatomy. He had eyes that snapped with vitality, a firebrand on the attack, putting every ounce of energy: mental, physical and vocal into his playing, giving everything in order to win.[74] He's a natural, he'll be a great one, Selee said to himself. Then his smile turned into a grin as he thought about this nineteen-year-old kid riding the rails all night, trying to catch a few winks in the smoker, chewing on black cigars to allay his hunger, then rushing into a uniform and playing a double-header. That took grit.

Selee knew that with Tinker, Evers and Chance, he had an almost perfect infield for 1903. Germany Schaefer, his third baseman, had a .196 batting average and he just had to go. Kling was his catcher. Jimmy Slagle in center showed his stuff with a .315 average. Davy Jones hit .305, his play in the outfield was okay. He'd have to find a new outfielder to replace John Dobbs.

Selee now pondered his biggest problem. Pitching. Jack Taylor did his job with a 23–11, but Pop Williams had to go. An 11–16 pitcher would not help carry the team to the top. Carl Lundgren was a disappointment at 9–9. Maybe next year would be better. Jocko Menefee, at age thirty-four, was over the hill. He was lucky to have finished with a 12–10 record.

Overall, Selee knew he now had a better team. Chicago fans agreed. They had read about the new players and attendance climbed from 205,071 to 263,700. The increase in revenues made owner James Hart happy. He readily agreed to have George Huff, at the University of Illinois, scout around for new players. Selee knew that with his friend George out there, new youngsters would be on the field next year.

Chance now saw himself as a permanent member of the team. He felt secure. He had a vision for the coming year, getting married. Having Edythe as his wife would be wonderful. Finding a larger apartment would be fun. Planning for and building a home of their own would be a real adventure.

1903

When the 1903 season got underway, Frank Selee's brilliance began to manifest itself almost immediately. His second baseman had taken his advice. Johnny Evers, a left-handed batter, now used a very heavy bat and choked up a good 6 to 7 inches on the handle. He was slamming it not only into right field, but also to center and at times to left. Selee knew the skinny little kid's measly .225 average in 1902 was on the rise.

Selee also knew that this young tyke had changed remarkably from the year before. He was no longer the shy, soft spoken lad who questioned his ability to play the game. He was a ballplayer who would take no guff from anyone. Johnny had become so high strung he would snap off the head of any player who so much as looked at him the wrong way. He had become fearless and defiant of umpires who made a ruling with which he did not agree.

Johnny Evers was now playing his position with an abundance of energy. He scuttled around second base low to the ground and sidled up to a ball as if he were all knees and elbows.[75] Because of his appearance on the diamond, his quick temper and sharp tongue, Charlie Dryden, a Chicago baseball writer, tagged him "The Crab" and it stuck as one of his nicknames.[76]

The fans often wondered where such a small body kept so much energy and righteous anger to say nothing about his high-powered thinking ability. Someone had finally decided that Johnny was all charged up with real electricity. The story spread like a field afire and many people actually believed it. Johnny later added credence to this tall tale by asking admiring fans not to give him a watch as a gift because the electricity in his body would not allow the timepiece to keep correct time.[77]

Frank Chance took delight in watching Johnny's underhanded throw but enjoyed even more his own fantastic feats. He socked one out of the park with such force the sportswriters were still talking about it. They were also talking about his speed on the base paths and wondered how a man his size could carry himself so swiftly. Selee knew that playing first base full time had invigorated this man. He seemed to enjoy his new posi-

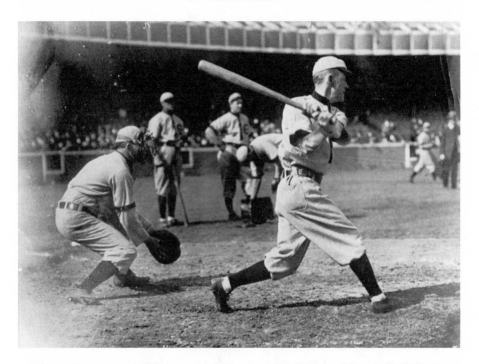

Johnny Evers not choking up on the bat in 1902 (National Baseball Hall of Fame Library).

tion and was probably glad he no longer had to struggle trying to catch foul tips.

Tinker too seemed to be having a great time. He, Evers and Chance were concocting plays and strategies while sitting in the dugout, while changing clothes in the locker room and even when riding on the bus on their way to another town. There seemed to be a bond between them. Slowly, everyone else began talking baseball. As these discussions widened, the team became aware that Johnny Evers was becoming a whiz on baseball. No one yet knew it, but every night he'd curl up in bed with two candy bars, *The Sporting News* and the rulebook. He was going to learn every rule a player had to know while playing the game.[78]

Doc Casey, the new third baseman, replaced Germany Schaefer and appeared to be a much better hitter. Johnny Kling was one of the greatest catchers Selee had ever seen. Certainly, no one had ever topped him. Throwing the ball while in a crouch, throwing it with a snap of the wrist, and throwing it with speed and accuracy was something that other catchers would be hard put to copy.

Jimmy Slagle in center was solid. Davy Jones could play right or left field. His new outfielder, Dick Harley, although good on defense, appeared to be a weak hitter. Maybe he would improve as the season moved on.

His two new pitchers, Jake Weimer and Bob Wicker, looked like winners. Along with Jack Taylor, the team might have a chance of getting near the top. And if Carl Lundgren began winning like he did in the Intercollegiate League, the team might even make it big time.

As month after month went by, most of the players lived up to Selee's expectations. Many sportswriters had now informally dubbed the youngsters, the Chicago Cubs. They were third, far ahead of Cincinnati in fourth and close to New York in second. Quite a showing for a team that finished a miserable sixth in 1901. Selee's rebuilding was making its mark on the national pastime.

The season ended with Pittsburgh winning (91–49), New York second (84–55) and Chicago third (82–56), a shade away from second. Their best finish in a dozen years. Attendance climbed from 263,700 to 386,205.

Tinker, Evers and Chance played a major role in moving the team to a new level. Chance, playing full time at first, had a .327 batting average with 24 doubles, 10 triples and 2 homers. He stole 67 bases! That was really something. The player closest to him in both leagues, with 46 steals, was the great Honus Wagner of Pittsburgh.

Tinker too, had a good year playing short. He was a natural for that position. He had a BA of .291 with 21 doubles, 7 triples and 2 homers and stole 27 bases.

Little Johnny Evers was also great, having taken over at second instead of Bobby Lowe. He batted .293 with 27 doubles and 7 triples and stole 25 bases.

As soon as the regular baseball season ended, the team found itself for the first time in a postseason City Series with the White Sox. This event was crucial to the building of the Chicago team that eventually rose to new heights under Frank Chance's management.

The series ran for 14 games, each side winning seven. Some of Jack Taylor's losing performances were suspect. Had he thrown games? Although never proven, Selee traded him that winter to the Cardinals as part of a deal that brought the Cubs the man who would become a remarkable pitcher: Mordecai "Three Finger" Brown. His nickname came about as a result of an accident with a corn shredder that had no mercy for this young man. That nasty piece of equipment tore off his index finger and damaged his pinky and middle finger. But fate took a strange turn. As a result of this injury, "Three Finger" Brown was able to throw a curveball with an exceedingly sharp downward break, forcing batters to hit ground balls that were to make Tinker, Evers and Chance legendary heroes.[79]

As soon as the City Series was over, Frank Chance told his teammates he was getting married to Edythe Pancake on October 3, and that he would be moving to 3234 Groveland Avenue. He was happy and excited.

Joe Tinker quickly followed with his announcement. He had captured the heart of Ruby Rose Menown of Kansas City, a rich girl of a fine family. Joe jokingly told how the young lady was first captivated by his fine appearance in a uniform.[80] They too were planning an October wedding. The thing he had to do fast was rent a new apartment. His one room flat would never do.

The couple finally found a place on the south side of

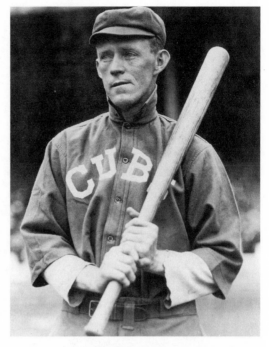

Johnny Evers choking up on the bat in 1903 (National Baseball Hall of Fame Library).

Chicago, at 484 East 45th Street. Although it was a distance to the West Side Grounds, they loved it. It had plenty of room, just right for raising a family. Joe knew he would have no trouble getting to the park. The elevated train would drop him off at Polk and Lincoln, a few steps away from the West Side grounds.[81]

Joe had a reason for living south. He had his eye on a vacant store at 555 West Sixty-Third Street, a perfect spot for a saloon. It would be hard trying to get along on a baseball salary. Joe had to have another source of income.

The word was out that Johnny Evers was also getting married. Johnny knew it wasn't so. Nevertheless, the October 31, 1903, issue of *Sporting Life* carried the story. It said that Johnny Evers was contemplating matrimony. Instead of congratulating him and wishing him well, it had the audacity to treat Johnny as if he were a fifteen-year-old. "He should be spanked," it said, "put to bed supperless, and told to play second base for five years more before thinking on the uncertain seas of matrimony. Him? At his age? Back to the ballfield, and out with Cupid for little John."

Frank Chance swinging away in 1903 (National Baseball Hall of Fame Library).

Johnny Evers was twenty-two at the time, hardly a teenager anymore. Yet his size and weight conveyed the impression that he was only a kid. Time would change all that. Even when it did, he always enjoyed telling the story about his diminutive size when he first joined the Colts:

"As I climbed aboard the team bus the first day, Jack Taylor the pitcher, looked me over very carefully and cut me to the quick with, 'He'll leave in a box tonight.' He meant that I wouldn't do at all. Some years later, I must admit it gave me great pleasure to still be with the Chicago club when Taylor was released and I refreshed his memory by remarking, 'Well, I'm still here, Jack, and I see you're getting the gate.'"[82]

This repartee was part of Johnny's character. The Irishman always had to have the last word. Having the last say in a matter was part of Johnny's restless nature. He was not content to just let matters lay.

When Johnny heard that Joe Tinker had opened up a saloon, he thought it was proper for a baseball man to have more than one source of income. Moving back to Troy after the 1903 season, he decided to become a leading merchant and looked around for a business venture. He chose shoes as offering the best opening to the guarded gates of wealth and bought out the local store of the Emerson shoe people.

The manager of the store, under the Emerson regime, was reputed to have engineered the deal for Evers. In gratitude for the aid given, he bestowed upon the erstwhile manager a half interest in the business as a simple gift. The two formed a partnership and business flourished. Evers himself knew little of shoes; his business was baseball. Shoes were but an incidental sideline and he was compelled to depend upon his partner to run the business. The latter was an experienced man, evidently capable, so Evers fell into the easy-going attitude of trusting his associate. In business, Evers was not the gladiator, the quick-tempered, sharp-tongued individual found at second base. He allowed his partner to run things absolutely, while he remained quiet and passive. This lackadaisical business attitude would come back to haunt him.[83]

CHAPTER 4

Getting Ready

1904

Frank Selee was pleased as he sat in the dugout watching the first game of the 1904 season contemplating his new acquisitions: "Three Finger" Brown, Frank "Wildfire" Schulte and Artie "Solly" Hofman. He had the feeling that his Colts could possibly make it to the top. The thing that had excited him more than anything else was watching Tinker and Evers during spring training exhibition games. He had never seen anything like it. As soon as the umpire hollered, "play ball," they were no longer two separate individuals, two separate players operating on their own. They suddenly became one.

Evers would make a lightening dash, scoop up a seemingly impossible grounder and make a throw to second for the start of a double play without looking to see if anyone was there. It was as if he knew Tinker would be there and that Tinker would not fumble the throw.

Tinker, with a wonderful burst of speed, would pull down a twisting drive, throw it to second for a lightning double play knowing Evers would be there, and that he would complete the play if it were humanly possible.

53

Selee knew that the Tinker-Evers combination was team play as it had never been done before. It showed the value of intelligent cooperation to its maximum. These two players were carrying their unique performance to the last degree of perfection. They were becoming masters of their craft. Both thought in terms of the best possible baseball and played together as one man. They simply knew instinctively how to do exactly the right thing, at exactly the right time, in exactly the right way.[84]

Then there was Chance, the third link in that combination, a sincere man in everything he did both on and off the field. Now that he had adapted to his new position, Selee knew that nothing short of murder could tear him away from that spot. Chance had but one goal, to win at any cost. So insatiable was his desire to get on base he refused to back away from a ball thrown at him. The trips to Cook County Hospital became more frequent.

As the first game of the season moved along, Selee's thoughts were still on his first baseman. He was worried about him—too many injuries. He was also worried about himself. Was his tuberculosis still under control? He wasn't coughing but he just didn't feel well.

A hot tempered raucous suddenly brought Selee out of his contemplative mood. Little Johnny Evers was putting up a fuss, talking up a storm, his face close to and looking up at James Johnstone, the umpire, who glared down at him. The ump had rendered a decision that favored Cincinnati and Johnny disputed that ruling in no uncertain terms. He wouldn't stop. He kept right on arguing until Johnstone's arm shot skyward. He thumbed Johnny out of the game. It was the first time the Trojan had been ejected.

Johnny now suffered tortures. Most banished players simply took a shower, sat in the stands or at a clubhouse window and watched the remainder of the game, but Evers stormed into the clubhouse. Without removing his uniform he sat in front of his locker moaning over his fate until the game was over and the other ball players trooped in. "I'd die a thousand deaths," he once said. "The umpires knew that. And that's the reason they didn't put me out as often as they should have, I guess."[85]

The season moved along. Selee's Colts were playing good ball but lost a few close ones. When the team rolled into Pittsburgh near the end of April, Chicago was fifth with a 5–5 record. The weather kept Selee's men idle and it looked as if there would be no play. A little sunshine on the last day enabled one game out of the scheduled series to be played. Selee decided to let Frank Corridon battle it out with Deacon Phillippe.

The Colts went into the lead in the second inning when McCarthy laced a double over Kruger's head in the outfield. Jones helped along with a single. McCarthy scored on Evers' hot grounder to Ritchey who fumbled it. The inning that promised to yield the visitors at least one more run came to a sudden end when Tinker hit into a double play.

It was 1–0 going into the bottom half of the sixth. Pirates player-manager Fred Clarke scored on a hit to tie the game, but a double play from Tinker to Evers to Chance prevented further damage.

The game went to the ninth a tie. Chance broke that tie. After two men were out he stole second. McCarthy came in to pinch hit and slammed a grounder past second giving Chance plenty of time to score. It looked like a sure victory for Selee's men at this point but Honus Wagner spoiled all the calculations.

He was first up and sent the ball over third base. McCarthy was unable to get it in time, so it rolled out to deep left. "Hans" was sitting on the bench when the ball came back. The crowd was wild. It was a critical moment for Selee's young pitcher and he was equal to the emergency. Tommy Leach made it look bad again by hitting a one-out triple to center. The infield was drawn in. Ritchey led with a popup that landed in McCarthy's glove just back of third. Phelps was an easy out at first.

The tenth started with Evers at bat. He was a victim for Clarke. Kling rolled a fast grounder to Ritchey, who was able to stop it but could not throw. A passed ball moved Kling to second. Tinker flew out and Corridon finished up a good day's work by sending the ball into center field, scoring Kling. Pittsburgh could do nothing in their half of the tenth. Chicago was a game over .500, and Selee knew that he had to win more of the close ones to make it to the top.

As the season continued, Selee's tuberculosis flared up again. Needing more rest, he began handing the reins of authority over to his first baseman. Frank Chance's leadership qualities had become apparent.[86] His time watching and thinking in the dugout and Selee's advice had begun to pay off. Frank became more adept at figuring out how to win games. This included getting on base no matter what price he had to pay.

On May 30, the Colts played the Reds in the first game of a double-header. Chance was hit three times by Jack Harper, suffering a black eye and a cut forehead. On one of the occasions, he was hit in the head and lost consciousness. On coming to, he continued playing. In the second game, he suffered two blows by Win Kellum, giving him a record of five hits by pitched balls for the day. Selee must have known that this would take its toll. But Chance was determined to win. He stood at the plate with that scowl on his face, waving that thin bat, as if daring the pitcher to get him out. There was no way of getting him to back away from a ball thrown at him.[87]

The Colts were holding their own in the pennant race. They had begun to win more of the close ones. On June 11, they came onto the field at the Polo Grounds knowing they would be facing "Iron Man" Joe McGinnity, who had an unblemished record. No team had been able to defeat him and New York was far ahead in the race. The fans poured into the stadium, breaking all attendance records with 38,805 fans anxious to see "Iron Man" do it again.

The fielding on both sides was magnificent. The game was scoreless. It was McGinnity versus Bob Wicker and the "Iron Man" worked like the Spartan pitcher he was. Wicker fought steadily and the Giants seemed under a spell. The team's best hitters, Devlin, McGann and Bresnahan, all struck out.

The quiet Wicker studied his opponents like so many mathematical problems, seeking out their weaknesses with splendid success. His control was wonderful. He shaved the edge of the plate again and again, mixed up his curves neatly, and changed his pace with no more indication of his intent than a graven image.

To all intents and purposes, not a hit was made off his delivery. If not for a scratchy safety by Devlin and a lucky drive by Mertes, his score would have been officially clean. It was the best exhibition of his baseball career. In spite of the partisan crowd, there was appreciation for his work. There was also appreciation for the work of Tinker as he scooped up hits on a gallop. As for the work of Evers, his reactions on the diamond were lightning fast.

In the seventh, it looked like the Colts were on the move. Evers slammed a pretty hit into the crowd in front of the left field bleachers. Under the ground rules he was awarded two sacks. Tinker sent him around to third with a neat single and a moment later started on the jump for second base. McGinnity wheeled quickly and hurried it to Dahlen. Tinker was yards away and looked like a sure out but Dahlen dropped the ball. Evers thought he could score but he was caught six feet or more from home.

In the twelfth the crash came. Chance, the first man up, smashed a single past McGann. Kling hit to Devlin who tried for a double play, shooting the ball to Dahlen at second. Chance beat it by great running but Dahlen whisked the ball to first, catching Kling by inches. An out at first moved Chance around to third. Selee's men scored what proved to be the winning run on Evers's smart single just out of Devlin's reach. New York's half of the twelfth was quickly over.

The *Chicago Tribune* reported that the fans were so excited about the Colts' win, they carried young Wicker, the opposing pitcher, off the field.

New York	AB	H	P	A	E
Bresna'n, cf	5	0	4	0	0
Browne, rf	5	0	1	0	0
Devlin, 3b	5	1	0	4	0
McGann, 1b	4	0	18	1	0
Mertes, lf	4	1	4	0	0
Dahlen, ss	4	0	4	6	1
Gilbert, 2b	4	0	2	4	0
Warner, c	3	0	8	4	0
McGinnity, p	4	0	0	6	0
Totals	38	2	41	25	1

Chicago	AB	H	P	A	E
Slagle, lf	5	0	2	0	0
Casey, 3b	5	2	1	8	1
Chance, 1b	5	2	5	8	0
Kling, c	5	0	0	0	0
Jones, rf	5	2	2	0	0
Evers, 2b	3	2	3	7	0
Tinker, ss	4	1	0	4	0
Williams, cf	4	0	1	0	0
Wicker, p	4	0	2	2	0
Totals	40	9	16	29	1

New York	000 000 000 000—0
Chicago	000 000 000 001—1

Run: Chance; two-base hit: Evers; sacrifice hit: Evers; stolen bases: Brown, Devlin, Chance, Tinker; first base by error: New York, 1; Chicago,1; struck out: by McGinnity, 2; by Wicker, 10; base on balls: off Wicker, 1; double play: Gilbert-Dahlen-McGann; left on bases: New York, 3; Chicago, 5; time of game: 2.25; umpires: Emelle and O'Day.

Notes of the Colts' Game. A foul tip off McGann's bat in the fourth inning went into the crowd and smashed a camera. The crowd was so enthusiastic over the Colts' victory it carried young Wicker, the Colts' pitcher, from the field.

So it went for the rest of the season. The Colts played excellent ball with a 93–60 record, finishing second to the Giants who were a sizzling 106–47. Selee was satisfied with the results so far. He saw that the team needed a 20-game winning pitcher to make it to the top. He also needed an outfielder who could slam the ball out of the infield. Wildfire Schulte looked like he might be that man. He would put him in as a starter for the 1905 season.

Selee was happy with his double play combination. They scrambled, schemed, slid, clawed and connived their way to victory. They worked out signals and combinations and sudden switches that continually confounded their opponents. They choked off runs and often turned sure defeat into impossible victory.[88]

Chance was great. He had a BA of .310 with 16 doubles, 10 triples and 6 homers. He swiped 42 bases, the lead number on the team. He played first full time but missed 32 games because of injuries.

When playing, Chance had learned to size up any ball thrown to him. He could dig it out of the dirt, leap high, grab it and still manage to nip the edge of the base with his toe after the ball was safely in his glove. Even when out with an injury, he was in the dugout helping to move a game along. Selee appreciated his help when he himself didn't feel up to managing the team.

Evers had a BA of .265 with 14 doubles and 7 triples. He swiped 26 bags. Best of all, he played in 152 games without an injury, performing brilliantly on the field. He and Tinker and Chance had turned into a machine designed to win ball games. They did it brilliantly with a smooth classy style. But Evers had begun to heckle umpires more and more. On many an occasion, Chance would nudge his powerful physique in front of the testy Irishman, quieting him down, preventing his expulsion from the game.

Tinker was Tinker. Even though his BA was .221, he got the hits when they were needed. That's how they won so many games. There was no better man at the plate when it came to clutch hitting. His 12 doubles, 13 triples and 3 homers helped push the team into second place. His 41 stolen bases were one away from tying Chance.

Selee knew that next year would be the year his boys would make it to the top. The only thing he wanted was to be around to enjoy it.

James Hart, the owner, was already enjoying the team's fantastic move upward. Attendance had jumped from 386,205 to 439,100. He was making a bundle.

1905

Frank Selee had done an excellent job rebuilding the team. However, the skipper was afraid he would not reap the harvest he had so diligently worked for. TB had taken hold of him. He knew he would have to turn to his husky first baseman for help.[89]

Frank Chance was ready. He knew the weak spots on the team. He knew the players Selee should keep and those he should get rid of. He also knew about George Huff, Selee's friend at the University of Illinois. Huff had tracked down and signed Ed Reulbach, a fantastic pitcher with a blazing fastball.

As the season got underway, Selee asked the players to elect a team captain knowing how they felt about Chance. Bobby Lowe, the former team captain, was now playing for Detroit in the American League. Such elections were unheard of in those days, but Selee wanted the players to have a voice in a very important decision. It was not only good for morale, it was important for the team to have a strong leader.

Prior to the start of a game, the players congregated in the clubhouse. Praise was voiced for three men. Votes were collected and the final tally was Chance 11, Casey 4 and Kling 2.[90]

The season opened. The team started off at about the same clip as the year before. There were days when Selee seemed to be doing well. Then there were days when he just didn't show up. At times he could not go along on a road trip. It was at these times that Frank Chance began to demonstrate his ability to manage the team.

Chance considered Frank "Wildfire" Schulte, his right fielder, as one of his finest players. Schulte was not only an inspired player in the outfield but a gem of a third batter, someone who could drive in runs with men on base. Yet Chance knew that "Wildfire" had a propensity to indulge when off the field. Each time Chance thought Schulte was drinking too much, he passed the word to sportswriter Ring Lardner, who covered the team for *The Chicago Tribune*. Lardner in turn tipped off Schulte, who would cut down his extracurricular activities long enough to avoid a fine and to pacify Chance.

It wasn't that Chance was against alcohol. In fact, after rained-out games, he often took the team to a saloon for a round of drinks but expected his men to be up and about by eight the next morning. If not, they suffered the consequences.[91]

The team had learned from the outset that their captain and acting manager was a firm believer in fines whenever anything was done that was detrimental to the winning of a game. They also began to learn that he was a stern disciplinarian, not averse to using his fists to bring a message home to an unruly player.

Frank Chance began to make his opinions known. He never backed down from an argument. He knew he was going to run the club with a clenched fist and would come down hard on any player who gave less than 100 percent. "Play it my way or meet me after the game," was his motto.[92]

The team did not resent the way he chose to manage because they knew he was sincere. Some may not have liked him, but they respected him. He was a fighter, not in the sense of pugnacity of temperament, but he was the boss and insisted his players give the best that was in them. He was the model to inspire nothing less from his men.

In one game at the Polo Grounds, when he was playing first against the Giants, he chased after a foul ball, crashed into the stands while making the catch and was knocked senseless. When the players dashed over and picked up his limp figure, the ball was still clutched tightly in his hands.[93]

This type of aggressive play, with determination and the desire to win, was the tone Frank Chance set for the team. He fired them up with his own blazing spirit and they came to love him for it. They knew he was going to be their future manager.

Selee's lungs had been eaten away by tuberculosis. It was only a matter of time. No one was surprised when Selee advised Jim Hart to put Chance in charge. The owner was perfectly willing to take the advice.

On August 1, the ailing Selee was forced to resign. That day, *The Chicago Tribune* carried the story of the team's success on the previous day in Philadelphia. The headline read, "Nationals Turn the Tide at Last." It told how the Chicago team captured a close game from the Phillies by a margin of one run:

> The victory of Chance's men was well earned, for they played better baseball at every stage of the game. Chance's men made the most of their opportunities and few chances were overlooked.
> The way the Phillies started after Wicker in the opening inning made it look like a Waterloo. Thomas fanned, but Gleason, Courtney, and Titus bumped singles to left field filling the bases. Then Wicker walked Magee forcing Gleason to score. Bransfield whipped another single to left and Courtney counted. Doolan fanned and Kling, seeing that Magee on second was taking too many liberties, whipped the ball to Tinker. Joe chased Magee up the line and Titus started for the plate. Tinker shot the ball to Kling who in turn threw to Casey, who ran the mustached one down, closing the inning. Chance's men got busy in the third and made enough runs to win the game. After that, the locals did not have much chance to count. Final score 3–2.

Throughout the month of August and early September, the team fought for the third spot. Spurred on by Chance's leadership, they won 40 of their last 63 games to finish a strong third at 92–61.

The Chicago Tribune reported their losses and hard fought victories, and the *Trib* began calling the team Nationals instead of Colts, also discerning them from Chicago's American League Club. Sportswriters from other papers increasingly referred to Chance's team as Cubs.

On their way to St. Louis toward the end of the season the team found themselves in Bedford, Indiana. It was September 13 and an exhibition game featured a duel between Wicker and Brigham. Before the game started, a loud brouhaha with fists flying erupted on the infield. Joe Tinker and Johnny Evers were slugging it out and they fell to the ground still trying to best one another. Chance and others had to pull them apart. Then and there, they agreed not to talk with one another, neither on nor off the field.

As the game played out, it became apparent that the Cubs were on their way to a rout. Bedford could do nothing against Wicker. The Chicago players were pounding the ball and Chicago won, 15–0. The following day saw what *The Chicago Tribune* reported, "Chicago Wins One Sided Game." No mention was made of the tussle on the infield.

When questioned, Tinker explained the incident:

> We dressed in the hotel and went to the ballpark in hacks. Evers got in a hack all by himself and drove off, leaving me and several others to wait until the hack returned. I was mad. I went up to him and said, "Who the hell are you that you've got to have a hack all to yourself?"
>
> One word led to another and presently we were at it, rolling around among the bats on the ball field. After we were pulled apart and it was all over, I said to Evers, "Now listen; if you and I talk to each other we're only going to be fighting all the time. So don't talk to me and I won't talk to you. You play your position and I'll play mine and let it go at that."
>
> "That suits me," said Evers.[94]

Evers had a different story:

> He threw me a hard ball. It wasn't any further than from here to there (Johnny pointed to a lamp about ten feet away). It was a real hard ball, and it broke my finger, this finger here (Johnny showed a finger on his right hand). I yelled at him, "You so and so." He laughed. We fought and we agreed to stop talking.[95]

The following day found the team in Washington, Indiana, for another exhibition game before the team moved on to St. Louis. Tinker and Evers worked side by side as if nothing had come between them. They were part of a new strategy that they and Chance had worked out. It was brilliant.

The focus was fielding: new defensive strategies to defeat the hit-and-run, the bunt, and the stolen base (the key run-producing technique of the dead ball era). They were also to put into play the first known version of the rotation play. This was a rehearsal in preparation for the 1906 season.[96]

Although Chance was kept busy playing his sack, he kept close watch on second and short. He knew that Tinker and Evers were as far apart off the field as two human beings could be. When on the bus, they gazed upon each other with ill-concealed disapproval. But on the field this changed. Though moving in the same silent aloofness, they again played together with faultless perfection, perfectly choreographed. It was beauty in motion, under the magic influence of the game of baseball. Under this influence, their differences were forgotten. They ceased to be human beings with the usual proneness of conflicting emotions. They became ballplayers, peculiar machines, having arms and legs and eyes and ears, but none of the emotions or animosities of the ordinary human. Frank Chance considered the apex of that diamond as the brightest jewel of the Cub machine. He was proud to be on the receiving end of that double play combination.[97]

Frank Chance was also proud of his team. He was looking forward to the exhibition game in Fresno that had been scheduled as part of a barnstorming tour. His players and the owner loved it because it gave them extra income. He loved it because he wanted to show his boys off to family, friends and other hometown folks when they played a local nine. He also loved it because it brought major league ballplayers to Californians who would have no other way of seeing such wonderful talent.

The exhibition game was with the Tacoma Tads, the short-lived Fresno Pacific Coast League team. It was here that Chance discovered Orval Overall who was to be one of the pitching mainstays of the Cubs during three pennant-winning years.[98]

Upon the completion of the game in Fresno, the team headed back to Chicago where Chance then led his boys to victory in an October series with Comiskey's White Sox for the city championship.

That winter, Charles Webb Murphy, seeing that attendance had climbed to 509,900, jumped at the chance to purchase the Chicago National League franchise and the West Side Grounds. He appointed Chance as manager.

Although the nucleus for a great team was there when he took over, Chance had to fill some very big holes. He concocted the scheme that parted the Brooklyn club from Jimmy Sheckard, a star left fielder. It was Chance who got Orval Overall, the fantastic pitcher, and Harry Steinfeldt, third baseman, from Cincinnati. It was he who negotiated to get Jack Taylor back from St. Louis. It was he who insisted on having another catcher to back up Kling and traded with Boston for Pat Moran. And it

Tinker and Evers executing a double play (National Baseball Hall of Fame Library).

was Chance who sent George Huff on a hunt for a twenty-game winning pitcher, finally signing Jack Pfiester for $2,500.[99]

Filling the third base spot with Steinfeldt gave Chicago the final ingredient it needed to break the lock the Giants and Pirates had held on the National League pennant for five successive years. Chance was grateful to Murphy for backing him up. He was looking forward to the 1906 season.

Joe Tinker was also looking forward to 1906. Ruby was about to make him a father and they were hoping for a boy. They even had a name picked out, Joe, Jr. They had his room ready in their nicely furnished apartment. The extra income from the saloon had made it possible for his wife to have the room decorated and to buy baby furniture. He wanted his wife and hopefully his future son to come out to the ballpark and watch the team play. It was something he really wanted.

Now that a tobacco company had come out with the Tinker Cigar, he would earn a bit more. These cigars, with his picture on the box, were something that attracted the attention of his customers as they sat around the bar drinking and smoking one of his stogies.[100]

He had never been happier. His wife was a beauty and he was madly in love with her. With both him and the team playing better baseball than ever, what more could he possibly want?

Johnny Evers wasn't exactly happy. He was content. The shoe business was bringing in extra income. His bank account kept getting larger and it felt good. If only he could find someone to love and someone who'd love him.

Johnny wanted a wife and a family. He knew his brothers and sisters were paying strict attention to the young ladies back home. For them it was fun. They would gather information, talk to friends, and once convinced they had found someone suitable, they approached the parents and put the question directly to them. That's how they found a handsome young man for his sister Anna, who married Daniel Kennedy. They were now living in the family home at 435 Third Street. Johnny wanted very much to meet the young man. Maybe he had a sister.

CHAPTER 5

The Glory Years

1906

Frank Chance was sitting at the kitchen table, holding a pipe in his right hand and the team roster in his left. His clear gray eyes had a solemn, contemplative look as he scanned a list of names, his head nodding ever so slightly.

Chance first, Evers second, Tinker short and Steinfeldt third, a perfect infield. The outfield was the finest: Schulte, Slagle and Sheckard. He had Solly Hofman, a star utility man, who could play any position be it infield or outfield and was almost as good as the regulars. Then there were the pitchers: "Three Finger" Brown, Jack Taylor, Ed Reulbach, Orvie Overall, Bob Wicker, Carl Lundgren, who had improved, and Jack Pfiester, a great southpaw. Quite a bunch of possible 20-game winners. With Kling catching, the pitchers were in the best of hands. If needed, he had Pat Moran to give Kling a hand.

Frank Chance had learned a great deal about baseball. He knew his team was ready. All they needed was a winning attitude. After his talk with them, they knew that every opposing team was the enemy. And you don't fraternize with the enemy. Every time they played they were at war, not at a "pink tea."[101] If a player shook the hand of a member of the opposing team, it would cost him $10. From now on there were fines if you didn't follow the rules.[102]

Joe Tinker was at home in his apartment, leaning back on the sofa. He was watching his wife and son rolling a ball on the living room floor. Joe was troubled. For a long time he could not figure out why Christy Mathewson, the pitching ace for the New York Giants, had him twisted up in knots. In 1904 he had gotten 2 hits in 30 times at bat. In 1905, with 16 at bats, not a single hit. Joe knew he was a pretty good hitter especially in a clutch, but he couldn't hit Matty. Those low curves on the outside had him swinging at air. Matty had been feeding him so many low ones he felt like an invalid, just standing there, unable to do anything before this mighty man.

From out of nowhere Joe had an idea. He picked himself up, kissed his wife on the cheek, slipped on a jacket and hurried out. He was going to order new bats for himself, longer ones. He was going to stand farther from the plate. If Matty pitched the ball on the inside edge of the plate, he would meet it. If the ball went to the outside, he'd have plenty of time to step into it. He knew he could now hit this ace pitcher by "out-guessing" him.[103]

Johnny Evers had no home in Chicago. His home had always been and still was in Troy, New York. That's the way he wanted it. That's the way he liked it. He wasn't married and had no responsibilities. When the season started, all he had to do was rent a furnished room and hang up his clothes. That was it. That's why there was no listing for Johnny Evers in the *City of Chicago Directory*. Yet people kept trying to look him up. When would they learn that he had no intention of listing his name with the city? Why should he? He was in Chicago to play ball, nothing else.

New men had strengthened the Chicago Nationals. Their opening series was in Cincinnati and it set a tone for the remainder of the season. The Cubs would let nothing go unnoticed even if it meant throwing a few punches.

On April 16, during a game with the Reds, Chicago was leading 2–0 going into the last half of the eighth. Carl Lundgren was pitching a great game. He looked like a sure winner. Suddenly he disconnected. His control was a thing of the past. He hit a batter with a wide curve, issued a walk and then a few hits changed the tally. This electrified the shivering fans. It was a mad bunch of Cubbies that came in off the field, especially the manager and Evers whose sharp tongue bedeviled umpire Jim Johnstone non-stop. Things had not been going smoothly between Johnstone and the visitors earlier in the fray and now they reached a climax. Walking over toward the Chicago bench, Johnstone waved Chance and Evers off the field.

The final score of 3–2 was in favor of Cincinnati, but further excitement was yet to come as reported by the press:

> Manager Chance and shortstop Tinker, of the Chicago team, were beaten up somewhat in a fight with spectators shortly after the game today, and had not the police interfered, both players would have received a severe drubbing. During the game it was noted that several of the spectators seated in the pavilion opposite to first base were continually hurling insults at Tinker, Evers and Chance. The players answered them on numerous occasions but nothing serious was thought of it.
>
> After the game however, these spectators found their way to the Chicago bus and proceeded to abuse Tinker in very vile terms. Tinker lost his temper, jumped from the bus and attacked one of the men. The man was too much for the shortstop however, and Tinker would have sustained a severe beating had not Manager Chance come to his rescue. Chance threw the man off Tinker. By that time, he himself was almost surrounded. He wielded his arms right and left and made his way to the bus. But by that time a great crowd had gathered. Luckily, the police got wind of the affair and three of them came running up. They soon put a stop to hostilities and the Chicago team was allowed to drive out of the grounds.
>
> Tinker was to blame to a certain extent for losing his temper. The spectators were blamed in general for following a conversation that started as a jest. Chance was to be congratulated, as his intervention probably saved Tinker from serious injury. It also helped stop what appeared to be a general fight among the spectators and other players that came running. Luckily, the affair happened after the majority of the crowd had left the grounds, or it might have turned into something serious.[104]

This entire affair followed a series where the Chicago Cubs trounced the Reds in a majority of the games. Charles Murphy, owner of the Chicago team, hurried home and made no mention of the nasty affair as he issued a press release to *The Chicago Daily News*: "Frank Chance says the team is getting better every minute. I really think we have a great club there. We would have won every game from Cincinnati if Seymour's hit had not become lost in the sun. I think Chance will switch Schulte back to left field and put Sheckard in right. Schulte is playing grand ball and he is the fastest young man I've seen work in a long while. He stole two bases yesterday. I am going crazy over Steinfeldt at third. He is hitting and fielding fast. He is a big, rangy fellow to throw at and altogether helps out a lot."[105]

Charles Murphy had hurried home not just for the press release but also to arrange for the homecoming of the team on the following day. He wanted publicity for his Chicago club. He wanted the attendance at the West Side Grounds to keep going up. What better way to do it than to have the world see his team. On April 17 a photographer from *The Chicago Daily News* snapped a picture of his team.

The opening day at the West Side Grounds found splendid weather, even though it was a bit on the cool side. The unfurling of the pennant was the feature of this Saturday afternoon. The ceremony attending the flag raising was simple. The Cardinals and the Cubs marched around the field to the music of a brass band and then stopped long enough to pull up the flag at the clubhouse while the crowd cheered the pennant as it swung in the breeze.

The game got underway and Chance decided to leave Schulte in right. It was a nip and tuck battle for most of the game. The Cubs took a slight lead and tried to hold it as the Cardinals threatened.

The Chicago Daily News told it best when on the following day, it reported: "John Evers was the hero of yesterday's game for the Cubs. Frank Schulte was a close second to the second baseman, for he pulled off a fielding trick that brought the crowd to its feet and saved the day for the locals when he made a brilliant running catch of a hard line drive to right field by Wagner. Evers contributed two timely hits and helped put the score out of danger. The score was 3–1 in favor of the Cubs."

So it went. The Cubs were winning close ones. On April 27, it was the Cubs playing the Reds at the West Side Grounds. In their half of the eighth, when the Cubs tied the score, Sheckard singled to right. Schulte hit a little fly to left that Hinchman never saw because of the sun. The ball struck the ground a yard in front of him. There was a delay while Manager Hanlon searched their baggage for smoked glasses but none was found. A pass to Chance filled the bases with none out. Then Steinfeldt hit to Delahanty who forced Sheckard at the plate and a double play was in sight. But Livingstone threw wildly to first letting Schulte score. Chance rounded third and stopped halfway home. Barry, who had retrieved the ball, hesitated where to throw it. Suddenly, Chance made a dash for the plate and scored the tying run. The next two batters were retired.

After nine, ten and eleven the score was still tied. Seymour opened the twelfth with a clean hit. Delahanty fanned and the next two were retired easily. The end of the game came quickly. Schulte opened Chicago's half with a single but was forced on Chance's effort to bunt. Chance stole second and it looked as if he was out, but he knocked little Miller Huggins senseless, knocking the ball out of his glove before he could tag the runner. The little visitor was groggy when he recovered but pluckily stuck to his post. When play resumed after a delay, Steinfeldt slammed a single sending the manager home with the winning tally. Final score: 7–6.

The following day found the Cubs again playing the Reds, a duel between "Three Finger" Brown and Jake Weimer. For eight and a half innings both teams found the going slow because of a heavy shower that preceded the game. Neither team had found a way to score. It was getting late. Because of the delayed start there was danger of darkness bringing about a draw.

Five times, Chicago had been denied scores when hopes were high for another tally but the fans were still confidently rooting. They cheered Chance lustily when he stepped to the plate to open Chicago's last half of the ninth. They stood and roared and waved jubilantly when the manager lined one straight to left, his second hit off Weimer. The noise grew as Steinfeldt laid down a perfect sacrifice putting Chance where a single would win.

Then began a duel between Weimer and Tinker. Jake wouldn't give Joe anything he liked, and Joe wouldn't hit anything he didn't like. After a dozen fouls, Tinker finally walked. As he took the base he glanced to his left and threw a wink and a nod to his beautiful wife in the first row, her hand on Joe, Jr. sitting on the rail holding a ball. Joe had every intention of having his son become a ball player.

Evers started for the plate. Chance sent him back to substitute a right-handed batter, choosing Moran for the pinch. He rapped a hot one to Delehanty and a double play seemed certain to retire the side. Delehanty shot to Huggins forcing Tinker at second but Joe blocked the play right there, preventing a throw to first. Huggins protested and began dancing around Umpire Bill Klem, demanding an out on Moran at first base on the grounds of interference. Chance had rounded third and seeing the opening, dashed for the plate while Huggins was off guard. A yell from the Reds woke up the little second baseman. He made a hurried heave to the plate to repair the damage but it was late, went high, and Chance slid under it safely with the run that was as good as a million.

The crowd that had waited through three hours of damp, uncomfortable conditions, shouted its acknowledgement that the game was worth the discomfort. Huggins and Delehanty roughed Umpire Klem a bit as he was leaving the diamond. The crowd started onto the field to protect him if necessary, but he needed none, as the players contented themselves with threatening and feinting, well knowing it meant a long rest for them if they started anything.[106]

Brown was as impervious as a seawall, pitching a wonderful game.

Joe Tinker's wife and son Joe, Jr., watching a game (courtesy Tom Tinker).

Not a man walked. Only one man ever reached second. After the game, Joe Tinker brought his son into the clubhouse to show him off to his teammates.

In early June, Manager Chance and his men headed for New York for a series with John McGraw's 1905 New York champions. Chicago was leading the pack and gaining ground with every game.

After the second game of the series on June 6, *The Chicago Tribune* proudly announced, "Nationals Trim Champions 11 to 3." Chance's men couldn't stop hitting as they collected 18 safeties off Dummy Taylor driving the Giants back into third place.

June 7 witnessed the third game of the series. After it was over the fans had every reason to be proud as they read the bold headline of *The Chicago Daily News*, "Chance's Men Get Awful Revenge." It read:

> Not content with the humiliation of the Giants on two previous days, Chicago's Nationals, remembering what McGraw did to them in Chicago, set out to annihilate the world champions today in the third game and succeeded. A score of 19–0: 11 runs in the first inning, 22 base

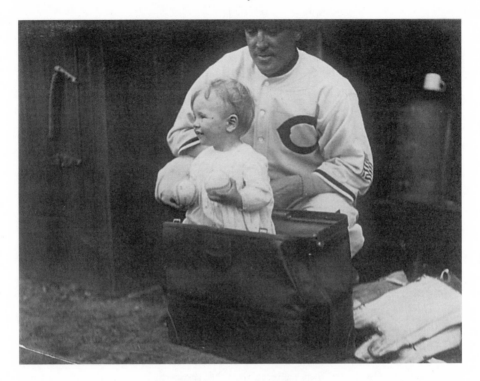

Tinker and his son in the clubhouse at West Side Grounds (courtesy Gloria Tinker).

hits and the scalps of McGraw's two crack pitchers, Mathewson and McGinnity, was the harvest of the Cubs. And they might have made it more.

Whitewashed and disgraced again, the world's champions were hooted and jeered at by the "loyal fans," who for three years have hooted and jeered all visiting teams alike at the Polo Grounds. They never dreamed of seeing McGraw at the head of as dilapidated and lifeless a band as the Giants looked today. The farce lasted considerably over two hours and at least half the 8,000 spectators left long before the end. Chance's men had to allow themselves to be put out on the bases after making their hits in order to get the game over.[107]

For John McGraw it was shame. After the Giants had won the pennant and World Series in 1905, he claimed to the day he died that his team was the greatest team he ever managed. The shirts of the road uniforms the Giants wore bore the legend, "World Champions." The legend was repeated on the yellow blankets that adorned the horses that drew the open carriages in which the Giants rode in splendor to the ball parks in the hostile towns.

But McGraw had become overconfident. He failed to see the feud that was to come. It was the Cubs against the Giants and Chance against McGraw. And on his side, Chance had Tinker and Evers.

As soon as the trio and the rest of the Cubbies took the field on June 7, it was as if a voodoo spell had been cast over the world champions. Steinfeldt's score in the first was made after an amateurish exhibition by the Giants.

Steinfeldt was at third when Evers tapped to Bill Dahlen, who threw home. Steinfeldt dodged back and forth to allow Tinker to get to third and Evers to second, then stood still, waiting to be put out. McGinnity ran up and touched "Steiny" but dropped the ball. The runner started for the plate. Devlin picked up the ball, hit him in the back and Steinfeldt was safe.

In 1906, the Cubs under Frank Chance, had put together a juggernaut that even McGraw's mighty New Yorkers could not stop. The lean and hungry Westerners rang up a record 116 wins, 36 losses for a still unsurpassed .763 winning percentage, leaving the Giants 20 games behind in second place. Even more humiliating to John McGraw was the fact that the Chicago team had taken 15 of 21 decisions against "his boys." Tinker's .400 batting average against Mathewson being no small factor in the record. In fact, it was Joe's double during that 11-run first inning on June 7 that sent Matty to the earliest shower of his career. Joe Tinker had really figured out how to outsmart Matty.

The leading hitter on the team was Harry Steinfeldt with a .327 and 83 RBIs, Chance was second with .319 and 71. Chance was the boldest thief in the National League with 57 stolen bases, Evers next with 49 and Tinker stole 30. Best of all, the team as a whole refused to swing at badly thrown pitches. It had to be down the pike or there would be a base on balls. Chance had 70, Sheckard 67, Slagle 63, Steinfeldt 47, Tinker 43, Evers 36, Schulte 31, Kling 23, Hofman 20 and Moran 7.

In spite of all the walks, getting on base wasn't the only way to win ball games. Chance insisted on playing smart. He originated the play to break up a sacrifice with men on first and second. Joe Tinker would pester the runner at second. When the ball was hit, the pitcher would bounce off the mound toward third and Chance would sprint in from first. The third baseman played close enough to the bag to take a throw for the force out. The strength of the maneuver lay in holding the runner so close to second that he couldn't get a jump to third base.[108]

Frank Chance again demonstrated his smarts on September 16, 1906 in Pittsburgh, as told by Harry Steinfeldt. "It was a corker," he said, "the last man wasn't out yet. Two were out in the ninth and the big crowd already was on its feet ready for the departing salute to the champions when Harry Peitz rolled a high bounder toward second which Tinker grabbed and hurled across to Chance. Peitz was five feet away and with a swoop the field crowd broke on the diamond just as Chance muffed the ball and let it roll away. Umpire Conway saw it. The crowd saw it. Everybody saw it, but Chance, thinking rapidly, gave Conway no chance. He grabbed the ball, and without looking, sprinted for the clubhouse with his entire team at his heels. The crowd rushed after them, and in the maelstrom of cheering humanity, Clarke and his men made a frantic kick to Conway, who, hesitating and stopping, finally decided it was useless to try to correct the blunder and let it go at that. We wanted to catch a train. And we did."[109]

This corker, as Steinfeldt had called it, was the Cubs' style of play. It was marked by its brilliancy, its speed, its remarkable headwork and its "inside play," perfected to a degree perhaps never known before. Frank Chance had indelibly impressed this on his team and taught his men by his own example.

Having led his team to such enormous heights, Frank Chance was named player-manager of the year and became known as the "Peerless Leader." Charles Murphy however didn't give a hoot what the sportswriters called his manager. His eye was on the bottom line. He must have really whooped it up when he saw that attendance had skyrocketed from 509,00 to 654,300. There was more money yet to be made! The Cubs were scheduled to play their cross-town rivals the White Sox for the world championship.

Chance's legacy of 116–36 has never been equaled. By comparison, the mighty 1998 Yankees, playing 162 games, had a 114–48. The 2001 Seattle Mariners tied the 116 wins but they lost 46 for an average of .716, not even close to the .763 for the Cubbies. They were a team without a weakness, with one of the greatest pitching staffs known. Every player was an acknowledged star. The 1906 Chicago Cubs rank as one of the best teams in baseball history.

They were about to be tested by the "Hitless Wonders." The name given to the Chicago White Sox because they were seen as a fluke winner of the American League pennant with a flimsy team batting average of .230.

Before the City Series was about to begin, Joe Tinker found himself struggling with a decision. On the one hand, he was earning extra income from his saloon on 63rd Street. Then again, with all the hoopla about their championship team and the exhibition games looming on the horizon, his baseball earnings would increase. And there was nothing better than baseball. In 1906, therefore, he decided to relinquish his liquor and tobacco license and close shop. Having made that decision, Joe Tinker was eagerly looking forward to the cross-town world championship games.

In contrast to the mighty Cubs, the Sox were a so-so team that should never have won a pennant. For most of the season they seemed doomed to stay in the second division, but with a sudden outburst of superb pitching they won 19 consecutive games in August and rose to the top. The national debate favored the Cubs to win the World Series.

The Sox outfought the Cubs through an intermittent snowfall, pushed across an unearned run and won the opener, 2–1, Nick Altrock beating "Three Finger" Brown. Most people dismissed the Sox win as another fluke. Although many sportswriters continued calling the team Cubs, *The Chicago Tribune* reverted to the nickname, Spuds. They headlined its story about the defeat, calling it "Mashed Potatoes."

Regardless of the name, Chance's men came back strong the next day and evened things out. Reulbach pitched a beauty, giving up one hit and winning, 7–1. Sox fans pointed to 2 Sox errors and 5 unearned runs and the plummeting team morale that gave the Cubs an easy victory. They claimed the Sox should've won it.

To prove their point, spitball pitcher Ed Walsh took the mound for Game 3 and did what Reulbach had done the day before. He completely shut down the Cub machine, giving them 2 measly hits, beating Pfiester with a 3–0 win.

Fortunately for the Sox, their starting shortstop had been injured and George Rohe, a player they were planning to get rid of, was forced into Game 3. He came to bat in the sixth inning of a scoreless tie with the bases loaded. As he stood at the plate, waving a menacing bat, chatterbox Johnny Kling tried to confuse him, saying, "You're the guy who likes fastballs. Well, you won't see anymore." But Rohe looked for a fast one, got one shoulder high and hit it solidly on the line, clearing the bases with a triple, giving the Sox a 2–1 lead in the Series.

Again the Cubs bounced back as Brown delivered a 2-hitter, nipping Altrock and the Sox, 1–0. The Series was knotted 2–2 and the majority of fans firmly believed that the moment had arrived for the Cubs to finally assert their power and their dominance in the Series. Most baseball writers agreed.

It wasn't to be. The Sox suddenly exploded. They astonished the baseball world by cranking up their hitting, pounding out 12 hits for an 8–6 win in Game 5. The Sox followed this up with a 14-hit slugfest in

Game 6, driving "Three Finger" Brown from the mound in the second inning, en route to an 8–3 win and the world championship.

After struggling with just 11 hits in the first four games, the White Sox came alive with their bats and pounded out 26 hits in the final two games, proving they were no longer "Hitless Wonders."

Baseball gurus continued to express their wonder at what the Sox had done. *The Sporting News* said, "Who would have thought that the Sox would show up the Cubs the way they did?" The *Sporting Life* chimed in, "By this remarkable crowning triumph the White Sox have proven themselves the most wonderful major league ball team on record."[110]

"They simply came out and beat us," Chance said, "that is the nature of baseball. It was fair and square." That was his statement for the record but privately he hated the Sox and hated admitting defeat. The skipper told "Three Finger" Brown, "How that goddamn ball club beat us, I'll never understand."[111]

In spite of his remark, he must have known why he lost. His pitching staff, those marvelous pitchers who had recorded an incredible staff ERA of 1.76 during the regular season, had lapsed. They allowed the Sox 22 runs in six games.

With the baseball season over, Frank Chance wanted to spend more time overseeing the completion of a new home that he had promised his wife. Their apartment on Groveland Avenue was small and they both wanted more room. A vacant piece of ground had been purchased, plans drawn up, and the two-story structure was close to completion. His wife Edythe had already notified Chicago officials to list their new address, 2671 North Robey, in the *City of Chicago Directory*.

Frank Chance loved the idea of being a homeowner. Even more, he was thrilled at the idea of owning 10 percent of the Chicago Cubs. He hadn't told his wife yet and wanted to surprise her when the team defeated the White Sox and became world champions. He would tell her now. As he thought about it, he was still amazed at how he became an owner of the club. It was in the final series with Cincinnati. Cubs' owners Charles Taft and Webb Murphy were in the stands. The Cubs were at bat in the ninth, one man out and here he was, the manager coming to bat with the owners watching. He was going to get on base even if the ball came at his head. It was waist high on the outside corner and he guided it through the infield for a single. Joe Tinker came to bat. Chance knew he had to steal. He took a nice lead, and as the pitcher started going through his motion, he was off. Tinker took a pitch for a ball and Chance slid in safely. From second base, Chance flashed a signal for Tinker to bunt, to "put" as Chance called it.

Tinker squared the bat before him as the ball left the pitcher's fist. Chance streaked for third. Tinker bunted. The Cincinnati pitcher scooped up the ball and glanced at Chance nearing third. It was too late to catch Chance, so the pitcher lobbed the ball to first to retire Tinker. The Reds relaxed. Taft and Murphy gasped. Chance had careened around third, heading for home. With a swooping slide he scored the winning run.

A week later, after the Cubs had completed their 116 regular season victories, Taft called Chance to his office. "Any manager with the brains to do what you did," Taft said, "deserves more than a salary. How would you like to buy 10 percent of the Cubs?"

Now Chance gasped. The Cubs had been baseball's most profitable club that season. "How much?" he asked.

"Ten thousand dollars," Taft said.

Chance wrote a check for $10,000.[112]

As a player and owner, Chance wanted to spend time thinking about his loss to the White Sox. He would talk with his team about the coming season. He knew he had the best damn team around and was determined to win it all in 1907.

1907

When the 1907 season started, Frank Chance had already reminded his players that he expected them to be tough and smart. That was the recipe for winning ball games. The new men: Del Howard, Newt Randall, Heinie Zimmerman, Chick Fraser and others, soon learned that Chance was boss. You either did it his way or you were out. If you did him dirt, you wouldn't be around long.

As soon as the new men joined the team, they heard what Chance had done to Jack Harper, a pitcher for Cincinnati. In the early part of 1906, this pitcher had deliberately hit him in the head. The manager showed Charles Murphy the kid's record, 23 wins in 1904 and 10 in 1905. Chance convinced Murphy that Harper would be an asset to the club. Having been convinced that the new pitcher would help the team win more games, Murphy traded for him.

When the kid arrived, Jack Harper found himself looking at a contract with a $3,000 cut in salary. Chance told him to sign or quit baseball. After he signed, Chance kept him in the dugout. He refused to let him pitch even though Harper threatened to go to the National Commission. Harper had no way out. He knew it. So he finally quit.

The incident was ironic because Chance always told his pitchers to keep the batters away from the plate.[113] They knew it meant throwing at the batter and they did. As a rule, batters moved away and were not hit by the pitched ball. Not Frank Chance! He never moved away! The ball pitched by Harper could've been the one that put the damage to Chance's head to a level where he began to have headaches and loss of hearing in his left ear.[114]

The season moved forward and the 1907 Cubs were hard to beat. The "Peerless Leader" insisted that the team talk baseball: new strategies, new plays, anything at all that would help win games. They did this on the bus, at breakfast, in the clubhouse or anywhere else. They had to eat and sleep baseball. If possible, dream baseball. When Joe Tinker came to him and talked about his difficulty in handling a ball on a wet and muddy field, they devised a new play. It was just too great a risk for Joe to throw the ball straight across the diamond.

"Bounce the ball to me," Chance said.

"I'll throw it so it will hit about ten feet in front of first base and you can take it on the bounce," Tinker replied.[115]

During one of their games, when there was enough rain to make the ball wet and slippery, they tried it, and it turned out to be a perfect play. The first baseman and the shortstop had to be in perfect accord. It was up to both players to know when the play was going to be made. The signals were very subtle.

Chance became quite proficient with a ball thrown into the dirt. He would either step back with one foot on the sack and take the throw waist high, or step forward and snatch it out of the dirt. It was great defense.

On offense, Chance and his players talked about getting that one run to win a ball game. That meant getting a man on base. Once on base he had to be moved along either by a hit, a steal or a bunt. The Cubs became masters in using the bunt. Instead of allowing the ball to hit the bat and drop in front of the plate, the ball was pushed. It became a slow roller, giving the batter more time to get on base. Once on base, it was commonplace to see Chance, Evers and Tinker steal. Every player was expected to do the same. Most of them did.

The season was going well. The team had become accustomed to talking strategy and became adept in devising new ways to defeat the enemy. Tinker was knocking Matty's curves for a .350 pace and no club was offering serious opposition to the Cubs. Sheckard began using a bluff bunt. He loved it. With the first ball pitched he bunted but deliberately missed. When the pitcher was in his windup, he squared away as if he were going to bunt again. The third baseman ran at top speed and instead of bunting, Sheckard poked the ball over his rival's head.[116]

That was the kind of heads-up baseball Chance expected from his men. He didn't demand perfection. He did demand that a player try. As long as you gave it your best shot, you were in. To do otherwise meant goodbye.

On July 8, the Cubs rolled into Brooklyn in the middle of the hottest spell of the season, but they didn't mind the heat one bit. They were in first place with a 53–17 record, far ahead of Pittsburgh's second place 40–20.

That afternoon it was Brown versus Pastorius. The stands were jammed with noisy people. For five innings the fans had little to talk about between peanuts. The sixth saw Pastorius jolted off the slab. Chance walked and Steinfeldt doubled. Tinker's hit sent in Chance but Joe was caught taking too much of a lead off first. Steiney scored on Evers's out. Kling doubled, Brown tripled and Slagle poked a single. Sheckard grounded to the pitcher.

The locals were helpless against Brown. He had the goose sign on them from the start. In the last of the ninth, Jordan and Maloney were out when the trouble started. The fans in back of first hurled vile epithets and pop bottles at the "Peerless Leader." He returned the same epithets and the same bottles, hitting one boy and a man in the bleachers. It was then a case of cops and clubs and loud excitement. When order was restored, the game was completed. Chicago won, 5–0.

As darkness fell, an armored automobile pulled up at the side gate of the ballpark. More than an hour had passed since the bottle-chucking episode but they were taking no chances. A crowd was lurking at the front entrance for a crack at the "Peerless Leader." Into the auto piled Chance surrounded by one police captain, two alert gumshoe men and Brooklyn President Charles Ebbets.

It was a nasty piece of business on all sides. For the first time in twenty-five years, so Ebbets said, his polite Brooklyn rooters took to throwing bottles. At the same time Manager Chance made matters worse by returning the glassware with the force of his mighty arm. He admitted it. He was sorry. He wished he could undo the fracas, especially the two bottles fired in the heat of passion at wide, open faces. Fortunately, no one was hurt. Chance nevertheless, was advised by Police Captain Maude not to return to Brooklyn during the series.[117]

Chance couldn't return as manager even if he wanted to. He was suspended pending an investigation. The team went back to Ebbets field the next day and trounced Brooklyn, 7–1. The rowdies were subdued. Crushed. Not a sound came from the open section. There was soda water everywhere but not a drop for the people in the bleachers.[118]

As part of the investigation it was learned that police regulations made riots possible at New York and Brooklyn ball parks. Officers were not allowed on the grounds. A heavy detail was stationed outside until someone was seriously injured. Then the cops would rush in and sweep up the remains.

The celebrated pop bottle case was hanging in the wind until all expert testimony was submitted. The report of umpires Carpenter and Emslie stated that the culprit endured great provocation. President Murphy submitted a long typewritten letter in which he spoke of the previous good conduct of the accused athlete. Before doing anything rash, Judge Pulliam said he desired to inspect all the points in the case. He journeyed to the Brooklyn ball park. After purchasing a score card and some peanuts, he asked that dotted lines be drawn through the air showing the exact route taken by the bottles hurled in the great combat. Mr. Ebbets wanted to know who would draw these lines. Mr. Pulliam said, "he didn't care a cuss who the artist might be so long as they produced some dotted lines for evidence." The investigation became stalled at this point.

Meanwhile, the "Peerless Leader" and his pards were anxious to have the affair settled as soon as possible. To prove he was not a fugitive from justice, Chance called on President Pulliam and related his side of the story before leaving for Philadelphia.[119]

The soda pop caper became quite farcical when, on the evening of July 10, at a roof garden show, George Cohan incorporated Captain Chance into a popular song. The comedian asked the captain in his ditty to tell them, "What he was trying to do."[120]

While people were having fun over the affair, the Cubbies were far from enjoying themselves. They had been playing ball at a .761 clip, but the pop bottle melee and all that it entailed resulted in a severe drop to a .500 level. They just had to have their leader back from the detention before they could climb out of the doldrums.

On July 15 it happened. Charles Dryden of *The Chicago Tribune* announced, "Chance Can Play Again Tomorrow." He told of a letter from Pulliam to Chance lifting the suspension. The welcome letter reached the "Peerless Leader" while he was at breakfast and the waiter brought him an extra piece of cantaloupe in honor of the event.

Pulliam regretted being compelled to inflict any penalty at all. The ten years' record of Chance for good behavior was all in his favor. Pulliam complimented the manly action of the player in calling at the National League headquarters and confessing his first and only mistake. For these reasons the president was inclined to leniency and limited the suspension to one week. Chance at once replied, thanking Pulliam and promising to be a good athlete in the future.

Dryden ended his column with very fitting remarks. "The Brooklyn club was more to blame than was Chance for the outbreak last Monday," he said. "There is absolutely no protection for players or the public. The presence of one cop would have prevented the trouble. Chance was goaded to frenzy by a bunch of filthy-tongued galoots and he stood it until they pelted him with bottles. Then he lost control and retaliated which would pass for human nature anywhere except in baseball. Mr. Pulliam should give Chance two errors in the official averages for missing the rowdies he aimed at. The only grave feature of the case was the danger of hitting innocent persons."[121]

The case was closed. Frank Chance was back. The team perked up and played their usual brand of baseball, remaining in first place and pulling away from second place Pittsburgh. Their archenemies the Giants were holding on to third place until the Cubs gave them a shellacking and pushed them down to fourth. The season ended with Chicago holding a 107–45 record with a .704 average, 17 games ahead of Pittsburgh. The Cubs again led the league in fielding, Johnny Evers leading all fielders with 500 assists. Joe Tinker had 390. Frank Chance was the team's best hitter at .293.

Chance did not forget the World Series of the previous year when the "Hitless Wonders" defeated his team. He was not going to allow it to happen again. With time to spare before squaring off with Detroit, Chance allowed himself to be interviewed by a *Chicago Daily News* reporter.

On the following day Chicago fans read: "Tomorrow is an open date for the champions, no game is scheduled. Manager Chance will not permit his players to spend it in idleness however, for he plans two sessions of hard practice at the West Side Grounds, one in the morning and another in the afternoon. This work will be given to keep the men keyed up to the highest pitch for the coming struggle in the World Series."[122]

The 1907 World Series between Chicago and Detroit got underway on October 8. It was a pitcher's duel until the fourth when it looked like Detroit would take the lead, but it was not to be. Evers made a sensational fielding play that undoubtedly shut off a run. Chance walked in the Cubs' half of the fourth and was moved to second on a sacrifice by Steinfeldt. Kling drove the Cub leader home for the first run of the game. Kling however, was slow in getting to second as Detroit tried to get Chance at the plate and Kling was nipped. It was a bit of tough luck because Evers laced out a single, which was ammunition wasted.

The 1–0 lead was shattered in the eighth when Detroit jumped into the lead scoring three runs on timely hitting and base stealing. Chance however, led off the ninth with a single to right. Steinfeldt walked. Kling popped to Rossmann. Evers was safe on Coughlin's fumble, filling the bases. Schulte was out, Rossmann to Donovan, Chance scoring. It was now a 3–2 score in favor of Detroit, two out and the tying run on third. Del Howard came in as a pinch-hitter and struck out, only to see the ball get away from catcher Charlie Schmidt, allowing the tying run to score. Thus reprieved, the Cubs went on to play a 3–3 tie, the game being called in the twelfth because of darkness. The Cubs then ran away with the series. Jack Pfiester made short shrift of Detroit, 3–1, in Game 2. The Tigers' attempt to switch to a new catcher, Freddie Payne, didn't work. He couldn't stop the Cubs from stealing five bases during the victory.

Fans whooped it up one day later as they watched their team maul Detroit, 5–1. Before the game started, Chance and his men got their batting eyes in practice, hitting southpaw Pfiester's curves. Little Johnny Evers was the batting star of the day with 2 doubles and a single. Although Tinker and Evers were still not on speaking terms, their on-field movements were flawless in mowing the Tigers down.

Two scratchy hits were all the Tigers got off Reulbach in five innings. But the Detroit squad started what seemed to be an inning of possibilities in the sixth. Three hits were bunched, Ed Killian, the pitcher, getting one of them. The Cubs broke up the Tigers chances with a fast double play. Only one run scored.

The series now moved to Detroit. When interviewed, Manager Chance said, "They have only Wild Bill Donovan to rely upon now and we will get to him tomorrow if they use him on their home grounds. We are going to make it four straight if we can and wipe out our defeat of last year by the White Stockings for the championship." The 1906 defeat by the Sox was still gnawing away at the "Peerless Leader."

"We're still in the saddle, though slightly disfigured," replied Detroit Manager Hughie Jennings. "We will show them a thing or two on our home grounds tomorrow. The boys are not down-hearted and believe they will get their batting eyes back when they return home."[123]

Critics pointed out that the Cubs were not better hitters. They pointed to the fleetness of the team in stealing bases, especially those stolen by Tinker, Evers and Chance. They pointed to the daring of Tinker and Evers when both were on base and Chance signaled for a double steal. That's why they were winning ball games.

The "Peerless Leader" did not like the critics' point of view. On October 11, *The Chicago Daily News* carried a story titled, "Cubs Quit Base Stealing Under Chance's Orders to Prove Hitting Superiority." It went on to say, "In order to convince baseball critics, he has told his club to abandon efforts to steal bases and concentrate its energy with the stick."

The team followed his order and beat the Tigers easier than before with a 6–1 win. Although Detroit took a 1–0 lead in the fourth after Ty Cobb ripped a hit to deep left, the Cubs passed the Tigers in the fifth. Evers started the rally by beating out a bounder to O'Leary. Time was called on account of rain with Schulte at bat. The band played "Wait 'Till the Sun Shines, Nellie." And the sun did shine.

The game was an easy win for the Cubs. Chance knew that the way his team was playing, he'd win four straight with "Three Finger" Brown at the helm on the following day. His expectation was correct as the Cubs took the last game of the series, 2–0. Frank Chance had his first World Series victory. But hits alone did not win this one. The club was pretty frisky on the bases. Evers and Tinker pulled off a double steal that dazed the Tigers by its boldness.

It started in the first inning. Slagle waited for a pass and stole second on catcher Archer, who Manager Jennings sent in behind the bat as a last resort in his effort to stop the Cubs from running wild on the bases. It remained for Steinfeldt to drive him in with a single.

Rossman's error was the basis for the second run made by the Cubs, Evers being safe on the play. Tinker's single put Evers on second. A signal for a double steal. Evers purloined third base quite handily while Tinker went to second on his end of the double theft. Evers scored when Slagle went out on a grounder.

Manager Chance couldn't play. His finger was dislocated on the previous day when hit by a pitched ball. He didn't know it until he called in a physician shortly before the final game. The finger was put under the x-ray and the middle joint was found to be out of place. The dislocation was reduced and the finger put in splints. Del Howard went to first base in Chance's place. The dislocation was nothing compared to his many other injuries over the years.[124]

The Cubs played 152 regular season games in 1907 and Chance had missed 43 of them. He continued to crowd home plate. He would not step away from a pitched ball. When the ball came toward his head, it was as if he remained frozen to the spot knowing the pain he was about to endure. His headaches became more severe and the hearing in his left ear was really going bad. But who cared about headaches? Who cared about hearing? He had won a World Series! He was happy.

Opinions of the best informed baseball men in the country were that the Chicago National League team stood out alone above any other organization the baseball world had ever known. Yet, they didn't know why.

It was several ingredients Chance had instilled into the team. The first was an attitude called team harmony.

The "Peerless Leader" knew as everyone else did, that Tinker and Evers were not on speaking terms. He knew how these men felt about one another. He knew that for each of them it was a personal matter. He also knew that what they thought about the team as a whole was something else. Although they may have hated each other, they loved the Cubs. Although they wouldn't fight for each other, they'd do anything for the team. The entire team felt the same way. That was one of the reasons for the Cubs' success.[125]

Another reason for the Cubs' success was the almost mystical way Tinker and Evers played together. It was as if they could read each other's mind by the mere shrug of a shoulder, the turn of a head or the subtle look they gave one another. Or also knowing what was called for by circumstances during the game. Whether it was a hot grounder hit their way or a man on second, they instinctively knew where to move and how to move to get opposing players out. They did it with style and class, without a moment of hesitation. It was this infield that made the club what it was.[126]

When Ty Cobb was on second during the World Series just ended, he took a lead off the base. Kling, one of the first Jewish players in the majors, was catching. Tinker said to Cobb, "Don't get too far away from that bag or the Jew will nip you off." With that, he in some mysterious way gave Evers a signal to take the throw. Tinker knew that Kling had also received the message. As Cobb turned to sneer at Tinker, Evers rushed to cover, took the throw and tagged Cobb out before he could get back to the bag. This one play helped win the game and the Series.[127]

A third, and perhaps most important reason for Chicago's success, was the excellent pitching staff Selee and Chance had put together. The "Peerless Leader" knew these excellent pitchers would be around for the 1908 season. With them and his other men he knew he had a winning combination. Chance knew he could win it all over again.

Now that the season was over, he and Edythe were heading back to Fresno to participate in one of the city's biggest events of the year. On November 9, The *Fresno Morning Republican* headlined a story, "Frank Chance To Play Ball Here." It told of a game of baseball between the Berkeley Elks and the Fresno Elks at Recreation Park on Saturday, November 30. Frank Chance, the peerless Fresno boy, Orvie Overall, the great California pitcher and "Hap" Hogan, also of baseball fame, were to appear before a Fresno crowd. It had been announced that Chance would hold down first while Overall and Hogan would make a battery that could not be beaten.

Chance leaps and stabs a high throw to first (National Baseball Hall of Fame Library).

Enthusiasm reigned supreme among local baseball lovers. The fans knew they were going to see an exhibition of baseball that had never been equaled in any game ever played in their city. They looked upon the November 30 as a red-letter day, one to be marked on the calendar. The townspeople planned to celebrate with a band that would greet the Fresno star as soon as he stepped off the train. Local pride and admiration for Chance had always been great. The desire of Fresnans to see the illustrious son of the soil perform was sure to draw an immense crowd.

Frank Chance felt great upon returning to the town where he played ball as a kid. He was looking forward to the event and spending time with family and friends. It helped him relax before heading back to the next baseball season.

1908

The 1908 season started with the team having undeniable respect for their leader. The respect was there not only because they had won the world championship in 1907, but also because of the way Chance had treated them while they climbed to the top of the league. Cubs backup catcher Jimmy Archer explained:

Chance's players respected him because he treated his players like adults. He understood the importance of allowing the players to blow off steam by having a few drinks. After home games, Chance took them to Biggio Brothers, across the street on the southwest corner of Polk and Lincoln. He'd always buy the first drink. When a player had had enough, the bartenders knew to refuse to sell him any more drinks.

When we'd get rained out, we'd be sitting around the clubhouse. Then Chance would come in. "What have I got here, a Sunday school club?" he'd say. We'd all go to a saloon. You couldn't buy a drink. Chance would buy them all. Then at 11:45 P.M., he'd say, "Drink up," and we'd head for our rooms. You had to be—not in your hotel—but in your room by midnight. He insisted that every player be called at eight in the morning, and if you weren't in the dining room by nine you didn't eat.

Chance also preferred his players to bet on horses and play poker. He didn't agree with many of his fellow managers that betting on horses was demoralizing to baseball players. He once told a reporter, "I figure that a little bet now and then results in moderate excitement which, I really believe, helps to stir up mental activity."

Johnny Evers agreed with Chance's point of view about poker stirring up mental activity. The second baseman felt it made a ball player sharper. He went on to say:

Chance made sure players did not gamble for high stakes and didn't trust a ballplayer who wasn't proficient at cards.

Chance never dabbled in psychological experimentation on a scientific basis, but he can discover how rapidly a ball player thinks more quickly in a poker game than in any other way. This saves the expense of carrying some player for months only to have him lose a game because his convolutions fail to revolve fast enough.

Chance permits poker playing with a 25 cent limit, but all games must stop by 11 o'clock. He stepped into a hotel room at midnight once and discovered five of his players and a newspaperman playing dollar limit.

"That will cost each of you $25," he said quietly, "not so much for playing as for deliberately disobeying the limit rule. I wouldn't mind you older players doing it," Chance continued, "but you're setting the worst kind of example to the young ones. As for you," he added, turning to the reporter, "I'll not give you a piece of news for a month."

"Can't I pay the fine and get the news?" inquired the reporter.

"Sure, that will punish you and not the paper," replied Chance.

Later on, Chance was playing poker beyond the time limit and fined himself $25. In doing this, the "Peerless Leader" demonstrated consistency and fairness, and this contributed to the respect they all had for him.[128]

The season moved forward and Chance quickly learned that lack of respect in the clubhouse had reached the point of causing a disaster. The Cubs had nearly completed their home games and were about to head east on their first road trip when a few hot words passed between Heinie Zimmerman and Jimmy Sheckard in the clubhouse. Zim, as he was called, had joined the team the previous year as a utility man and was considered to be a hothead. One word led to another. Zim picked up a bottle of ammonia and hurled it at Sheckard. The bottle struck Sheckard in the forehead between the eyes. It exploded! Fluid splashed into Sheckard's eyes, streamed down his face and several players rushed him to Cook County Hospital across the street. The fear was that he would be permanently blind.

Manager Chance was thoroughly enraged. He tore into Zim and wrestled him to the ground. Zim received a beating that made it necessary to cart him to the hospital as well. Afterwards, the players took sides in the matter and the affair created bad feelings all around. Sheckard and Zim were out of the game for several weeks. That weakened the team. When Wildfire Schulte also had to quit on account of illness, the Cubs could not gain ground against the Pirates and the Giants.[129]

On July 17, two master mechanics, Brown and Mathewson, fought it out on the field. Three-Finger found himself in a jam in the second with bases loaded and none out. He pulled out of that mess and Tinker's one hand stop in the fourth rescued him again. There was no score until the fifth when Tinker hit a long line drive over short. Tinker was at third before Seymour caught up with the ball.

As Tinker weathered the third corner, Zimmerman, coaching there, threw the hooks into the sprinter and rammed him toward the bag. Joe thought the ball must be right on top of him but when he saw the backs of the relay men strung across the field, he dug out for home and beat Bridwell's heave, which came a bit wide. When it was all over, Zim explained his high tackle by saying he lost track of the ball in the sun and didn't know where it was.

The Cubs had finally won a close one. The tension had been so high that two fans, eager to see the game, fell to their death outside the park.[130] *The Chicago Tribune* played it up big, showing Joe Tinker in the "West Side Melodrama."

The popularity of Tinker and Evers had skyrocketed in Chicago. Their fame spilled into the offices of Will Rossiter, a Chicago music publisher. He had a new song, "Between You and Me." He wanted to publish it under the names of Johnny Evers and Joe Tinker. Fortunately for Rossiter, although Joe and Johnny had not yet shaken hands, they were now on speaking terms. On July 25, 1908 the song was published.

HERO TINKER IN THE WEST SIDE MELODRAMA.

This Tinker caricature denotes his hero status with the Chicago fans (*Chicago Tribune*).

By mid-August the Cubs trailed the Pirates by 6 games and the Giants by 3. It took the heroics of Joe Tinker, who drove in the winning runs two days in a row, to keep the Cubs as close as they were.

At the end of August the Giants came to town. With the Pirates doing a fade, it appeared likely that the pennant would come down to either Chicago or New York. In the opener, left-hander Jack Pfiester, in his first year with the Cubs, shut out the Giants, 19–0, and became known as "Jack the Giant Killer."

Before a Chicago-Pittsburgh series, Pirates Manager Fred Clarke advised his players that $25 would be waiting for the man who did the most damage to a Cub. Chance's team retaliated in kind. The game became a bloody mess.

Chance approached Clarke when the carnage was done. "Look here, Fred," he said. "What say we quit cutting up each other and give the Giants the business? After all, they're the common enemy." They shook hands. It was a rough season for John McGraw's Giants.[131]

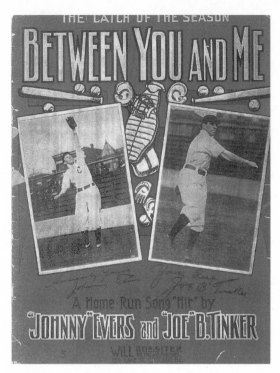

Sheet music for the song Will Rossiter published in 1908 under Johnny and Joe's names
(courtesy Max Weder).

Chicago continued its
love affair with the exciting,
irresistible Cubs. New York
won the Saturday game but
the Cubs came back on Sunday when Brown beat Math-
ewson, 3–2. The next day,
"Pfiester the Giant Killer"
defeated the Giants, 2–1, as
a double play from Tinker to
Evers to Chance killed the
lone New York rally.

On September 21, after
the teams split a double-
header, the Cubs trailed the
Giants by three and a half
games. The results that day
made it appear as if the championship had been decided.
The Cubs, returning to the
hotel in carriages, were silent
and downhearted. Not a word
was spoken for a long time.

Suddenly   Tinker
remarked to Chance: "Well,
Cap, I guess it's all off. Let's
break training and make a good night of it." For an instant Chance was
silent. Then he said, "No. We were good winners last year. Let's show them
we are good losers and play the string out. We may win yet."[132]

On September 22, the Cubs beat the Giants in a doubleheader, 4–3
and 2–1. At this point the Giants led the Cubs by a game and a half. The
Cubs had 11 more games to play. The Giants had 17, including 8 with a
mediocre Philadelphia team.

On September 23, the race was very close. Everyone's nerves were
on edge. In the final game of the Giant-Cub series, Jack Pfiester started
for the Cubs against Christy Mathewson. A large crowd of 20,000 filed
in knowing the importance of every game. The crowd took their baseball
with a deadly intensity.

It became a pitching duel between Mathewson and Pfiester. It was
a scoreless tie going into the fifth. Joe Tinker, facing his favorite pitcher,
hit an inside-the-park homer, taking advantage of the long center field

power alleys at the Polo Grounds to leg out his sixth homer of the year. Tops on the team.

With one man on in the last of the sixth, Turkey Mike Donlin singled over Evers's head to tie the score, 1–1. Three New York rallies threatened to take the lead but they were felled by Cubs double plays from Tinker to Evers to Chance.

In the last half of the ninth the score was still knotted, 1–1. There was one out and tension was rising. Art Devlin singled to center to get the Giants going. The winning run was on first. Moose McCormick hit a slow grounder to Evers who relayed it to Tinker in time to get Devlin at second but too late for the double play that would have retired the side. Up to bat with two out and McCormick on first came a nineteen-year old rookie first baseman, Fred Merkle. Pfiester studied the young right-hand hitter and delivered. Base hit, right field. McCormick raced to third.

Al Bridwell was the next batsman. He took Pfiester's first pitch and lined it to center for the game-winning single. McCormick raced home with the winning run. The fans poured onto the field yelling their elation at the Giants' 2–1 triumph. Merkle, seeing the crazed New Yorkers heading his way, stopped running toward second and made a beeline for the clubhouse beyond right field.

Evers, known for having one of baseball's most agile minds, began screaming for center fielder Solly Hofman to throw him the ball. Hofman's throw went over Tinker's head and rolled to where Joe McGinnity, the Giants pitcher, was standing. Joe raced for the ball. Joe McGinnity realized what was happening, outwrestled the Cub shortstop for the ball, and with Tinker on his back, he heaved the ball into the crowd.

Rube Kroh, a second-line Cubs pitcher who was not even in the game, saw who caught the ball. A tall, stringy, middle-aged gent with a brown bowler hat. Rube demanded the ball. When he wouldn't cough it up, Kroh hit the fan on top of that stiff hat, drove it down over his eyes and as the gent folded up, the ball fell free. Kroh grabbed it and tossed it to Tinker. Evers was yelling and waving his hands out by second base. Tinker fired the ball to him. Evers stepped on the base and made sure umpire Hank O'Day saw him.

When the hit was made the crowd swarmed upon the field. O'Day, remembering the Pittsburgh game several weeks earlier, where the same play had come up, raced toward second base. He saw Merkle turn and go to the clubhouse, waited until Evers received the ball, then saw the second baseman touch second base.

"The run does not count," O'Day said, as the crowd swarmed over him. Fans shrieked, struck at him, pulled him and threatened his life. He made no attempt to continue the game because of the confusion.

When hundreds of drunk and angry Giants fans learned what the Cubs were trying to pull, they headed for the Chicago clubhouse intent on revenge on both umpires and the Cubs. Chance was the target. Though he was a pugilist, the crowd would have treated him harshly but for two fat policemen. Surrounded by them and some of his players, the Chicago manager argued that he would protest the game and called for O'Day. He complained that because the Giants fans had invaded the field and prevented the continuation of the game, the Cubs should be declared winner by a forfeit. Umpire Bob Emslie refused to take a stand for or against O'Day. "I didn't see the play," he insisted. That was all he said on the matter.

Mathewson and a couple of the Giants had dashed for the clubhouse and tried to get Merkle back to second, but Evers was standing there with the ball before they got him out of the door. They saw it was too late. McGraw kept screaming bloody murder, hollering that the Giants had won. A couple of cops McGraw had scattered around to protect the visiting players took a few pokes at Chance under the guise of keeping the crowd back. Fistfights were going on as the team finally got out of Polo Ground.

When the umpires emerged in their dress clothes, Bob Emslie repeated that he hadn't seen anything. Hank O'Day shouted back over his shoulder, "Merkle didn't run to second, the last run doesn't count. It's a tie game."

When Giants Manager John McGraw began to protest with his customary vitriol, O'Day told him if he didn't like the decision he could take it up with National League President, Harry C. Pulliam. The next day, the furious Giants appealed to Pulliam. So did Chicago. Giants owner John T. Brush wanted O'Day's out call nullified, giving the Giants the victory. Chicago owner Charles Murphy demanded the Cubs be awarded the game by a forfeit. The world waited for Pulliam's decision.

Regular season play continued. On September 30, the Reds landed a blow that hurt the Cubs. Trailing 5–4, they pushed across two runs in the ninth for a 6–5 win that forced the champions into third place. Two days later, Pulliam handed down his ruling. He upheld the umpire's decision citing the O'Day report. "The people had run out on the field," the umpire stated "I did not ask to have the field cleared, as it was too dark to continue play."

Pulliam said he was upholding the umpire on a question of fact. O'Day had ruled that the game had ended in a 1–1 tie. So it would stand. As neither club had an open date, Pulliam ruled that the contest would not be continued. The Giants appealed Pulliam's decision to the Board of Directors.

On October 4, the Cubs beat the Reds, 16–2, with Tinker leading the charge. When the Cubs returned to Chicago they discovered the city had gone Cubs crazy.

On Monday, October 5, the Cubs hosted the Pittsburgh Pirates before 30,247 fans, the largest crowd ever to watch a baseball game anywhere in America. It was a crucial game. The Cubs won, 5–2.

Hugh Fullerton wrote a detailed description of the game and its aftermath in the *New York American*:

> The game was grandly played, the stops by Tinker and Evers setting the crowd mad with applause. But the major honors was reserved for Chance, for in the eighth, by one of the most astounding plays ever made, he stopped the Pirates.
>
> Leach hit a fierce line drive straight over first and it looked like a sure double until Chance, with a running jump, shoved out one hand, turned backwards and clung to the ball. Against that kind of defensive work Pittsburgh had no chance.
>
> In the ninth, with one out to go, "Chief" Wilson hit a hard bounder straight at Tinker and the ball flashed to Evers on top of second forcing Alan Storke. The game was over and the crowd broke. Thousands poured down in the battleground in the wildest, craziest demonstration of the year. Brown was carried aloft on the shoulders of admirers. He was carried across the field. Hundreds of men and women hurled cushions high in the air, screaming and flinging hats.
>
> An hour after the game, a thousand fans still waited outside the park. As Chance backed his automobile out, hundreds swarmed around him, cheering wildly. Evers escaped in a cab with a hundred men trying to unhitch the horse so they could pull the cab themselves. As for Tinker, not a soul could figure out how he had escaped the throng that had waited for him.

On October 5, 1908, the Board of Directors of the National League met for eight hours with no intermission for dinner. When it looked as if the decision might be rendered in favor of the Giants, Jack Ryder of the *Cincinnati Enquirer*, broke into the meeting. He delivered a tremendous speech in favor of the Cubs, claiming there was no choice but to play the game over and vowing that the league would make itself a laughingstock if it let the Giants get away with a pennant on a bonehead play.

The Board met again on Tuesday, October 6. A decision was not released. On that day the Giants beat Boston, 4–1. With the Cubs season over, the Giants still had one game remaining against the Boston Braves. If the Braves won, the entire matter would be moot.

In Chicago, the *Tribune* was offering prayers that the next day's Giants-Boston game be rained out, preventing the Giants from finishing in a tie with the Cubs. Such was not to be. The season ended with the Giants and Cubs in a tie, 98–55.

The Board decided to replay the Merkle game. There were choices to be made. They could play a single game or the best out of five. Charles Murphy liked the idea of five games because of the extra money a series would bring. He didn't want to risk everything on a single game against Christy Mathewson, the best pitcher in baseball. So he opted for five games. McGraw didn't give a hoot about money. He cared only about winning! He had Mathewson and chose to play one game.

On October 7, the *New York Herald* wrote: "The coming showdown is going to be a war. Never before have two teams been tied at the end of a season. Never before has the race been so close. Never has it been necessary to play off the tie of six months' baseball in a single gigantic battle. That the game will be a struggle to the death is certain."

Joe Tinker made a statement that was widely quoted. Joe said, "If you didn't honestly and furiously hate the Giants, you weren't a real Cub."[133]

Evers reported threatening phone calls. The message was always the same. If he played, they would kill him, cut off his ears and send them to his mother. Some thoughtful tramp even called his mother in Troy and repeated the warning to her. She called her son and begged him not to play. He promised not to, knowing she wouldn't find out until she got the papers that night or the next morning.[134]

When Frank Chance led the Cubs into New York the morning of October 8 to meet the Giants that afternoon, Mordecai Brown had a half-dozen letters in his coat pocket. "We'll kill you," these letters said, "if you pitch and beat the Giants."[135]

It wasn't the only Giants' hanky-panky afoot. McGraw cooked up a scheme to get Frank Chance thrown out of the game. Joe McGinnity was to pick a fight with Chance early in the game. Frank always hit Matty pretty well and McGraw felt his team had a better chance of winning with the "Peerless Leader" out of there. They were to have a knockdown, drag-out fight and both would get thrown out of the game. McGinnity did what he was supposed to do. He called Chance names, stepped on his shoes, pushed him, actually spat on him, but Frank wouldn't fight. He was too smart.[136]

McGraw concocted another scheme to beat the Cubs. He planned to cut their batting practice time from thirty to fifteen minutes. Then, if the team protested, to send his three toughest players charging out to pick a fight. The wild-eyed fans would riot! Blame would be put on the Cubs for starting it and the game would be forfeited to the Giants.

As McGinnity stepped to the plate under orders to begin knocking grounders to the Giants for fielding practice, Chance tried to brush him away and the "iron man" raised his bat menacingly. For one instant it looked like the beginning of a riot. But players rushed in and surrounded the belligerents, smoothing out the incident quickly. When the thing was explained to Chance, he smiled contemptuously and acquiesced. The Cubs proved later that they didn't need the extra fifteen minutes of batting practice.

The game was one of the most fiercely fought in the history of baseball. It was Mathewson versus Pfiester, the same pitchers that dueled it out during the 1–1 tie in the Merkle game.

The Cubs started with their first three men making easy outs. In the Giants half of the first, the first ball pitched by Pfiester was a sign of disaster. Tenney was hit on the arm. With two strikes on Herzog, Pfiester lost control and passed him, putting Tenney on second. Bresnahan struck out but Kling dropped the third strike. Bresnahan was out anyway because first base was occupied. Seeing Herzog taking a long lead, Kling fired a throw to Chance nailing Herzog for a double play.

Despite Kling's play, the Giants scored the game's first run. Donlin pulled a liner over first base close to the foul line scoring Tenney. Chance argued the ball was foul. The crowd hooted and the tensions rose to such a high pitch, a fireman out beyond center field fell off a telegraph pole and broke his neck.

Seymour was given a base on balls. Chance removed Pfiester from the slab and Brown replaced him. Brown's first act was to strike out Devlin leaving two men on base.

Chance came to bat in the second. The fans met him with a storm of hisses; he responded with a single. The ball came back to Mathewson. He looked at Bresnahan behind the plate, then wheeled and threw to first, catching Chance off guard. Chance slid. Tenney came down with the ball. Umpire Bill Klem threw up his arm. Husk was out.

Chance ripped and raved, protesting. Most of the Cubs rushed out of the dugout. Solly Hofman called Klem so many names that he was ejected. The stands went into a panic. The roar became even wilder when Matty went on to strike out Steinfeldt and Howard.

Chance was grim when he came to bat in the third. Tinker had led off the inning with a long ball to center over Cy Seymour's head. Kling then singled on a line to left center, sending Tinker across the plate. Brown bunted toward first for a sacrifice and was retired by Tenney unassisted, putting Kling on second.

Johnny Evers came to bat and Mathewson deliberately pitched four wide balls, sending Evers growling on his way to first. Schulte was next. His fighting Dutch was just as good as Johnny's Irish, hitting a liner over third base into the crowd in left field giving him two bases and scoring Kling with the run that put Chicago ahead and driving Evers to third.

It was now Chance's turn with the crowd howling. Gripping the bat, he put into his swing all the vim and vengeance that had been welling up in his heart, all the enmity and disgust for the petty tricksters who had been yapping at his heels, trying to do him out of a pennant. He met a curve squarely in the middle of its break, driving the ball far out of reach of Mike Donlin. With that swat two more Cubs crossed the plate, borne by Evers and Schulte. Frank made it to second with a great slide that beat a great throw by Donlin. As Chance stood on second with a smile on his face, the Cubs were ahead, 4–1.

The Giants fought back in their end of the third and got runners on first and second by way of hits with only one out. That situation nearly precipitated disaster, for Joe Tinker slipped as he gathered in Donlin's chop hit and fell to the ground. He lost an easy chance to end the inning with a double play, but recovered in time to force a runner at second and save the day. Seymour's long fly to Sheckard closed the threat.

For three innings the battle ran along smoothly, as if the great stakes had been forgotten. Then in the seventh, came the final Giants rally and the final successful repulse. Devlin started the attack with a whistling single to left center. McCormick poked a grounder just beyond Evers's reach into right field, and Bridwell would not let Brown outguess him at the plate. Instead he drew a base on balls to load the bases with nobody out.

Once more the raging mob, which had been chewing the bitterest cud known to baseball fandom, rose to the occasion. Once more they saw a new pair of pennants floating in center field in place of the torn and stained emblems of 1905 when the Giants were the whole thing in baseball and then some. The yelling was rasping and raucous, with the anger of hope deferred and of anxious moments of fear and dread.

Here Manager McGraw seized the opportunity by sending Larry Doyle to bat in place of Mathewson, to try to bring home the runs and complete the downfall of Brown and the Cubs. Instead of sticking his hip into a pitched ball, as this same Doyle had done once before to steal a game from the Cubs, he hit only a pop foul. As Kling went to catch it, the fans sailed derby hats, bottles, and paper, anything and everything to confuse him. But Kling had nerve and he corralled it. That was one out, but those three Giants still panted on the bases and unless they were kept there, Chicago's lead would be wiped out.

Tenney was next. He lifted a fly so far into right field that Schulte was content with pulling it down and made no effort to stop Devlin's score. Instead, he fired the ball back to Evers to hold McCormick on second. Two were out and only one run of Chicago's lead had been lost. Still there were Giants on first and second and the gate was still open. Herzog grounded out: Tinker to Chance.

New York could do nothing against the great "Three Finger" Brown in the last two innings. Four pitched balls in the ninth and the game was over. For the third successive year the Chicago Cubs were the National League champions.

As the ninth ended, the Cubs ran for their lives, straight for the clubhouse with the pack at their heels. Some of the boys got caught by the mob and were roughed up. Tinker, Howard and Sheckard were struck. Pfiester got slashed on the shoulder by a knife. Chance was hurt more severely when a blow struck him in the neck. Before the Cubs manager could wheel to defend himself, the coward was swallowed up in the tremendous throng and escaped punishment. A hurried examination of the manager in the dressing room by a surgeon in attendance disclosed that the assailant had probably broken a cartilage in Chance's neck. The injury would not likely keep him out of the World Series, but Husk's voice would be gone for a few days during Series play.[137]

Finally, the whole team made it to the dressing room and barricaded the door. Outside, wild men were yelling for their blood. As the mob got bigger, the police came and formed a line across the door. They even had to pull their revolvers to hold the crowd back. When it was safe, they rode to the hotel in a patrol wagon with two cops on the inside and four riding the running boards and the rear step. That night, they left for Detroit and the World Series by slipping out the back door and were escorted down the alley in back of the hotel by a swarm of policemen.[138]

Back in Chicago the *Tribune* had shown the game on the Electrical Baseball Board at Orchestra Hall for the benefit of the Tribune Hospital Fund. Seats were 25¢, 50¢ and $1 for boxes. A howling, shrieking, ball-mad crowd, wild in its enthusiasm, sat through it all.

When the Giants were retired at the close of the ninth, the cheering reached a pitch. A beautiful young woman whose eyes shone and cheeks flushed turned to the gray-haired woman by her side and said, "This is our anniversary day, mother. He had to win. It's wonderful, isn't it?" And she laughed and cried at the same time. If the crowd had known that the wife of the great Cub leader was in their midst, Mrs. Frank LeRoy Chance would have been given a standing ovation.

Another Cub wife was in the throng. With a party of friends, Mrs.

This caricature represents McGraw's feelings toward the Cubs (*Chicago Tribune*).

Joe Tinker sat only a few rows behind Mrs. Chance waving a Cubs banner. Upon leaving the building, she shouted over and over, "Four to two, four to two."[139]

Frank Chance issued a brief statement on the following day, "My boys were nervous at the start of the game. The circumstances naturally account for that. But they braced up and you know the rest. The team is the finest in the history of the sport."[140]

Praise for the Cubs poured in from the baseball world. Even President John Brush of the Giants had something nice to say. Bellyaching comments from John McGraw, however, showing he would never forget, were consistent with a caricature by Briggs in *The Chicago Tribune*.

Tinker, Evers and Chance had become household words. They were in the news from coast to coast. The song that Johnny and Joe had signed their name to had become a smash. Everyone was singing "Between You and Me."

Tinker and Evers were in demand for advertisements and earned more money. They posed in their uniform, each player standing in the center of a large garter that said:

Johnny Evers   Joe Tinker

25¢   50¢

Boston   Garter

Velvet   Grip

Holds your sock smooth as your skin[141]

Little Johnny Evers was in heaven and not because of all the publicity. He was getting married to Helen Fitzgibbons. It had all been arranged. He looked at the photo and was in love. He had a friend type in beneath the photo, the new name of his bride to be. He liked it.

Cubs owner Charles Murphy was delighted at the publicity his players were getting. It meant higher ticket prices for a World Series that was certain to be a complete sellout. He was, however, incensed at John McGraw's bellyaching that the Giants had been cheated out of the pennant. Deciding to rub salt on the Giants' wounds, he issued a press release referring to Fred Merkle's failure to run to second base on a base hit. He said, "We can't supply brains to the New York Club's dumb players." The complaints from McGraw

Mrs. John Evers

Johnny fell in love and married Helen Fitzgibbons (Baseball Magazine).

suddenly vanished from the sports pages and were replaced by World Series news.[142]

October 10 brought out a Detroit crowd to root for the home team in Game 1. For eight innings they had something to scream about. The Tigers were ahead, 6–5, going into the ninth. Three more outs and Ed Summers, a rookie knuckleball pitcher would have put one away for Detroit.

With Evers out, Schulte sped down the path, beating out a hard drive to deep short. Then came Chance with a vicious single to center, putting Schulte on second. Steinfeldt came to the plate and lined a single to McIntyre in left. So quickly did he field the hit, the fleet Schulte had to hold third. Solly Hofman, a great utility man, took two strikes and waited out three balls. It was a guessing match between batter and pitcher. It came, a fast one over the heart of the plate and away it sailed into left, scoring Schulte and Manager Chance, Steinfeldt taking third on the throw.

Joe Tinker bunted on a squeeze play. It worked. Steiny scored. While they were trying for Steinfeldt at home, Tinker got to first. Hofman was on second. Then Tinker and Hofman worked a double steal. The Cubs were playing rings around the discomfited Tigers. There seemed no way of stopping them. Kling delivered a single to center to score Hofman and

Tinker. Brown sacrificed and Sheckard, the man who got three hits the first three times up, flied to Sam Crawford.

The agony was over. The Tigers were subdued. The first game, which carried so much with it in a short series like this was won, 10–6. A happy group of Cubs left the field to prepare for the next day's game in Chicago.

Prior to the second game, Charles Murphy infuriated the fans by raising World Series ticket prices. Usually a team charged double the regular season price. Murphy charged five times as much. Instead of the sell-out crowd of 25,000 that was expected, only 17,760 showed up at the West Side Grounds.

For seven innings, they saw Orval Overall and Bill Donovan duel it out in a scoreless game. With one out in the eighth, Hofman beat out an infield hit, Chicago's second hit of the day. Donovan threw Tinker a wide, slow pitch. He hit it deep to right. It sailed high, far, and over the fence. It was the first Cub home run in World Series play. Donovan, unnerved by the two runs that had scored, allowed 4 more hits and 4 more runs in what became a 6–1 loss.

After the game, Cobb blamed the wind for the defeat of the Tigers. He said that Tinker's hit would have been a sure out had it not been for the wind in back of the ball, and there would have been no runs scored in that terrible eighth inning.

"Tinker's hit was a high one," he said. "And I rushed back and got set for it. I saw the ball was sailing on over my head and I rushed back to the fence and backed up against the wire netting, believing that I would surely get it. I was surprised when the sphere went on over the fence. I jumped for it but I could not touch it. On an ordinary calm day the ball would never have gone so far and I could have easily caught it and held Hofman on first. That would have made two outs and Kling's two-base hit would not have scored two runs. The inning would have ended in a tie at the most, and we could have gone on to win."[143]

Hughie Jennings, the Detroit manager, also found reasons for the loss and vowed that the Tigers would come from behind and take the lead as they had done in the past. In Game 3 there was a hint that his vow could become a reality. Ty Cobb banged out 4 hits and the Tigers beat Jack Pfiester, 8–3.

The Series returned to Detroit. Tigers fans were confident that they had now seen the real Tigers and were expecting more of the same. But Mordecai Brown took the slab in Game 4 and he was the whole show. Tinker, Evers, Chance and Steinfeldt gave him sparkling support, but it was Brown's pitching that beat the hardest efforts of the Tigers. Brown laid down a thick coat of whitewash in a 3–0 win. Tinker carried off the fielding honors with two of the prettiest stops and throws of the series, but in one of them he had assistance from Manager Chance who stabbed a high throw to get the runner out. The Tigers now had to win three straight against the Cubs to stay in the game and even the most loyal Detroiters believed this to be an impossible feat.

So it was. Overall took the mound for the Cubs and proceeded to toss another shutout over the American League champions, by a score of 2–0. Manager Jennings was the first to congratulate Manager Chance, rushing to the Chicago bench the minute Kling caught Schmidt's foul fly in the ninth inning.

It was a brilliantly played game, full of pretty fielding and some timely hitting on the part of the Cubs. Evers, Tinker and Steinfeldt worked some sensational fielding plays

A cartoon of the Cubs' World Series win over the Tigers, 1908 (*Chicago Tribune*).

and the Trojan was there with the bat, figuring prominently in both Chicago runs. He started the work in the first round and scored the first run and his clean two-bagger in the fifth brought Kling home with the second. Of the 10 hits made by the Cubs, 7 were made by Tinker, Evers and Chance. The "Peerless Leader" led the team in hitting with a .421. The Cubs thus became the first team to win the Series two years in a row.

On October 15, *The Chicago Tribune* said it all, "Cubs Supreme in Baseball World." The *Tribune's* caricaturist expressed a similar feeling.

In an article titled "Evers Gobbles 'Em Up," the October 14 *Chicago Daily News* had something else to say: "To Evers fell the lot of accepting the hardest of the opportunities offered, and twice he helped Overall keep the hits down to three by reeling off his copyrighted stabs and throws on sharp grounders which were tabbed for hits."

The Cubs were overjoyed knowing they would soon receive another championship medal with rubies and diamonds in addition to a nice piece of cash. In the midst of this celebration, Joe Tinker and the baseball magnates were suddenly hit with court citations that threatened to tie up that cash. Ban Johnson, Harry C. Pulliam and Garry Herrmann in addition to Joe Tinker, had to appear in debtors court because Joseph B. Tinker allegedly failed to pay a cigar and liquor bill when he quit the saloon business in Chicago. The members of the National Commission were named because they were in control of the World Series' receipts of which Tinker would have a share amounting to at least $2,000.

The citation was issued by Municipal Judge Hume on the petition of Charles Ginocchio, a liquor dealer who had been attempting to collect a judgment for $350 against Tinker. The debt was contracted while Tinker was a saloonkeeper in Chicago. The plaintiff asserted that Tinker had declared himself without funds. Ginocchio was now attempting to attach the player's share of the gate receipts to satisfy the judgement. The matter was settled out of court.[144]

With Joe's issue set aside and monies doled out to the players, Johnny Evers was heading back to Troy. He was getting married to one of Troy's prettiest and most charming girls. The date was set for January 13, 1909. Besides buying a ring, he wanted to buy his wife a pair of diamond earrings, a wedding present from him to her. He also wanted to keep the wedding a secret until he and his bride were out of town.[145]

One matter that required his immediate attention was to talk with his partner who had been managing the shoe business in Troy and doing quite well. Up until now the store had been called "John J. Evers."

Johnny wanted to close the Troy store and move the business to Chicago. He wanted to open a large shoe emporium called "Manning and Evers."[146] Johnny was firmly convinced that an emporium in Chicago was a great idea. The entire city knew him by name. His name on the window would attract a flood of business, especially if he was in the store at times to greet customers and to give them his autograph. With the extra income, he and his wife could afford a few luxuries, perhaps a nice automobile.

Joe Tinker had other plans. Exciting plans. He was going on stage. Jake Strand, a booking agent for big time vaudeville, signed him to a contract for eight weeks of winter headlining. The publicity was a natural. But Jake Strand had a problem. Joe hadn't sufficient experience to do a "single" and it was essential to bring him on stage in his baseball uniform to arouse immediate enthusiasm. So Jake decided on a playlet and engaged twenty-one-year-old Sadie Sherman, a seasoned and attractive singer and trouper, to bolster the act.

The problem was how to introduce Tinker in baseball uniform into a strange lady's parlor and why. It stymied Jake's regular staff of writers so he phoned Charles Adelman, a theatre critic and a friend of Joe's. He asked Adelman to meet him and Joe for lunch. Adelman came up with a plot. After appropriate orchestral din, the parted curtain discloses Sadie watching through her window the final play of the crucial Cubs-Giants game and describing it with intense excitement to a friend over the phone.

Sadie works up to the crucial climax when Doyle socks Mordecai Brown's fast one. Then Sadie screams, "It's all over! We lose! What a blow! That ball is never going to come down!" Of course it does. It smashes right through Sadie's window. Is the game lost? Of course not.

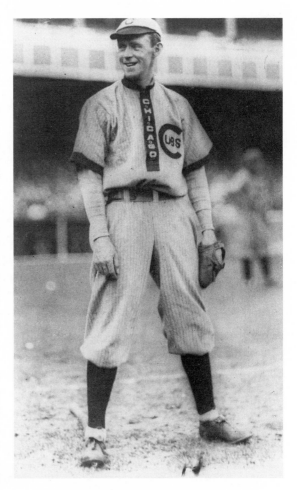

Evers at the keystone sack, West Side Grounds (National Baseball Hall of Fame Library).

Footsteps are heard rushing up the stairs accompanied by a frenzied roll of the drums. In skids our hero, spearing the ball with one hand and shouting, "He's out!"

Triumphant screams from off stage. Sadie throws her arms around his neck and kisses him. Fifteen minutes of pertinent dialogue and a couple of songs follow. When Joe attempts a duet on the last one, the entire orchestra rises, hurling imitation baseballs at him, whereupon he carries Sadie triumphantly off stage.

The rehearsals went very well. On a miserable, cold, muddy day in early November, the tryout of *A Great Catch* was played at a matinee in a small vaudeville house in Blue Island. Fortunately, it was a small audience, mostly children. There were no reporters present. Wily Jake had seen to that because if there were any bugs in the act, the tryout usually exposed them.

Joe had a slight cold and assorted butterflies in his stomach. All worked fine up to the climax when the ball crashed through the window and Joe rushed across stage to spear it. The bugs all came out at once. With the new surroundings and the floodlights in his eyes, the world's greatest shortstop missed the ball by a foot and it dribbled into the pit. Of course the curtain was hastily dropped. Joe was shaking with rage and fright.

"I couldn't even see it," he yelled.

Jake whispered to Adelman, "Can you imagine if that happened during a real performance? It would ruin the guy."

Several hours followed of intensive practice catching the ball from any angle. To make doubly sure, Jake's assistant, who traveled with the show, lobbed the ball through the window himself while the regular stagehand only kicked the box of broken glass at the proper moment. Also, an indoor baseball was substituted for size and it was painted a contrasting tint.

The act was a great hit all around the circuit, especially Joe's first entrance. Needless to say, he never muffed again. A *Chicago Journal* review recognized Tinker as "a refreshing change from most athletic champions who took to the stage—good looking, bore himself like a gentleman, and neither clumsy nor obstreperous."[147] *Variety* gave Joe rave reviews.[148]

While Tinker was prancing about on stage, and Evers was off attending to business and preparing to betroth himself to the lovely Helen Fitzgibbons, Frank Chance and his wife celebrated by buying their first automobile, a Stutz. This was an early version of the 1914 Stutz Bearcat.[149] They headed toward Glendora, California, where Frank and Edythe had already hired contractors. They were eager to see how their magnificent estate was coming along. They had named it, "Cub Ranch."[150] They loved the name and loved the idea of living in a home surrounded by orange groves.

When Chance arrived home however, he was fuming. His negotiation over a new four-year contract with President Murphy did not go well. The discussion resulted in an argument. So Chance called in the press and said he was quitting baseball and offered to sell his 10 percent ownership in the Chicago Cubs.

Harvey Woodruff, representing *The Chicago Tribune* on behalf of the fans of Chicago, went to California in February 1909. With Chance at one end of a telegraph wire in Los Angeles and President Murphy on the other end in The *Tribune* office in Chicago, a compromise was reached for a new contract.

Mr. Woodruff had more to say in a *Tribune* article. "Personally," he said, "Chance is one of the most likable fellows in the baseball profession. His friends are legion. He has no enemies. His players swear by him, and it is their sense of loyalty to his many fine qualities, which has been a great factor in the success of the Cub machine. The retirement of Frank Chance would have been a distinct loss, not only to the Chicago Cubs and the Chicago public, but also to the game of baseball."[151]

1909

Prior to the start of the 1909 season, Frank Chance knew he had problems. Johnny Kling would not be back. He had invested $75,000 in a business venture, had nobody to oversee it and had to stay in Kansas City. Johnny asked President Murphy for an indefinite leave of absence. Murphy granted it in writing.[152]

Chance had Pat Moran as a back-up catcher and could use him part time but he

Sadie Sherman at a party as Mae West, December 22, 1950 (courtesy Gloria Tinker).

needed someone to replace Kling. Unfortunately, he did not find another Johnny Kling. He accepted Jimmy Archer, who had not played ball in 1908. Archer's record was a year with Pittsburgh in 1904, where he got 3 hits out of 21 at bats and a year with Detroit where he came to bat 42 times and hit 5 safeties. Archer was not the razzle-dazzle catcher that Kling was. The Cubs now had a serious weak link on the team.

Another worry was Tinker's insistence that he be given a raise of $1,000 before he agreed to play. He didn't think $1,500 for the season was

Frank Chance and his wife in 1908 in an early version of the Stutz Bearcat (*The Sporting News*).

enough. So Joe did not start the season. He went off to play the vaudeville stage at Havlin's Theater where he could make some real money. Heinie Zimmerman took over Joe's spot for 12 games but the money issue was quickly settled when Joe accepted an increase of $200.[153]

The "Peerless Leader" had another problem that was indeed tragic. He lost Jimmy Slagle. The lad became ill and the doctors said he would never again play ball. So Chance was forced to put his star utility man, Solly Hofman, into the outfield and use John Kane, a new man, as the utility man. This was another weak spot on the team. Kane had a BA of .213 for '08 and would not contribute much hitting power to the team.

There was an even more serious problem. Frank Chance was having agonizing headaches. Although he had missed only 28 games the past year, not the 43 he missed the year before, the pain was getting worse.

Del Howard could take his place at first, just as he did in '07, playing in 33 games and batting .230. In '08, Del was on first in 5 games and in the outfield 81 with a BA of .279. Not bad. Frank knew that Del had had a much better record with Pittsburgh in '05 when he covered the first sack 90 times with a BA of .292. Frank was looking for Del to repeat his '05 performance.

The season started with Frank on the bench because pain was shooting through his head. He couldn't play. His physician told him to get away from baseball for a while, but he refused. There was a pennant up ahead and it couldn't be won by deserting. He was the manager, and he could still issue orders, bawlings out, advice, prayers and protests.

The season moved forward and Frank found he could play more days than not. When not playing, he found it helpful to kick the ball bag. It was a small handgrip in which he carried new and old balls used by his players in warming up before a game.

Kicking the ball bag helped. When his pitcher had two strikes on a batter, then mislaid his control and handed over four balls to the same batter, especially in a close game, the pitcher was not within kicking distance. Bang! There it goes, and the balls that the bag contained scattered hither and thither in the vicinity of the bench, some making it half way to the foul line from the impetus given them by the "Peerless Leader's" right foot. The peerless mind was relieved. It then became the duty of someone on the bench to return the balls to the bag. He put the bag within kicking distance again.

How could Frank Chance not become angry? A pennant was not too far away. He may not have been playing as much as he would like but his presence on the bench made a lot of difference. Cubs didn't feel like loafing or growing careless when "Papa Bear" was watching their every move. They had to be on the jump, or else act as audience to a series of lectures, delivered with much vehemence and containing words easily intelligible and not complimentary. These lectures would be delivered when it was Chicago's turn at bat. When the Cubs were in the field the addresses were prepared and the ball bag helped in the preparation.

When something happened that ought not to have happened, the conversation between Chance and a member of his team started as a dialogue and wound up as a monologue.

"What were you doing on that ball, Heinie?"

"I thought Artie would get it."

This from Zimmerman, and that was where the dialogue part of it ended and the monologue began: "If that's the way you think, you'll be doing your thinking from the bench pretty soon and you won't be getting any money for it either. You fellows are getting balled up like that all the time. What's the matter with you anyway? If they'd scored on that, I'd have put a 'plaster' on you that you'd remember for a while. Now you wake up! Get those fly balls! Keep after them. Artie and Schulte will tell you when they don't belong to you."

A "plaster" was a fine. A "plaster" of the remembered kind amounted to about $50. It came out of the offender's salary on the subsequent pay-day, and usually was returned to him at the end of the season.

Ball players criticized Chance for "soaking" his men too heavily for offenses such as the one cited. The question then arose, if a manager doesn't fine his players, how can he enforce discipline? There were some ball players who played their hardest all the time, who could be managed by orders from the boss. There were others who let up once in a while and upon whom mere words had little effect. Chance could "lick" most of the men on his club. But would that be better than taking their money? Furthermore, the ones who criticized usually forgot to mention that most of the fines were remitted if the "plastered" athlete showed a disposition to try harder in the future. As a matter of fact, the players who had aroused the ire of the "Peerless Leader" to such an extent that he had fined them considerable sums, should have been grateful to him for the good he had done them. He had led them to three pennants and two World Series championships in which they had earned amounts several thousand times the aggregate "plasters."

Some could have argued that it was all luck. That the Cubs had the ability to win all those honors regardless of who was managing the team. That they would have done the same without managing and that Chance couldn't help being a successful leader with such a bunch of talent. It would have been all right to argue those things if they were talking to a convention of milliners. No baseball man would have believed them.

Something besides luck and talent was needed to manage the ball club, even as capable a club as the Cubs. It wasn't luck that kept the men going at top speed all the time. It wasn't luck that selected the pitchers, took them out and put them in with such successful results. It wasn't luck that conceived plays for the undoing of the team's strongest opponents and the upsetting of the most formidable kind of hostile attack and defense. No! It took managerial ability to win even with a good ball club.

Yet, there were times when a game was lost. That's where the ball bag had to suffer pains to show how deadly earnest the "Peerless Leader" was. It actually hurt him to see one of his pitchers slip up in a close game. It hurt him to see a fly ball fall safe between two fielders when one or both of them could have made the catch. It hurt him worse to see one of his Cubs make a brainless play, "pull a bone" when the error resulted in a run. For the error of commission was, in his mind, an accident, while the "bone" could have been prevented if the culprit had been thinking base-ball.

Frank Chance was not popular with all his men, but he had everyone's respect. His players were well aware of the fact that their manager knew baseball from top to bottom, that he was a great ball player himself when well enough to play, and that he could think as quickly as anyone in the game. If there had been any doubt in their minds to his ability, they wouldn't bow so gracefully to his authority.

In fact, Chance was among the most popular of managers. He was the personification of good fellowship off the field. His Cubs liked nothing better than to be invited to smoke, eat or drink with him or to listen when he was in a conversational mood. He was a good talker, a good "mixer" and good company.[154]

The managerial ability of the "Peerless Leader" in 1909 led the Cubs to another terrific season with a 104–49 record, winning 5 more than in '08. But it wasn't good enough. The Pirates were far ahead by Labor Day and there was just no catching them.

It was a firm belief in the Chicago camp that had Johnny Kling played ball that year, the Cubs would have once again taken it all. Del Howard's BA of .197 and Jimmy Archer's .230 were weak spots on the team. Another weak spot was Chance missing 61 games. His headaches had become so severe they incapacitated him. Had he been able to play more games, it could have made a difference, especially in the close ones.

Although the team could not capture the pennant, Johnny Evers must have felt pretty good. He and Joe made up, shook hands and called off the war.[155]

With the season over, Frank Chance went home. He wanted to rest up at his "Cub Ranch." He wanted to read the sport pages from beginning to end, spend time with his wife and walk his dogs.[156] His ranch was the one place where he did not need a ball bag.

While Chance enjoyed sunny California, Joe Tinker signed a contract to play vaudeville. His name could be seen on the marquee of the Empress theatre in Chicago.

Johnny Evers needed more income. He was now the father of a newborn son.[157] Although the Troy store was a good establishment, and Johnny and his partner were seen as promising businessmen, Johnny knew he could earn a lot more in Chicago.

His partner rebelled! He did not like this move to Chicago. He didn't want another place, so Johnny compromised. He continued with the shoe store at Troy and talked with Charley Williams, the secretary of the Cub organization, about Chicago. They decided to become partners. Johnny then began making plans for a large shoe emporium the following year. They decided to call it "Boots and Shoes."

Frank Chance and his wife at their Cub Ranch (courtesy Tom Tinker).

1910

On April 14, 1910, the umpire stood in his place at the West Side Grounds and shouted, "Play ball." Manager Frank Chance and his men were pleasantly surprised to find a remodeled home. Rumor had it that "penny pinching Murphy" had spent a bundle. If true, the players were convinced that he had been put under some kind of voodoo spell.

The "Peerless Leader" smiled at these remarks. The owner of the Cubs had definitely become more reasonable in his expenditures for the team. He also smiled when Johnny Kling came back from his pool hall sabbatical and magnate Murphy signed him to a new contract. Frank Chance was delighted, but his delight soon turned to dismay. Kling couldn't throw the way he used to. He couldn't hit as well. He wasn't as fleet footed as before.

Chance knew that Jimmy Archer would have to back up Kling more than had been originally planned. Archer would also have to cover first when he, the manager, found it impossible to play. The incapacitating headaches troubled him greatly. It bothered him even more when he thought of Tinker, Evers and Chance no longer playing together as often as in the past. He had become accustomed to and fond of the Tinker to Evers to Chance mantra and was determined to be in there as much as he possibly could.

As Chance thought about the rest of the team, he was satisfied with his outfield. He still had Schulte, Hofman and Scheckard. He had a solid infield, men who could play every day. His pitching staff was superb: "Three Finger" Brown, Overall, Reulbach and two new men, Harry McIntire and King Cole. Frank Chance had confidence in his team's ability to reach the top. He also had confidence in his long ball hitters slamming out more home runs since a cork-center ball had just been introduced in an effort to increase hitting.

The Cubs started slowly. The New York and Pittsburgh teams started with a bang. By mid-May, Chance found himself in fifth place. The team then began to play smart

Tinker on stage after refusing a contract without a raise, 1909 (courtesy Tom Tinker).

baseball and had inched into first place by May 25. The momentum continued and the Cubs pulled away by winning close ones. The feats on the diamond were stunning! The cork center ball began to pay off with four-baggers, Wildfire Schulte pacing the way. The Cubs had a commanding lead in July and a fortuitous event was about to create a legend that would forever enshrine Tinker, Evers and Chance in the hearts of baseball fans throughout the land.

Franklin Pierce Adams, known as F.P.A., was the "Lion King" of newspaper columnists in his day. He was born in Chicago and was a die-hard Cub fan. At the age of twenty-two he moved to New York City. Here he worked for the *New York Evening Mail* and had his own column,

"Always in Good Humor." His column was chatty, easygoing and thoroughly charming. Within one week it gained the important right-hand space on page 6, the editorial page. It was syndicated in six newspapers, read by everyone.

In summer, he would journey to the Polo Grounds with his friends, Grantland Rice, Damon Runyon and, when he was in town, Ring Lardner. Often, he bet gleefully against the Giants. On July 11, he and friends watched the Cubs beat the Giants at the Polo Grounds. The one play that F.P.A. must have loved most was the double play in the eighth inning:

Doyle walked. Murray forced Doyle, Tinker unassisted, but when Tinker tried to double up at first and threw wild, Murray took second. Seymour singled to left, sending Murray to third. Becker ran for Seymour. Al Bridwell singled over second, scoring Murray, putting Becker on second. It was Al's third hit of the game. Devlin then hit into a double play, Tinker to Evers to Chance.

F.P.A. won his bet. He left the Polo Grounds feeling good about his favorite team. One week later, July 18, the composition room called telling him his column was eight lines short. Remembering the Cubs-Giants game of the previous week, he quickly scrawled out a poem that was published that day.[158]

> These are the saddest of possible words:
> "Tinkers to Evers to Chance."
> Trio of bear cubs, and fleeter than birds,
> Tinker and Evers and Chance.
> Ruthlessly pricking our gonfalon bubble,
> Making a Giant hit into a double—
> Words that are heavy with nothing but trouble:
> "Tinker to Evers to Chance."

F.P.A. made "Tinker to Evers to Chance" a national catch phrase. It became a diamond chant by loyal fans who trooped out to the West Side Grounds shouting with glee, not allowing patients in the county hospital across the street to finish their afternoon naps.[159]

Years later, on November 24, 1946, F.P.A. wrote Ernest Hemingway a letter that now resides at the National Baseball Library in Cooperstown. It said: "I wrote the double play thing for the *New York Evening Mail* in July 1910. I was the only Cub rooter in the Polo Grounds press box. I wrote that piece because I wanted to get out to the game, and the foreman of the composing room at the *Mail* said I needed eight lines to fill. The next day, T.E. Niles said that no matter what else I ever wrote, I would be known as the guy that wrote those eight lines. And they weren't much good at that."

On July 11, 1910, as the Cubs walloped McGraw's Giants, the team they hated most, they could not have known that the double play combination, Tinker to Evers to Chance, was one week away from becoming immortalized.

After the poem came out, the Chicago Nationals were fighting for first place. It was a tug of war between the Cubs, the Giants and the Pirates. The race was still in doubt by October 1. The Cubs needed a win against Cincinnati to clinch a tie for the pennant. During that game, the Cubs suffered a crippling blow as described by the *Cincinnati Enquirer* on October 2, 1910: "Evers came to bat and got a base on balls. Sheckard sacrificed him to second. Hofman then cut a clean single through to center and Johnny Evers set sail for the plate. Miller's throw home was slow and Johnny saw, while still a few feet from the pan, that it would not be necessary for him to go to the ground. He was all ready to slide however, and the change of mind cost him the use of his leg. As he checked himself, his spike caught in the hard earth near the plate and he toppled over on his side. Even in that position, and with the sharp pains shooting through his broken leg, Johnny's first thought was to touch the plate and score his run. He put his hand on the rubber making sure of the tally and then ejaculated, 'Oh, Lord, my ankle's all gone to hell.' The snap of the breaking bone was plainly heard in the stands and the fans realized at once that Evers had suffered a serious injury. The bone protruded through the flesh and Evers was carried off the field on a stretcher."

The Cubs won that game, 9–6, but Johnny Evers was out of the lineup for the rest of the season. With only two weeks of regular season play left, Chicago romped home with the pennant, 13 games ahead of the second-place Giants. Their pitching staff had an ERA of 2.51. It was Chicago's fourth championship in five seasons and the first time a major league club, after winning three times in a row, then losing, regained the title within a year. It was an excellent show of strength.

The World Series was another matter. For the fourth time in five years, the Chicago team charged into the World Series as heavy favorites. On the other side of the diamond sat the Philadelphia A's, featuring the "$100,000 infield" and four pitchers, each having won more than 15 games that season. The A's needed only two pitchers, Jack Coombs and Charles "Chief" Bender to dispose of the Cubs in 5 games.

The Chicago team avoided a clean sweep by pulling out a tight win in Game 4. Trailing 3–2 going into the bottom of the ninth, they knotted the score on a triple by Chance before putting the game away in the tenth with a two-out single by Jimmy Sheckard. The team batted .222 compared to Philadelphia's .316.

The Series was over. The Cubs were defeated. That was a bitter pill for Chance to swallow, but more bitter was the talk that followed. To hear his club spoken of as "outclassed" almost broke the manager's heart. Nevertheless, he proved a good loser by maintaining silence in the face of all the wild conversation. He knew there would have been none of this talk of difference in class if his pitchers had been at their best. The team looked bad because the Athletics hit as they pleased. He was perfectly willing to admit that the American League champions had won the title because they played better ball, but it was hard not to burst forth in wrath when the "critics" said that the Cubs had no business on the same field with Connie Mack's crowd. The "Peerless Leader," however, held his tongue.

If only Johnny had been able to play, Chance must have wondered. Would that have made a difference? He certainly was badly needed. Heinie Zimmerman had taken his place and he was only 4 for 17 with one extra-base hit and no runs scored for the entire Series. Having "Crab" around wouldn't have hurt.

With no exaggeration, Evers was the heart and soul of the Cubs. His energy had that inexhaustible source of enthusiasm. His tireless activity was a mental tonic for the team. His resourceful brain, a never failing factor of strength. His ready wit, his keen insight, his comprehensive knowledge of the game, his aggressive style of play was an ongoing nerve stimulus to his teammates. He had the ability to wear out the opposing pitcher, to weary him with aggressive, exasperating tactics. He had the speed on the bases and ground covering ability to make him the liveliest wire on the diamond. His aggressive and coordinated efforts with Tinker made it difficult for opposing batters to get on base when a ball was hit on the ground. He and Tinker were better together than they were separately, and that pair could not be duplicated on any other diamond. Without Evers, the infield was sadly shaken.[160]

Suddenly, after the loss to the Philadelphia A's, the Cubs appeared to be an aging team. They seemed to have lost the confidence and the dash that had been theirs prior to the 1910 World Series. The Cubs had grown old, seemingly overnight.

Then again, perhaps it wasn't aging. The "Peerless Leader" played in 87 games out of 154. He was doomed to kick the ball bag as a way of letting out anger and his frustrations. Yet, in spite of blinding headaches, he ended the season with a BA of .298. He had stolen only 16 bases, far from the 67 in '03 and the 57 he had swiped in '06.

Joe Tinker too was not his old self, missing 23 games, needing Heinie Zimmerman to cover short when he was unable to play. Joe managed to finish the season with a BA of .288.

With the season over, Frank Chance returned to the "Cub Ranch" in Glendora, California. Joe Tinker once again signed a contract to tour the vaudeville circuit. Johnny Evers, although on crutches, remained in Chicago. He and Charley Williams had planned on opening their shoe emporium in fall. They anticipated a brisk business. Things however, went badly. The stock did not arrive until the middle of October, causing Evers to miss the valuable fall trade. There was nothing left to do but prepare for the spring trade that was yet to come.

A cold blustery December descended upon Chicago and Johnny was still troubled at having missed the World Series. His leg just didn't seem to be doing well. The doctor could not say he'd be well enough to play again. Maybe yes, maybe no. He tried to resign himself to a future without baseball, but the idea that he was dead timber devastated him. Johnny wanted several more years. He didn't want to be robbed of more time in the game by such a little accident.

During the weeks, when he hobbled around on crutches, it gave him comfort to think about the good years in baseball and the money he'd made. "I'm pretty well fixed," he said to himself, "even if I don't play anymore. I shall be independent the rest of my life." This in itself gave him peace of mind.

Then it happened. On December 16, 1910, Johnny Evers received a telegram from the manager of the local Troy establishment. It said, "If you want your store open next Monday you can open it yourself."

His partner had signed the ultimatum. Johnny received the telegram too late to get the night train for Albany. Had he done so, he would have had the store open on the proper date. As it was, he did not arrive until the night of the day in question. He was still on crutches but went directly to the store. A boy, who did the work there, gave him the key and he went in. The first thing he did was to examine the books. Johnny found that whole pages had been cut out. There were so many conflicting statements; he could make nothing of them. He was forced to call in an expert accountant.

The man spent four days untangling the wreck. When he was through and had sorted out the figures, Johnny found that he had lost $9,600. Other items that appeared later swelled the total past $10,000. All of it wasted through culpable mismanagement.

His former partner had fled south with his family. Manning could be sent to the penitentiary for a year or two, but Johnny decided to do nothing. The money had been gambled away and mere revenge would not bring it back. This initial loss was only the beginning.

A shoe clearing house in Boston gathered information about the

credit of those in the shoe trade. This information was transmitted elsewhere. The news of the serious difficulty of the Troy establishment spread
rapidly. The credit houses, from which Johnny had obtained his stock for
the Chicago emporium, swooped down upon him. They feared that
Johnny was about to declare bankruptcy or would flee for parts unknown.
He told them he would pay if they gave him time. They refused. Within
three months, Johnny Evers was broke. When he figured up his losses, it
amounted to $25,000. His leg injury and the loss of every dollar he had
saved caused him to suffer a complete nervous breakdown. It looked as if
he would never again play baseball. Evers, in his own words, was in a bad
way:

> It might interest those people who are always throwing the harpoon into
> Murphy to know that at this juncture, when it looked as though I might
> never play again, Murphy sent me the best contract for the ensuing sea-
> son that he had ever sent me. He tried to get me to take an ocean voyage
> at his expense. He offered me a great deal of encouragement. I am not
> claiming that Murphy is a saint by any means, but I am saying that many
> things that Murphy has done for which he has been criticized, have been
> duplicated by every other magnate in the game without that criticism.
> Murphy has his faults but so have the rest, and fair play is only fair play.
>
> I won't disguise the fact that that was a dark winter for me. The com-
> fort that I had gained from thinking, that whatever happened to me I
> was comfortable, was gone. It is no pleasant thing to find the savings of
> the best years of your life swept away and yourself in a crippled and
> uncertain physical condition to face the long climb again, once more
> penniless and without resources.[161]

CHAPTER 6

Downhill

Johnny Evers, 1911

Johnny Evers's leg was healed by the start of the 1911 baseball season. He was able to once again occupy the keystone sack. His spirit had been renewed by his ability to play baseball and by the generous contract he had received from Charles Murphy. He no longer felt like a pauper.

Bad luck, however, continued to haunt him. After the season started, Johnny was driving his car with a party of friends, including George McDonald, a newspaperman with the *Chicago Journal*. In crossing a street, a trolley car collided with the auto, smashing it. The entire party was shaken; McDonald was killed. Evers, though having the heart of a gladiator, was devastated. Evers said it was an event that took a long time to get over.

> I was driving the car, and McDonald was sitting in the rear seat. I had been talking to him just a moment before, the next instant he was lying on the ground, fatally injured. He died the next morning. The collision was bad, though I wouldn't have minded that so much. But the shock of that sudden death was more than I could stand. I again had a bad case of nervous prostration and was laid up for a very long time. I wasn't inter-

ested in anything after that. It didn't seem to me that anything mattered. They didn't blame me for it. It was an accident. But even so, a man can't help blaming himself. I felt like a murderer.

Chance and Murphy tried in every way to get me into a more cheerful frame of mind. I used to sit up in the grandstand with Murphy, watching the game, for I couldn't play. I couldn't seem to get interested in it anymore. It is needless to say I wasn't interested in anything else. I don't believe anyone who has never suffered from nervous disorders will understand the moods or actions of one who has. A person will do peculiar things in such cases. I know in my own experience, I couldn't bear to sleep above the second story in a hotel. I could not play but I accompanied the club on the road. When I took my room I had to have one near the ground. It wasn't that I was afraid of fire or anything else, I merely had a nervous horror of being carried up in an elevator. At Boston I was worse than ever. I had gotten into the dumps and went three nights without sleep.

I went to Chance and told him I couldn't play. He said to me, "I know you can't, John, but I was waiting for you to come and tell me so. I didn't want to speak about it, for I didn't want to hurt your feelings." Chance was very kind to me during the season. He let the fellows stay up with me late for company when I couldn't sleep, and was very thoughtful. He sent me away to the mountains to rest. I never knew who did it, but when I arrived at Troy, there was a big automobile waiting for me that took me direct to Camp Totem, where I spent several weeks. I lived out in the open air, went to bed every night at eight o'clock and slept. I had smoked many cigars a day before that time. I couldn't seem to get along without them. But here, the proprietor used to come to me at 7:30 every night and say to me, "Here's your cigar, John," and he would give me one cigar to smoke before I went to bed. I used to miss them very much before that time, but after a while I grew used to it, and the single cigar would satisfy me.

I was in the camp for several weeks and was greatly improved physically when Chance had his famous run-in with Joe Tinker. He suspended Tinker, fined him $150 and had all kinds of trouble. He wired me, "Tinker is out of it for rest of season. If you can play, come back at once." I knew nothing of the circumstances, and supposing that Tinker had broken his leg, wired back, "Will come at once. How badly is he hurt?" Chance replied to this, "He is hurt very badly as to feelings. Come at once." When I arrived I found Tinker back in the lineup playing as good as ever. Expecting to find him badly injured, I need not say how much surprised I was. I played a few games that season but I did not really get into shape until 1912. Then I made up my mind that the only thing I could do under the circumstances was to do my best, and I did. In many ways it was my best season. The story of my appointment to the managership of the Chicago Cubs is well enough known. At first I did not think I could carry the burden of managing. I thought I would break down under it, and I will not deny that I thought so for the first month or two of my work. But you can get used to anything. I am used to the worries of managing now. It doesn't bother me much, and I never felt better in my life.[162]

By the time Evers had been appointed manager of the Cubs in 1913, much had already happened.

Frank Chance, 1911

At the start of the 1911 season, Orval Overall retired, a polite way of saying he quit. He packed his gear and walked out of the clubhouse because of the way Charles Murphy treated him. Johnny Kling was traded to the Boston Braves. Johnny Evers had had a nervous breakdown and couldn't play. Chance too was ailing. The headaches were more severe. A hot day catapulted him into sheer agony. By sheer force of will he struggled through it all and managed the team.

Changes had to be made. Frank Chance wasn't satisfied with Harry Steinfeldt at third and decided to use Heinie Zimmerman. After Johnny broke down, Zimmerman was shifted to the keystone sack. Chance was desperate for a third baseman. George Huff was still scouting for the Cubs and he uncovered two young stars. Jimmy Doyle went right in at third and the position was his the first day he tackled it. The other rookie was Vic Saier, who played first. Joe Tinker was the only veteran on the infield and the outfield was still intact. Jimmy Archer now handled the pitchers from behind the plate.

Considering the drastic changes, and considering the absence of that fantastic double play combination, the Cubs had a good year in 1911, winning 92 games, finishing 7½ games out of first. They just couldn't catch McGraw's Giants.

Although Chance tried, he played in 29 games, had a BA of .241 and swiped 9 bases. Evers played in 44 games, most of them prior to the May automobile accident in which his friend was killed, had a BA of .226 and 6 stolen bases. This was the worst season both of them ever had.

Joe Tinker, 1911

Though the Cubs didn't beat out those hated Giants, the players rose to their finest moments whenever they played John McGraw's men. They derived a great deal of pleasure in defeating the New York team and Joe

Tinker always played a key role in that defeat. This year he had something to brag about, something he would never forget:

> The game that gave me the greatest thrill was on August 7, 1911. I had 4-for-4, 2 singles, a double, a triple, scored 3 runs, executed 2 double plays and stole home on Christy Mathewson. That's something a man tells his grandchildren.
>
> The Cubs, with four pennants and two world championships in five seasons still were on top of the National League on that August day, but closer to a complete collapse than any of us knew. The old lineup had broken up, and young Vic Saier had taken Husk's job at first.
>
> I guess my memory of the game is made keener by the fact that two days before, I'd had a terrific argument with Chance and had been suspended. On Saturday—that'd be August 5—we were playing Brooklyn and out in front 2–1 in the third. There was a strong wind blowing to left field, two were out and two on. The Dodger batter pumped one over my head. I went back and yelled to Jimmy Sheckard, I'll take it. Well, the wind blew the ball out. It dropped safe and two Dodgers scored.
>
> By the seventh we were ahead again, 4–3, and once more the Dodgers had two on and two out. At that time the wind had changed and was coming in from left field. When the batter popped another one over my head, Sheck started in and I didn't move. The wind drove the ball back toward the infield but I thought Jimmy would get it and let it alone. Jimmy couldn't reach the ball and two more runs scored.
>
> When I got back to the bench, Frank, his face red with fury, snarled, "I'm damn sick and tired of you letting those flies drop."
>
> I was just as mad because the Dodgers had scored, so I screamed right back, "I'm sick and tired of you yelling at me."
>
> Husk told me to turn in my uniform and fined me $150.
>
> Well, there was no game on Sunday and Charlie Murphy sent for me to come to his office. He said he wanted Frank and me to straighten things out and I said it would be all right with me.
>
> Now Monday also was an open day but the Giants were coming through and McGraw had agreed to stop off and play a postponed game. So Husk agreed to reinstate me for that game. Chance was a great guy and a square manager. And smart.
>
> Only two games out of first place and going into August, the game looked like the spot for New York to pick up some ground. McGraw had Matty ready to pitch. Chance countered with Brown, who always gave Matty a battle.
>
> There was a good crowd at the old West Side Grounds to see Matty and Brownie. The game was in an uproar before it was one minute old. Brownie hit John Devore in the head with his first pitch and they had to carry the Giant left fielder off the diamond.
>
> McGraw sent Red Murray in to run for Devore and Brownie was nervous. He passed Larry Doyle, and Fred Snodgrass singled to fill the

bases. It looked for a minute as if Brownie wasn't going to last. Then Sheck took Beals Becker's low liner so fast that Murray had to stay on third. Merkle slammed one hard at me and I could have forced Murray at the plate but I tossed the ball to Zim and he whipped it to Saier for a double play.

Sheckard opened our half with a triple on Matty's first pitch. Then Matty guessed wrong when Schulte's bunt didn't roll foul. Archer hit to Matty and Sheck was run down, but Schulte went all the way to third and was nailed at the plate trying to score on Zim's roller. You ran the bases and took the chances for Chance. Zim and Archer tried a double steal but catcher Chief Meyers broke it up easily and we were all square.

I was up second in the next inning and hit a single to left. When Murray decided to throw to first, I went into second and scored on Saier's double to put us one run ahead.

We got all tangled up in the fourth when the Giants tied the score but we got two runs in our half of the inning.

In the sixth I hit off the left field fence for a triple. It might have been a homer inside the park except that Zim got a slow start off first and I had to pull up at third. I think Matty thought I was winded and would rest awhile. But I broke on his next pitch and scored standing up.

When I came up in the eighth, Matty threw me one of those low, outside curves. I hit it for a long double to score Zim and Archer. That was the ball game. We won, 8–6, and made 14 hits. When we got back into the clubhouse, Chance came over to me with a big grin and said, "Damn it, I ought to suspend you every day."[163]

Although the team won many close ones, they could not maintain the pace as the season drew to a close. They finished with a 92–62 record, coming in second to the Giants who won the pennant at 99–54. Considering the inability of Chance and Evers to play as in the past, the team had done fairly well.

Johnny Evers knew that the team would have done better and could have even won the pennant had he been able to play. He also knew that he had to pull himself together. His wife would soon make him the proud father of their second child and he could not let the family down.

CHAPTER 7

Good News and Bad

1912

Good news! Johnny Evers was back full time, feeling great. He was now the proud father of a son and daughter and ready to play ball. Bad news. Jimmy Doyle , star third sacker, suddenly died during spring training from an acute attack of appendicitis. More bad news. Chance would never play again.

The reason Chance had to quit playing spilled onto the pages of the *Cincinnati Commercial Tribune* in an article by Hugh Fullerton

> He and I had a long talk last fall on the eve of his departure for home and he never again would play. He told it to me sadly, for Chance hates to quit, worse perhaps, than any player in the game. His love of baseball is wonderful, and being essentially a leader, he cannot bear to sit and watch anyone else try to fill his place. The job of bench manager is much harder for him than playing would be and the nervous strain of sitting on the bench last season wore him out. Only those inside the club know what suffering Chance endured after he was compelled to stop playing. The fact that his head was almost splitting with a headache that lasted for three months was not the half of it. He raved and raged on the bench, although toward the end he forced himself to be calm and sup-

pressed his feelings, which really was worse than breaking loose and raving.

I was with Chance when his sufferings were worst. For a month after Suggs hit him on the head with a pitched ball, he suffered enough to kill an ordinary man and for weeks remained in the game in spite of it. I begged and pleaded with him night after night to rest, and the big, earnest fellow would only say: "They can't make me quit by hitting me on the head." He did not average two hours sleep a day in that period. He walked the floor many nights, unable to lie down because of the pain.

At times, he would sit in one chair and lay his head on his hands in another and get a few moments' rest before the pain again drove him to pacing the room. The only sleep he got was due to utter exhaustion—sometimes not getting to sleep until almost noon and then going out and playing ball.

One day at St. Louis, he played. He made a base hit that won the game but did not see the ball he hit. A thrown ball from Tinker went past his head, missing it only an inch or two. He never saw it. That night, with a sorrowful kind of a smile he said, "Let's go in to Tony's."

We sat for a long time, almost without talking. Then he said, suddenly and sadly, "I've quit. I had to. I can't see the ball anymore."

The doctors told him he might die at any moment if he continued to play and that another blow in the head meant the end. He didn't care about that. He quit only when he knew that his playing had hurt the team. Death for himself didn't concern him.[164]

Chance finally decided to manage the team from the bench. In mid-summer, while in St. Louis during a hot spell, he suffered so much that he left the team and returned to Chicago. It was soon after this experience that he had a brief talk with President Charles Murphy.

On the night of September 1, while riding from Chicago to Pittsburgh, Chance told several newspapermen of hinting to Murphy that he had better be on the lookout for another manager. He said nothing about giving him a formal notice of quitting. Murphy passed the remark off lightly, saying he expected Chance to be back on the job.

At the same time, on a trip east with the Cubs, Chance told of his examination by a New York physician. This physician had expressed the hope that an operation would restore his health. He said Murphy was in New York and was present at the time of the examination.[165]

On September 12, in a game against the Reds, the Cubs were playing ball as if ordered to lose. Grover Lowdermilk's attempts to pitch were pitiful. He was a badly licked guy, surrendering 11 walks and 10 hits and his mates made 6 errors behind him.

Ralph Works, the ex-Detroiter, pitched in fine style for the Reds, allowing only a double by Vic Saier in the seventh inning. A wild pitch that bounded into the stands let the runner get home. After seven innings the umpire called the game because of rain, darkness and disgust, the Reds winning, 12–1.

On September 19, peevishness among the Cubs was evident just after Brooklyn had trimmed them, 9–6, in the first game of a double-header at Washington Park. When they realized that victory had been tossed away because they couldn't solve Elmer Knetzer, the Dodgers' relief pitcher, the Chicago team growled and snarled at one another until there was open warfare on their bench. According to the story circulated after the trouble, Joe Tinker, who was acting manager in the absence of Frank Chance, called Johnny Evers down for loafing on the bases during a force play. Tinker argued that Evers was tossed out at second, although more aggressive running would have beaten infielder Enos Kirkpatrick's heave.

When the last man had been retired, there was a sudden rumpus on the Chicago bench. Tinker was seen in the act of swinging a blow in the direction of Evers. In the mix-up, it looked as if these star players had clinched. Other members of the team grabbed Tinker's arms and the next moment a plain-clothes detective jumped between the belligerents. It was all over in a minute. During the second game, which the Cubs won by a score of 12–4, Tinker and Evers indulged in several heart-to-heart talks while covering their positions on the field.

On another occasion, Zimmerman caught a fly ball that Archer had called for. They came together with a bump. After some hard looks, Zim threw the ball down in a rage.

On the following day, a Brooklyn newspaper headlined the story, "Chafing Cubs." The secondary headline was as long as it was damning: "Lack of Harmony in Team Publicly Displayed. Acting Manager Tinker's Authority Resented By Infielder Evers to the Point of Fisticuffs on the Bench During a Ball Game."[166]

By the end of the 1912 season, Murphy was feuding with Chance, whom the owner had once called "the greatest manager in the past quarter century." His manager was demanding a new four-year contract and Murphy was reluctant to give it to him. Though the Cubs had won 91 games that year, the team finished third behind the Giants and the Pirates. That the team had done as well as it had despite the death of Doyle and the worst season of Mordecai Brown's career (5–6 record with just 8 starts) was a testament to the "Peerless Leader's" managerial genius. If Chance had to put up with Murphy's interference and mouth, he wanted security and salary to make it worthwhile.

On September 27, 1912, while Chance was recovering in a New York hospital, having undergone an operation for a blood clot on his brain,

Murphy attempted to undermine him when he announced that Chicago did not win the pennant this year because the Cubs were too careless in their habits. He charged some of them with drunkenness. He declared that the players would have to get along for the rest of the season without liquor and that an anti-booze clause would be included in the contract for all Cubs next season.[167]

When Chance was told of Murphy's charges against his players, he didn't hem and haw or decline to speak for publication like most managers do who fear they will lose their jobs if they offend their bosses. Chance boldly came out with a hot retort. He said, Murphy was an "ingrate" and a "cheap liar," that it was his habit to insult the players when they failed to win. Chance went so far as to say that if he remained with the Cubs in 1913, there would be no prohibition clause in their contracts.[168]

Murphy issued a strong statement to the press: "If any member of the Cubs does not like the prohibition clause in our contracts and expresses this opinion either privately or to the newspapers, I will make it a point to trade him off."

With these words, Charles W. Murphy, owner of the Chicago National League baseball team, reiterated his command that his athletes must abstain from intoxicants and then took it two steps further. He demanded that they be in their rooms by midnight and prohibited smoking. The penalty for a violation would be a fine, a suspension, or both.[169]

This statement put Murphy and Chance at loggerheads. Murphy could discharge Chance for insubordination. The sportswriters, however, did not believe Murphy would do so because "without the 'Peerless Leader,' the Cubs would quickly go to pieces." They also believed that if Chance were to leave the Cubs, it would be at his own volition. He had talked of it the previous winter when on his ranch in Southern California, stating that it was an option if the operation on his brain proved unsuccessful. He had finally admitted that he could no longer tolerate the violent headaches. They were simply too much to endure.[170]

In September 1912, Chance rose from his sickbed and defended his players as industrious and sober. He denounced Murphy and revealed his one-tenth interest in the team had been sold (for $150,000). Chance had also agreed to write a column for *The Chicago Tribune*. He asked the fans to support him:

> At the request of *The Chicago Tribune* I have consented to write articles about what may be my last series of games as manager of the Chicago Cubs.... Chicago has been good to me and I have tried to give the best I had. I promised the gentleman who bought my one-tenth interest in the club that I would come back as manager if Mr. Murphy

offered me a fair contract. I am ready to do so. It's up to Mr. Murphy. I have not resigned.

Since my operation I feel much better. The doctor tells me I will be as good as ever next year. Consequently, it is up to Murphy whether I manage the team next year. However, he must give me either a contract as manager or my absolute release.[171]

Above all things, if I do continue to manage the Chicago team, I shall continue to protect my ball players against unjust accusations as I did when they were champions of the world.

The sporting editor told me the fans would want to know just what I thought of the chances of the Cubs against the White Sox...I always expect my own orders to be obeyed by my players, so here it is. I think the Cubs will beat the White Sox.

Naturally, that is what everyone would expect me to say. But I do expect to win. So do our players. We always feel that way. It is one of the reasons why we won four pennants. We expected to win the pennant this year. And I still think we would have won except for hard luck, the worst of which was the injury that put Archer out of the game. I knew all along that if something happened to Archer, we were gone. We cut the Giants' lead down from 16 games to 4 games. Then just when we had them on the run we slumped ourselves and lost our chance.

It was because we expected to win and never gave up fighting that took the pennant in 1908.... I wouldn't give lead money for a ball club that didn't expect to win. A really game club should expect to win every game all season.

I make these statements because I want the fans to know the Cubs.

What we feel is what some of the regular baseball reporters call our "fighting spirit." The Cubs have just as much of that spirit now as ever.[172]

Chance returned to Chicago to take charge of the team in the City Series against the White Sox that began October 8. The Cubs were leading three games to one with only one more game needed for them to claim the town's championship. The Sox took the next two and the series was tied 3–3. During the final game, the White Sox scored 6 runs in the first inning and went on to hammer the Cubs into a disgraceful loss of 16–0. Murphy was so furious he came down from his box seat to the bench and fired Chance. Although the city series was as emotionally charged a competition as the Cubs played all year, the most successful manager in Chicago history was fired after a loss in what amounted to an exhibition game. It was the end of an era.

Johnny Evers was asked to succeed Chance. Murphy offered Evers the five-year contract he had refused to give Chance at a salary of $10,000 a year. Johnny did not immediately accept the offer. He was troubled by the humiliating manner in which Murphy got rid of Frank Chance, someone the Trojan had always admired and looked up to, someone he had called, "the greatest first baseman of all time," someone who had lived up to the demanding title of "Peerless Leader."

The meeting took place at Murphy's residence in Chicago and was opened by Murphy saying, "John, I want you to manage my ball club." Evers expressed surprise and at first he balked. He had always been loyal to his manager and felt uncomfortable in being party to the termination of Frank Chance. He proceeded to ask, "What about Chance?"

The Trojan was then assured that Chance would never again be a member of the Chicago club. If he didn't want the job as manager, there were several others who were ready to step in. Murphy told Evers in substance that he knew he would be severely criticized for letting Chance go as he did, but the criticism would not hurt the owner. Murphy said he did not care if he did not take in a cent at the gate; he had sufficient money to run the club and would play every game the schedule called for.

Under the conditions of the case, Evers thought he should not pass up the opportunity to advance in his profession. Evers remained troubled. He remembered the days when he sat with Tinker and Chance in the clubhouse figuring out new plays. He remembered Chance throwing his fists in every direction when fans at opposition stadiums stormed out of the stands or waited at their bus to assault members of the team. He remembered how he felt in winning four pennants and two world championships with the "Peerless Leader" at the helm. And he felt uncomfortable in taking over a job that belonged to Chance for so many years.

Finally, after Evers assured himself that he was doing no wrong to Frank Chance, he accepted Murphy's offer. It was simply a case of him or someone else getting the job. Evers clearly displayed devotion and loyalty to Chance.[173]

Once Murphy announced that Chance would not be coming back in 1913, Chance gave vent to his feelings: "No manager can be a success without competent players, and some of these I have are anything but skilled. In all the time I have been with this club I have had to fight to get the players I wanted. Murphy has not spent one-third as much for players as have other magnates. How can he expect to win championships without ballplayers?"

According to Chance, when he told Murphy what the other owners were spending for new players, Murphy told him, "If they want to be suckers and pay for it, they can, but I won't."[174]

Before he left, Chance said that he had had to operate under Murphy's cheap reign for the past three years. He said his players would often complain of the low salaries that Murphy was paying them. Chance revealed that in 1906, the year the Cubs won 116 games, he was making $5,500 a year when his less successful rivals John McGraw ($18,000) and Fred Clarke ($10,000) were making far more money than he was. As a farewell statement, Chance brought up Murphy's often-made promise to build a new ballpark. "I'll bet a thousand bucks he never does," said Chance.[175]

Murphy, in his own defense, tried to tell everyone that Chance had resigned. The fans knew differently. On December 7, they read the following story in the *Sporting Life*:

Joe and his wife make a night of it after he asked to be traded in 1912 (National Baseball Hall of Fame Library).

During the past week, the former Cub Manager, Frank Chance, had his household effects shipped to Glendora, California. His house is to be sold in the near future. When the former Cub leader and his wife left Chicago in October, he still was the property of the Chicago club and under promise to return and manage the team if offered a satisfactory contract for next season. This promise was extracted by the purchaser of Chance's tenth interest in the stock of the local club. To keep faith with his purchaser, Chance was unable to follow his own wishes and retire voluntarily from the game. He had to wait to be fired or released from the Cubs."[176]

On December 15, Murphy rid the city of another high-priced star, selling Joe Tinker to Cincinnati. Tinker did not wish to play ball with the Trojan as his manager and asked to be traded.[177] Joe then signed a contract to tour the vaudeville circuit starting the first week of January, just as he had done in the past. He liked the stage. It paid good money. In celebration, he and his wife went out for a night on the town.

Why did Murphy select Evers and not Tinker as manager? One could argue that after conquering his financial problems of 1910 and emotional difficulties of 1911, Evers bounded back onto the diamond in 1912 with an abundance of energy, once again on the attack, giving it his all to win. He and Tinker connected immediately. The chemistry was still there. When Tinker scooped up a ball and flipped it to second without even looking, he knew that Evers was ready with his pivot and they were about to execute a double play.

In regard to hitting, Tinker had done quite well, ending the season with a BA of .282, a 31-point increase over his career average. Johnny Evers, on the other hand, pounded out an amazing record for himself. He finished the season with a career high average of .341, a remarkable feat for the second baseman with a ten-year average of .261. It was as if he was making up for the previous year when he didn't have the energy or ambition to put on a uniform and play ball full time.

It seems reasonable to assume that Charles Murphy saw what a fantastic comeback Evers had made and was confident that he would do the same for the Cubs.

CHAPTER 8

Adrift

Johnny Evers, 1913

The "Trio of Bear Cubs," one of the greatest infield combinations that ever smothered an enemy threat, went their separate ways. These rough, tough, heroes who fought with each other as they fought their enemies, who rode their teammates savagely after every losing game, were indeed adrift, looking for new challenges.[178]

Johnny Evers was now manager of the Cubs. On December 21, 1912, long before the new season started, a general verdict about the Trojan's ability was published in the local press: "Johnny Evers doesn't have the right temperament for a leader. But the responsibility may work a complete change in the great second baseman. Evers's greatest difficulty will be in handling the players, and getting together a ball club that will possess even first division possibilities next year now that the once powerful machine has been left with so many worn out remnants. Victor Saier has developed into a high-class first baseman, but Johnny will have to get a new shortstop to replace Tinker, and his own days of second basing may be shortened by managerial responsibility. His pitching staff is a wreck, and he has only one good catcher. His outfield needs rejuvenation. All in all, Johnny has undertaken no enviable task, but we wish him well."[179]

During spring training in Florida, Johnny issued an order in spite of Charles Murphy's ban on alcoholic beverages. "One beer a day for the Cubs," he said. This order was to let the players know that he was in charge. The Trojan, or "Keystone King" as Murphy had named his new leader, then told the players that he meant to be boss; he was the leader and they must obey his orders implicitly. He said he would adopt many of the rules of his old boss, Frank Chance, and reminded the veterans that they must set an example for the recruits.[180]

Just before the season started, an April 19 article in Chicago's *Gazette Times* did not paint a good picture of the new era in Cubs baseball:

> Don't imagine that managing a big league ball club is an easy task. Likewise, don't think that John Evers's initial flier into the ranks of pilots is a "joy ride" for the little second sacker. It is anything but that, and to know that the Cub leader is already worrying over his job, one need only to take a good look at him and note the change that has come over him since the Cubs went into training less than two weeks ago.
>
> Evers has actually aged. The lines in his face have deepened, and it is evident that he is finding the burden of a big league ball club a little more than he reckoned with before he took the job vacated by the former leader. Not only has the ball club itself been a nightmare to the Trojan, but he is bothered by the fact that he is being penned more or less by scribes who are peeved by Murphy's ousting of Chance, and who are venting their feelings on the successor of the "Peerless Leader."
>
> All this works on the mind of Evers, who even as a player was highstrung and sensitive. With the added responsibilities, he is irritable, nervous and lacking in patience. He has shown this by his actions on the field when players would not obey his commands as quickly as he wished. Not that Evers wishes to be a stricter disciplinarian than his predecessor, but nature did not endow him with the disposition of a natural leader, hence his tendency to crab.[181]

And crab he did. The pitchers of the past were gone. Evers expended so much energy on the mound in persuading pitchers to put the ball over the plate, that when pitchers did give the Cubs fielding chances to save a game, the Trojan assisted in blowing the chances.

Evers saved his worst vitriol for umpires and suffered numerous suspensions. Charles Murphy offered him a new suit if he would go two weeks without being ejected from a game. Evers won that suit but was thrown out of a game the day after he collected his prize.[182]

His worst arguments were with Bill Klem, with whom he got into a real doozie of a screaming match. There were other suspensions that had nothing to do with the umpire's decision-making ability. At times, it had to do with the umpire's past life, something that was not very flattering.

Johnny got one on umpire Cy Rigler but was obliged to wait six weeks before he had an opportunity of landing it on the umpire. While in Chicago, Evers was told that before Rigler entered the big show he was employed in a little town in Illinois where he used to take care of the baseball grounds in the morning and then umpire the games in the afternoon. Evers did not forget it. He waited for a chance to tell Rigler he knew of his former duties and the chance came one afternoon in Chicago. The Cubs were in the field with Ed Reulbach pitching and an opposing base runner on third. The Cubs were signaled to play in to cut the man at the plate. Suddenly, the visitors protested claiming that Reulbach's foot was not on the rubber. Rigler ran to the box, pulled a little broom out of his trousers' pocket and proceeded to sweep off the rubber. While the umpire was engaged in sweeping, Evers, only a few feet away, whispered: "Well, Rig, I see you're back at your old job taking care of the grounds." Infuriated, Rigler stopped sweeping long enough to banish Johnny from the field.[183]

Johnny Evers always had it in for umpires, especially poor umpires, those he considered not knowledgeable enough about baseball to make a proper ruling. Evers knew the game backwards and forwards, going to bed every night with two candy bars, *The Sporting News* and the rulebook. Johnny was considered to be the brainiest player in baseball. He was also considered the most obstinate man in the game. He earned the nickname "Crab" because of his untiring devotion to the proper way of playing the game—and not letting anyone forget it.

He was now trying everything he could to move his team forward and his loyal fans in Troy loved him. So on May 10, they invaded New York to hold an "Evers Day" parade at the Polo Grounds where the Cubs were scheduled to play against John McGraw's Giants. Final arrangements had been completed on May 7.[184]

Brigadier General John McGlynn and his army marching band of fifty pieces boarded the train in the morning while 2,000 rooters had already gone down the Hudson the evening before. Plans called for Mayor Cornelius F. Burns to lead the entire Troy contingent across the big ballpark in the afternoon, and for two of the leaders of the delegation to pose with Johnny.[185]

With the festivities over, the umpire hollered, "Play ball." Evers played a brainy, clever game. In the sixth, with the game scoreless, he slammed a hit through Buck Herzog. Mike Mitchell reached base, Art Phelan sacrificed and Vic Saier drove a long fly to score Evers. The Troy crowd roared and the band struck up, "When Johnny Comes Marching Home Again."

New York tied the score in the seventh, but Chicago won the game in the eighth. Ward Miller rapped an easy one to Herzog, who threw low to Fred Merkle. The ball rolled to the stands and Miller went to second. Evers placed a hot liner down the third base line about two feet from Herzog and only six inches inside fair territory. It rolled to deep left while Miller scored. Evers was subsequently thrown out at the plate on Phelan's easy grounder but the run was enough to win the game by a score of 2–1.

Sitting on the Giants' bench was Joe Evers, Johnny's brother. John McGraw had taken him to the spring training camp to see if he had the potential of becoming a star.[186] It was Joe's first and only game as a major leaguer and he was used as a pinch runner. He was in a terrible predicament. Being a Giant, he could not root for the Cubs. Being Johnny's brother, he could not pull for the Giants. A scoreless tie would have suited Joe fine, but it was not to be.

Johnny Evers saw to that. Of the three hits which Al Demaree, the opposing pitcher allowed, Evers made two, scoring the first run himself and driving in the winning run.

Johnny was surrounded at the plate as his long-time friends and neighbors took turns shaking his hand. The family grocer had his place in line and gave Johnny the tightest grip of all. Girls in the grandstand that Johnny saw home from parties in the olden days, looked envious because they couldn't take the little Trojan Cub by the hand and tell him how glad they were to be there. Orders from the megaphone helped clear the field. This gave the Giants a chance to complete the game. After it was over, John McGraw was given a silver trophy.

Mayor Burns then addressed his remarks to Troy fans and to the idol of Troy: "I have been delegated to present you with this handsome, silver loving cup, which is symbolic of our esteem. We wish you well Johnny Evers. May your success continue."[187]

For a while it did. On July 4, *The Chicago Tribune* reported, "Timely Cub Hits Beat Redlegs, 5–1." On July 6, *The Chicago Tribune* headline announced, "Cubs Pound Ball in Comedy Game; Beat Reds, 12–6." It went on to say, "In a game of many base hits and many blunders, the Cubs crushed Joe Tinker's remodeled Reds yesterday at the West Side. Fourteen base hits for a total of 22 bases tell of the prowess of the Trojans in figures, and accounts for most of the 12 runs.

"In the last of the fourth the Reds crumbled. With two on and one out, Manager Evers clouted one to the fence in left center and by splendid leg work made a homer of it, sending in two others ahead of him. A base on balls, an error, a couple of stolen bases, two singles, and a triple

Troy delegation leaders honor Johnny's first appearance in New York as the Cubs' manager (National Baseball Hall of Fame Library).

followed the drive before Johnson could retire the side. This whole mess netted seven runs."

By July 9, just days later, the Cubs were not doing well. Johnny Evers tried to extract some kind of magical effect from his pitching staff, but they simply didn't have the stuff. In a game against the hated Giants, the Cubs started lambasting Jeff Tesreau in great style in the sixth. They combined five clean, lusty swats, two of them for extra bases, for four richly deserved tallies. They looked quite ample, until Jimmy Lavender's hurling fell apart. Evers held extended confabs with his pitcher without result. Lavender remained groggy and the Giants won their third in a row.

Two days later, the Giants crushed, ripped and wrecked the Cubs, 14–4. Not only were the Cubs trounced, they were thoroughly disorganized and routed at the finish, being deprived of their leader early in the fray when Evers was ejected after a close decision at second base in the third inning.

The struggle to maintain a challenging position in the race became more difficult when Cub catcher Jimmy Archer injured a finger. On July 18, he reported to Evers that he couldn't play against Boston because his split finger was still in bandages. So the Trojan pushed on with the players he had. For the opposing team, he continued to be the most annoying of base stealers. He took long leads, up on his toes all the time, doing a little dance and edging toward the next base.[188]

When the Cubs moved into Pittsburgh on September 25, Evers led the onslaught with 2 doubles and 2 singles in 4 times at bat and scored 3 runs, trouncing the Pirates 7–1. In addition to being seen as the sparkplug of the club, he was also seen as a "snarling, aggressive grouch" by the New York press.[189]

The turmoil Evers was under was easily seen by the weary look on his face and his wan complexion. He was far too thin for the proper build of an athlete but he played like a baseball maniac, with an unquenchable fire of enthusiasm. His wiry frame was capable of standing a world of fatigue because his gameness knew no limit. He simply continued on. It was sheer determination, dogged perseverance and grit that made him great.

Unfortunately, his boss didn't see him that way. According to Sam Weller of *The Chicago Tribune*, he had had several run-ins with Murphy, and only the success of the Cubs during the last six weeks of the season kept Evers from being fired. Wrote Weller: "Long before the season was over Evers had confided to some of his friends that he didn't feel sure of his job, and in reality was manager in name only because he dared make no move of consequence without the sanction of Murphy. He explained that his financial condition compelled him to stick to the job no matter how unpleasant it might be."[190]

Chicago finished the regular season at 88–65, nipped out of second place by Philadelphia with an 88–63 record. The Giants marched to the pennant at 101–51. Now came an exhibition game in Champaign, Illinois, and the inter-City Series with the White Sox.

The old White Sox spirit was still there and it kept Chicago in a whirl until it came to a climax on October 13, when the "South Siders" crushed the Cubs by a score of 5–2. The Sox won the series by terrific and timely batting. When the Cubs went out in front by counting once in the first half of an inning, the Sox came right back in their half with a storming assault and drove in more than one run. Although the Cubs lost, the team went on to divide $14,530, their share of the take for the series.

Charles Murphy also received extra money from the games but it was not enough to salve his anger over his team's third-place finish. He fired Evers several months later and hired Hank O'Day, the umpire who sided with the Cubs in the Merkle game in 1908. Johnny was as mad as a wet hen when he heard he was replaced by an umpire and made no pretext to hide his true feelings. "Frank Chance had the right dope on Murphy," said Evers, "only Chance did not put it half strong enough. I will not play for Murphy again under any conditions, and that goes!"[191]

The first intimation that Murphy intended to depose Evers came days before the firing when Murphy discussed at some length the advisability of having a bench manager instead of one playing the game. He closed his discussion by declaring that Evers's bad judgment had enabled the White Sox to defeat the Cubs in the fall series of 1913.

> We ought to have beaten the White Sox easily and would have licked them if the team had been properly handled. Evers's bad judgment cost us the series. The worst case of bad judgment was in the fifth game, the one that Benz pitched against us, and won in eleven innings by a score of 2–0. Cheney was pitching for us and neither side had scored when we went to bat in the last half of the ninth. We had made just one hit off Benz, but Archer opened the last of the ninth with a base hit. Right there is where Johnny erred. He should have put a fast man in to run for Archer and a pinch hitter for Cheney. That decision cost us the game.[192]

According to Evers, he asked Murphy for a new contract, which the owner construed as the manager's resignation.

> Murphy claimed I was responsible for the loss of the City Series. The reason for this was that I allowed a pitcher to bat in turn instead of sending in a pinch hitter. If my judgment was poor, Connie Mack's judgment during the last World Series was worse—and there you are!
>
> Murphy, however, called it bad baseball and said that I had cost him at least $10,000 in cash. This was because the series only went six games instead of seven. The proceeds of the extra game, as Murphy figured it, would be about $10,000.
>
> But I made him $250,000 when I pulled the play on Merkle in 1908. If not for that play, Murphy would have lost the big money he made in the great playoff game with the Giants, the receipts of the 1908 World's Series and the big receipts the club took in 1909 with its prestige as world's champions.
>
> The beginning of my dismissal dates back to the signing of the contract. I thought it gave me an appointment for five years. I was glad to be honored with the managership of what had been the greatest club in the world, and signed willingly enough, scarcely reading the contract at all.
>
> William Locke, the unfortunate president of the Phillies, who died last year, was witness to the contract. He told Ban Johnson, the president

of the American League, that I had signed over a trap door. As he explained it, the contract permitted Murphy to terminate the agreement in accordance with his own sweet will.

The "Evers Deal" was one of the turning points in baseball history. Charles Murphy, a disturbing element in the National League, flouting an ethical contract, fired his manager with scant ceremony. In doing so, he overreached himself. It was Murphy who was banished from the game. Evers, far from being a loser, in one bold stroke won back the $25,000 he had lost in the disastrous shoe venture.[193]

Lucky Johnny. After being fired, he learned that Murphy was going to trade him. He threatened to jump to the Federal League, a third major league that was then being formed. The rest of the National League club owners, already gearing up to do battle with the newcomers (whom they viewed as brazen interlopers and worse) were appalled at the idea that one of the league's top stars was essentially being forced into the ranks of the "outlaw" league. So Murphy was summoned to a meeting in the office of league president John Tener. Present at the meeting was Charles Taft of Cincinnati, who had originally bankrolled Murphy in the Cub venture. Tener, Taft and various league officials informed Murphy that baseball no longer needed his services. Murphy's dignity was comforted by approximately $500,000 that Taft coughed up for Charley's 53 percent interest in the club. Taft then appointed Charles Thomas to run the club for him.[194]

When the dust had settled, Evers, who had been fired as manager, considered himself a free agent. So Johnny sold himself for $25,000 to the Boston Braves.[195]

He could have made much more had he signed with the Federal League. They had offered him a five-year contract at $15,000 a year and a $30,000 signing bonus. To try to sway him, the Federal League official offering the contract, counted out thirty $100 bills in front of him in the Knickerbocker Hotel in New York. That money could not buy Johnny's integrity. He insisted on maintaining his loyalty to the National League.[196]

Be that as it may, he had money. So he took $15,000 from his small fortune and announced that he was going to build a home in Troy such as he wanted all of his life.[197]

Joe Tinker, 1913

As Johnny Evers tried to deal with his ups and downs, so did Joe Tinker. He had been traded to Cincinnati where he became player–manager for the Reds. This happened at Tinker's instigation, not wanting to play in Chicago under the managerial tutelage of Johnny Evers. Tinker had nurtured a friendship with Garry Herrmann, the Cincinnati owner, and arranged his own trade. He left his wife and kids in Chicago until he was certain about his future.

Tinker had taken on the unenviable role of player-manager for the hapless Redlegs. Between 1901 and 1912, the team finished in the top three only once, that being in 1904 when they came in third behind Chicago's second-place finish.

Even before the season started, Tinker knew he had a difficult task in trying to move the team forward from its fourth-place finish in 1912. The problem was pitching. George Suggs, who had a 19–16 record in 1912, didn't seem to have the stuff to equal his record of the previous year. Rube Benton had an 18–21 record in 1912, but his control had gone south. Tinker, however, now had "Three Finger" Brown, his former teammate. He was hopeful that Brownie could again become the dominant pitcher he had once been. Tinker also had Johnny Kling, another former teammate. He was hopeful that with Kling and Tommy Clarke behind the plate, they could help the pitchers deliver the right pitches at the right time.

It was not to be. On July 4, *The Chicago Tribune's* headline announced, "Timely Cub Hits Beat Redlegs, 5–1." On July 17, *The Tribune* again announced, "Giants Take All From Tinkers, 5–3." It went on to say: "The Giants made a clean sweep over Cincinnati, winning the fourth game of the series 5 to 3. The visitors got a two-run lead in the second inning, but Suggs blew up in the fourth, and the locals scored three runs on singles by Burns, Fletcher and Merkle, Doyle's double, and a wild throw by Suggs.

"Packard relieved Suggs in the fourth and pitched well, although New York made use of all its three hits, scoring one run in the fifth and tallying again in the eighth.

"Tesreau pitched an unsteady game for New York but tightened in the pinches and received fine support. Manager Tinker, of the visitors, was ordered out of the game in the fifth inning for objecting to Umpire Orth's decisions."

Joe Tinker was under tremendous stress prior to this game. It says something of his character that he was even there. On July 15, The *New York Times* carried an article titled, "Tinker's Blood for Wife." The paper reported the serious condition of his wife:

> Joe Tinker, the shortstop and manager of the Cincinnati Reds expects to leave for Chicago today with the object of having a transfusion of his

blood to his wife, who is seriously ill. It is understood that Tinker will not be able to play for several weeks.

The Cincinnati team is playing a series with the Giants at the Polo Grounds, and before the game, Tinker received word from his wife's physicians. He knew what was ahead of him but he played through the game. Up to a late hour he had received no word, but is ready to start for Chicago at noon today.

Last week the Reds played in Brooklyn, but the manager remained in Chicago for a few days and his wife's condition improved. The physicians decided that any serious development would necessitate a transfusion of blood to save her life. Tinker volunteered. The message yesterday telling Tinker to be ready for a call today was a sad blow to the ball player, for he knew that the critical turn was near. He patiently waited last night for a message calling him to his wife's bedside but none came. The other players fear that Tinker, unable to stand the anxiety, will leave for Chicago today anyway.

This is Tinker's first season as manager of the Reds. The club is in last place in the National League race and only lately has started to play winning ball. The team has shown great improvement under his management. He has had a hard time weeding out the dead wood and adding new players. An able player and a natural leader himself, baseball men believe that the club would be well up in the league race before the close of the season if Tinker could hold on.[198]

Ruby Rose Tinker made it through a difficult time and Joe returned to Cincinnati. He tried to move the team upward by walloping the ball harder than ever. When the Reds played the Giants, Joe continued to hit Christy Mathewson as if he owned him, but even Tinker's bat could not prevent Matty's team from taking five out of five against the Reds. By going undefeated against Tinker's Reds in 1913, Christy Mathewson, in one sense at least, gained a bit of revenge against the Kansas farm boy who had so often befuddled him.

The Reds finished the season in seventh place with a dismal 64–89 record. Tinker had gained more batting power after he turned thirty. He hit 20 doubles, 13 triples and 1 homer and led the team in batting with a career high of .317. In the field he posted a .968 average at shortstop, more than 30 points above the league norm. The team as a whole had a BA of .261, but the real problem was pitching. George Suggs dropped from a 19–16 in 1912 to 8–15 in 1913. Art Fromme went from16–18 to 1–4. "Three Finger" Brown never caught fire like in the old days with the Cubs. His 1913 record was 11–12.

With the Reds having slipped from fourth place in 1912 to seventh in 1913, regardless of why, Tinker was viewed as a poor manager. Herrmann sold him to Brooklyn owner, Charles Ebbets for $15,000 and agreed to pay Tinker $10,000 for signing a Brooklyn contract. Although Joe was unhappy about going to Brooklyn, he perked up when he heard about the $10,000 cash bonus that he was to receive.

Cincinnati's board of directors challenged club owner Gary Herrmann's right to sell Tinker and repudiated the deal. Ebbets promptly denounced the board and wanted to know whether Herrmann was president of the club or an office boy. Herrmann angrily demanded to know the answer to that one, too. While the battle was in progress, Murphy, who still owned the Cubs, stepped in with a crack that, having had Tinker once before, he would like to have him back.

Ebbets accused Murphy of tampering with the player and hurled threats of drastic action against him. Tinker told the Chicago newspapers that he would rather return to that city than go to Brooklyn. After a few days of lively firing on all sides, the Reds directors apologized to Herrmann and approved the deal. Murphy backed off. Ebbets sent a check to Cincinnati for $15,000 and dispatched his Manager Wilbert Robinson to Chicago with a check for $10,000 to Tinker, plus a contract for Joe to sign. When Robinson got off the train he was met with the news that Tinker had signed with the Federal League.

Ebbets got his $15,000 back from Herrmann, branded Tinker a traitor and swore the shortstop would never be allowed to play in organized baseball again. Tinker, unmoved by his wrath and that of the other owners, took over as manager of the Chicago Federal League club. His presence in the new league caused other headline players to follow him, some having been recruited by him in person. Ebbets's colleagues were unanimous in decreeing that the renegade must be barred forever.[199]

Tinker told *The Sporting News*: "I wanted to know where I stood, as to whether the story of the $10,000 bonus was really true. I wired Ebbets and asked him if he would be in Indianapolis on the following day but got no response. The deal with the Federal League had been completed and I decided to cast my fortunes with them."[200]

In regard to his being disbarred from organized baseball, Tinker told *Baseball Magazine* that he now owned a motion picture theatre in Kansas City and a big fruit farm about twenty miles from Portland, Oregon.[201] Joe Tinker had let it be known that regardless of what happened, he was fixed financially and his family would not starve. It was Joe's way of demonstrating his independence and defiance of organized baseball.

The new league had declared war on major league clubs on October 14, 1913. The Federal League directors at Indianapolis were hammering out their future. Edward Steininger, president of the St. Louis Federal League baseball club, asserted that war on the major leagues was under-

DEPARTMENT OF BUILDINGS

CITY OF CHICAGO

CITY HALL

APPLICATION FOR BUILDING PERMIT

Commissioner of Buildings,   *March 5th* 191*4*

City of Chicago.

Dear Sir—

Application is hereby made for permit and use of water for building to be erected on

Lot......*Entire*......Block *14 of Loflin Smith + Dyra Subdivision of the N.E. 1/4 (except 1.28 acres in N.E. Corner) of Sec 20 T. 40 NR 14 E*

Street and Number *1000 to 1052 Addison St. + 3601 to 3605 N. Clark St*

Owner *Chicago Federal League* Address *1052 Addison St.*

Architect *Zachary C. + Charles G. Davis.* Address *Steinway Hall Chicago*

Mason Contractor *Blome Sinek Co* Address *City Hall Square Bldg*

Carpenter Contractor......*do*......Address......*do*

Use to which buildings will be put *Grand Stand* No. of Stories *One*

Length *800* Breadth *100* Height *56* Brick or Frame *Steel + Concrete*

Number of Brick *160 M* Number of Cords of Stone......

Number of Cubic Feet of Concrete *452m* Number of Cubic Feet of Hollow Tile *1900*

No. of Yds. of Plastering *1700*

Total Cost of Building *$250 000*

Remarks:...

....

....

....

The applicant hereby certifies to the correctness of the above.

Signature *Blome Sinek Co*

Address *City Hall Square Bldg*

The application to build Weeghman Park, now known as Wrigley Field (Raymond Kush).

way: "We are going to invade the majors and take some of their players," declared Steininger, "There are players who are dissatisfied with the salary and the treatment they have received this season and we have every reason to believe we will secure what players we choose to take into our organization."[202]

Federal League owners geared up for action. Ballparks were on the drawing board. In Chicago, an application for a building permit had been completed. Plans were made to hire 350 men to work on the structure and 140 on the landscaping. The estimated time to complete the new field, to be called Weeghman Park, was just seven weeks.[203]

Frank Chance, 1913

While Joe Tinker and Johnny Evers were trying to find their ways as managers, Frank Chance decided to continue as a manager, albeit in a different location. He signed on with the New York Highlanders, who changed their name to Yankees.

Chance had every reason to believe that he was now in excellent shape. A news release in New York on December 25, 1912, confirmed what he had been told by Dr. W. G. Frolich, the surgeon who had operated on him. The doctor reported

I will stake my reputation in asserting that Frank Chance is in better health than for the past six years. The operation I performed in September completely cured him of a nervous trouble which had caused frequent headaches and compelled him to give up ball playing. This ailment had been caused by being hit on the head by pitched balls. Chance was not treated for mental troubles. He recovered from the operation rapidly and before he left me he promised to come back if there was a return of the ailment.

As Chance's health continued to improve he notified me while in Chicago in October that he felt so well that he decided to go to his home in California. I have heard stories possibly circulated to injure Chance, but you can quote me as saying they are entirely without foundation and have been prompted by malice. Chance is not only able to manage the Highlanders with all of his former skill, but I believe he will be playing ball again next season. He has a rugged constitution and a remarkable will power.

His ailment was never serious and I have treated many similar cases successfully. In justice to Chance I make this statement, absolutely sure of my ground. This opinion coincides with that of several specialists who have examined Chance in California. President Farrell has received positive assurance that the "Peerless Leader" is once more the same robust man who led the Cubs to victory in four pennant races and two world's championship series."[204]

Frank Farrell, owner of the American League club, signed Chance to a three-year contract. Neither Chance nor Farrell stated the terms, but estimates of Chance's annual salary ranged from $10,000 to $25,000, with the probable figure being around $12,000. Chance was also to receive 5 percent of the net profits of the club, which would net him about $50,000 for his three years of service.

The signing of Chance was viewed as an excellent move by Farrell, whose team was still years away from becoming a dominant force in the American League. Chance, he hoped, would give the team the kind of leader it needed to bring the club to a higher position than it had held for many years.[205]

Without talent to work with, the "Peerless Leader" began looking for ways to reshape the team. The hunt was on for new players. His success in rebuilding the Yankees can best be told by a newspaper report of the game between the Tigers and Chance's team on September 16, 1913. It said: "Detroit, by winning from New York, 7 to 5, evened up the series and prevented Chance's men from moving into seventh place. Detroit won in the ninth when Willett doubled with two out and drove in Gibson and Louden. Outside of the battery, Chance did not have a man in the lineup who was on the team at the opening of the season."[206]

Frank Chance tried to instill a winning attitude in the team as he had done with the Cubs, but the chemistry was not there. Tinker and Evers were not there to spread the *fire* and *spirit* needed to win ball games. Chance even missed the constant chatter from the second base spot and would have given anything to once again listen to the nervous, intense "Crab," jawing it out with the umpires. He even missed the arguments he had had with Tinker, whose temper flared during the intensity of the game. He definitely had nobody like Tinker, who could come up with a clutch hit and drive in the winning run in tight games. Tinker was the greatest clutch hitter he had ever seen. Yes, Chance missed both of them.

He even missed treating them harshly when the occasion arose, and was determined to treat his new players no differently than the old. He remained a strict disciplinarian and dealt with players severely when they did him dirt, like the day he discovered first baseman Hal Chase was making fun of him.

Chance was deaf in his left ear. So when he and the players were on the bench, Chase made sure he sat on Chance's deaf side, mimicking his manager's throaty commands and imitating his facial expressions, a pastime for which Hal had a real gift. When a player loyal to Chance told him what Hal had been up to, Chase suddenly found himself traded to the White Sox. Chance could have pummeled the man, but it was the rare player who offended Chance sufficiently to cause a fight.

In exchange for Chase, New York acquired Rollie Zeider and Babe Borton, two players who, Frank Chance believed, would bolster the team. Not so. The "Peerless Leader" soon filed a letter of protest to the league, claiming that Zeider was not in proper condition to play baseball. Borton, on the other hand, couldn't hit. Chance lost his protest. Later however, Borton was transferred to minor league Jersey City.[207]

The season ended with New York managing to squeak ahead of last-place St. Louis, finishing seventh with a 57–84 record as compared to the 57–86 Browns. Chance returned to his Cub Ranch in Glendora, California, and took comfort within the beautiful orange groves that surrounded his home. At times, he just didn't feel well. His illness finally took hold of him and he could not tend to the orange groves or other responsibilities that went along with managing the ranch. His brother-in-law Karl Pancake moved in to manage his affairs.

CHAPTER 9

Landing on
Foreign Shores

Frank Chance, 1914–1915

Frank Chance returned to his managerial role for the New York Yankees in 1914. The team was in even worse shape than the 1913 version. Russ Ford, one of his "better" pitchers, with the unenviable record of 11–18, was gone. Ray Fisher had signed on, but the record books could not predict a promising career for this young man coming off an 11–17 mark in 1913. The other pitchers had been even worse.

As the season moved forward, Chance found no reason for optimism. The Yankees again finished in seventh place and Frank Chance was forced to retire because of ill health. Before returning to his ranch in California however, he traded in his worn and weary Stutz for a new Bearcat. He wanted to drive home in comfort and style.[208]

The identity of Frank Chance's first automobile became an issue after finding literature claiming that Frank bought a Blitzen Benz in 1908. According to Stan Peschel of the Daimler Chrysler Corporation in Stuttgart, Germany, where the Benz line was manufactured going back to the early 1900s, the radiator and hood proved the car was not a Benz.[209]

Robert Rosencranz of Highland Park, Illinois, an antique car hob-
byist, agreed. He said that Frank's car did not have a chain drive. Benz
autos had one. Robert went on to say that the filler cap on the radiator
and vertical slats on the side made it look like an early version of the
Stutz.[210]

Johnny Evers, 1914

While Frank Chance struggled to create a capable New York Yankees team, Johnny Evers, the new captain of the Boston Braves, was busy
creating a miracle.

On March 1, 1914, he was interviewed by a *Chicago Tribune* reporter
who wrote: "Johnny Evers, deposed manager of the Cubs, will leave tomorrow morning for Macon, Ga. to join the Boston Braves in their training
camp. He finished packing the household goods yesterday and had them
shipped to Troy, N.Y. where he will take up his permanent residence once
more. 'I'll be back in May,' said the Trojan, 'but it will be with the visiting club and I'll be fighting to beat my old club. I'm perfectly satisfied
with my new place and besides getting a lot more money than I would
have received here, I'll be relieved of the worry of managing the team.'"

In 1913, under new manager George Stallings, the Braves had ended
the season in fifth place, their best finish in eleven years. By mid-1914 however, they were in last place, 15 games back. They even lost an exhibition
game against employees of a soap company.

Then the miracle happened. With a come-alive double play combination of young, fun-loving Rabbit Maranville and old, irascible Johnny
Evers, and a red-hot pitching staff anchored by new acquisitions, Bill
James and Dick Rudolph, the Braves won 52 of their last 66 games. They
swept past the defending National League champion New York Giants
so fast that they clinched the pennant in early September and went on to
win the flag by 10½ games.

The fans in Boston were jubilant. They stormed onto the field and
held Evers high while they crowded around him and shouted for joy. On
September 16, there was an "Evers Day" in Boston. With the team on the
infield, Johnny was presented with a silver tray and tea service in appreciation for what he had done to help the Braves win the pennant.

The Braves were far from done. They toppled the world champion
Philadelphia Athletics (the team with the "$100,000 infield" and pitch-
ers like Chief Bender, Eddie Plank, and Jack Coombs) in four straight
games in the World Series.

**Boston fans hoist Evers on their shoulders after the miracle Braves clinched
the pennant in 1914 (University of Notre Dame).**

The two main players given credit for this miracle were Captain
Johnny Evers and pitcher Bill James. These two were involved in a bitter intra-club feud that never was settled. The pitcher, graying and bespec-
tacled James, at age 72, told the story to *Baseball Digest*:

"Evers's temperament was as famous as his second base skill. He was
a legend in mid-career because of having keyed the Cubs' immortal Tinker to Evers to Chance triumvirate. He never doubted his value to the
Braves.

"He was good for our club, we needed him. He gave the club spunk.
His spirit caught fire and I think that was largely responsible for our success, but ... we never got on very well together. I got off to a bad start
with him at the beginning of the season and he never forgave me."

At the beginning of the season, James was a 22-year-old pitcher with
only one big league year of experience behind him and it was a mediocre
one at that. Admittedly he had a lot to learn.

"We were playing the Cubs in Chicago where Evers was king,"

Johnny Evers receives a silver tray and tea service for helping the Braves win the pennant (R.W. Sears, International News Service photograph).

related James. "Because of the slide in my delivery the hitters weren't getting around good and they were hitting to their opposite fields. I motioned for Evers to move over, wanting him to change his position. Evers was humiliated that a greenhorn player would openly direct him before his worshipping fans."

Evers obliged James by moving, only to make mockery of it by returning to his normal position before James could release a pitch.

"The batter swung and the ball sailed right through the spot where I had asked Evers to play," James continued. "He grew madder and I was furious. Manager Stallings removed me from the game immediately."

After showering and suiting up in civilian clothes, Evers and James met as they exited from the clubhouse.

"I was happy once more; we won the game," said James. "I figured Johnny had calmed down. I had, but I couldn't help getting in the last word. I said, 'Well, Johnny, you have to admit I was right.' Evers blew a fuse and I never was able to make him like me."[211]

What Bill James didn't understand was the essence of Johnny Evers. He did not take criticism lightly, especially when it came to playing baseball. He had been trained under the leadership of Frank Chance who bossed a hard-bitten crew with an iron fist. The "Peerless Leader" was a strict disciplinarian who demanded the very best from every man on the team. And the worst critic of other players and himself was Johnny Evers.

Rabbit Maranville had two anecdotes about the 1914 season to prove this. Early in the season, he drew Evers's wrath by allowing a runner, sliding into second base, to force him into making a poor throw which allowed the game's winning run to score. Maranville's uninspired play drew a blast of curses from Evers. "You big sissy," Evers said, "the next time anyone comes down at you to stop a double play, hit him between the eyes."

When Evers made a mental error in a World Series game that cost the Braves two runs, he returned to the Boston bench crying like a baby at his own mistake.[212] In spite of the error, Evers played a key role in Boston's stunning sweep of the A's with a .438 average. A committee of baseball writers voted Evers winner of the Chalmers Award, that period's equivalent of the National League's Most Valuable Player. Evers, who beat out Maranville and James for the award, received a Chalmers automobile.

On Saturday afternoon, October 17, the *Troy Times* announced "The Evers Celebration." It went on to say:

> Mayor Thomas Hislop will be the Grand Marshal of a parade with more than 5,000 people in line. Several organizations intend to put on special features, and it was expected that the illumination from thousands of torches and redfire sticks to be burned will give the appearance of a second burning of Troy. But it will be burning with enthusiasm for Johnny Evers.
>
> Following the parade, the town has plans for a banquet. Men, women and children, irrespective of race, politics or creed, are prepared to cheer themselves hoarse. They will contribute in diverse ways to make the reception of Johnny Evers, captain of the Boston Braves, one of the most memorable in the history of the municipality. It will be a joyous celebration.[213]

For Johnny Evers however, there would be no joyous celebration. He was still mourning the loss of his three-year-old daughter, Helen, who had suddenly come down with scarlet fever in early August and died.[214]

Joe Tinker, 1914

Joe Tinker was now at the helm of a new Chicago Federal League team, the ChiFeds. The major leagues called them "outlaws" and filed suits to stop them and Joe Tinker. So Joe fired a broadside at the National League even before the 1914 season began.[215]

William Shettaline, secretary of the Philadelphia National League club, arrived in Shreveport, Louisiana on April 1, seeking pitchers Tom Seaton and Ad Brennan, two of the ChiFeds' stars, with intentions of taking them back to the Phillies. He went at it quietly, slipping into a secluded hotel where he phoned the two pitchers. The "outlaws," staying at the Hotel Youree, succeeded in leading the enemy, through a ruse, right into their hotel. A pitched battle of words took place. Organized baseball was horribly defeated in the first skirmish with Joe Tinker's club.

Manager Tinker led the attack, and it was a hot one directed at organized baseball in general and the National League and the Phillies in particular. All the ball players and guests at the hotel, numbering at least 100, formed a big circle around the two leaders and listened to every word. Shettaline looked up, gave the audience the "once over" and remarked, "You have a crowd around you, I see."

Tinker's reply was sharp and to the point: "Yes, and we'll have a crowd around us all season too. The public likes to see the ball player get what is coming to him, and that is why the Federal League exists. We are going to pay the players some real money, money they are worth, and we are going to treat them right."

"Why, the players surely have prospered under organized ball and have been treated all right," broke in Shettaline.

"You think they have?" answered Tinker. "What did the Philadelphia club do to Tom Seaton last season? Didn't it keep a telegram away from him in Chicago, a message asking him to come home at once because his wife was dangerously ill? They kept that message away from him and made him pitch a game that afternoon and made him miss two or three trains for home."

"Yes, and you had that telegram before noon," said Seaton, who was right there listening.

Shettaline professed ignorance of the whole affair.

"Didn't you make Killifer miss several days of the season last year because you refused to pay him the measly $250 that had been promised him and which he had coming, and didn't he have to quit the team later in the season in order to get that money?"

Again, Shettaline professed ignorance.

Then Tinker followed with another tirade against the National League, the national commission, and all of organized baseball, and recalled a dozen cases of mistreatment in such rapid succession that the Philadelphia man was bewildered. Once, when Tinker dropped the remark that the Philadelphia club hadn't been square, Shettaline misunderstood and took it as a personal insult and came back angrily.

The battle in the hotel lobby lasted the best part of an hour, and the audience stayed to the finish. Finally, Shettaline was dragged to one side by the scribes and calmly said he had come to have a talk with Seaton and Brennan, especially Seaton. He explained that Seaton had agreed to terms with the Phillies by telegraph before he signed a Federal League contract. "But it looks," concluded Shettaline, "as if he's satisfied here and wants to stay." And stay he did. Although defeated in the war of words, Shettaline remained to watch his former players practice with the ChiFeds. There were no further words.[216]

The baseball public expressed their feelings toward the new league during exhibition games as demonstrated by a caricature in *The Chicago Tribune*.

After this verbal attack on organized baseball, Joe Tinker became an "even handed" kind of manager. He called his team to his room for a lecture before starting the season. He announced that it was "his intention to have numerous round table talks during the season."[217]

The ChiFeds began the season in Chicago on April 23. *The Chicago Tribune* headlined the story, "Chicago Welcomes Feds, Who Triumph Over Packers, 9–1, Wild Enthusiasm Marks Start." It was quite a day for the new team.

Chicago took the Federal League to its bosom yesterday and claimed it as a mother would claim a long lost child. With more frills and enthusiasm than ever prevailed at a baseball opening here, Joe Tinker and his ChiFeds made their debut before a throng of fans that filled the new north side park to capacity, and the Chicago boys trounced George Stovall's Kansas City team, 9 to 1. All Chicago cheered and the north side was maddened with delight.

The windows and roofs of flat buildings across the way from the park were crowded with spectators. The surface of elevated trains leading to the north side was overhanging with people in the early afternoon. Four separate and distinct automobile parades unloaded several thousand gaily-decked rooters at the gates. Owners Weeghman and Walker of the north side club and President Gilmore of the new league were so overjoyed with the spectacle that they almost wept, and there is little doubt that it was an epochal day in the history of the national game.

Before the game, a squad of women from the Ladies of the G.A.R.

This caricature reflects the wild enthusiasm of the fans over the new league (*Chicago Tribune*).

marched upon the field bearing a huge American flag. Led by a band and followed by the members of both ball clubs, the women carried the national colors to the flagpole in far center field. Rockets and bombs were fired as they approached it, and when the emblem was drawn to the top of the staff, the throng of fans arose with bared heads and cheered while the band played, "Columbia the Gem of the Ocean."

With the flag pole ceremonies over, the band led the paraders back to home plate where there were several cart loads of flowers in the form of horseshoes and bundles of American beauties. Most of them were for Manager Tinker who was compelled to smile amid the blooms for the benefit of the moving picture machine. Some were for Mrs. Tinker and some for President Weeghman.[218]

The 1914 season opened with franchises bucking the established competition in Brooklyn, Chicago, St. Louis and Pittsburgh, and with teams in the AAA cities of Baltimore, Buffalo, Kansas City and Indianapolis. New parks had been constructed in all eight cities and were ready for the openers. Chicago's entry was a beautiful new Weegham Park, which remains a gem today, although with a different name: Wrigley Field.

Tinker must have felt like celebrating his new fortune. He went out and bought a new car.[219]

On April 16, Tinker and his crew left for Kansas City to start the race for the Federal League Flag. Game one went to the Tinkers, 3–2. As the season progressed, the new league put some bruises on the Cubs, cutting the older team's attendance in half from what it had been in 1913. The White Sox also suffered a considerable drop at the gate. The Feds' gate however, was boosted by a spirited pennant race in which almost every team at one time or another contended.

Under Tinker's leadership, the ChiFeds stayed close to league-leader Indianapolis. They raced neck and neck into the final week until Chicago lost a slight lead over the Hoosiers on October 6, by dropping a double-header to the Kansas City Packers. This allowed Indianapolis to finally grab the brass ring. Chicago finished with an 87–67 record (.565), a hair away from first place Indianapolis with an 88–65 (.575). The team's bat-boys included Tinker's two sons, Joe, Jr. and Roland (Rollie).

Weeghman Park, new and nicer than the dingy West Side Grounds where the mediocre Cubs were playing, attracted fans by the droves. The ChiFeds became the most successful team in the Federal League, and organized baseball did everything it could to fight this "outlaw" league. But Weeghman was a tough competitor. He had Joe Tinker send wires to major and minor league players all over the country: "You are invited to come to the Federal League quarters in Chicago and discuss terms. Even if you decide not to sign a contract, the Federal League will pay all your expenses."[220]

Major league teams tried injunctions, with little effect, as the year closed. The Feds continued to wave hefty contracts under stars' noses.

**Joe Tinker and his sons, Joe Jr. (right) and Rollie, batboys for the ChiFeds
(National Baseball Hall of Fame Library).**

Although it was a tactic that eventually harmed the league, the players
welcomed the money. They had been frustrated for a long time by a closed
market and found the Federal League profitable.

The Chicago fans loved the new league and its new ballpark. They idolized Joe Tinker. On August 22, the Royal Arch Masons gave Joe, who was a Mason, a silver loving cup.[221]

Joe loved his new job. He also fell in love with a new sport that allowed him to get away from the city in the off season. He, his wife Ruby and friends, enjoyed duck hunting. It was something he and his wife could do together. She seemed happy being with him in the forested area. Here, she was finally able to smile, no longer depressed.

Joe (second from left) and his wife Ruby (left) with friends, duck hunting (courtesy Tom Tinker).

Joe Tinker, 1915

The 1915 season started with President Weeghman sponsoring a "name the team" contest. The name Whales was selected out of 350 entries but no one was quite sure why. One speculation was that Weeghman wanted to make his team look big. After Tinker announced his plans, it looked as if the Whales were *really* going to make it big.[222]

Busy as Joe was in preparing for spring training, he had an uncanny ability for remembering a friend's birthday and for acknowledging it in a very special way. On March 8, Joe paid the following tribute in a letter to Hans Wagner, on the legendary Pirate's forty-first birthday:

> My Dear Hans,
>
> It might be possible for the world to get along without sunshine and we poor mortals might struggle along without food, but when the great game of baseball loses your services, the gap will never be filled by one of your equal.
>
> I have played against you for years, and make this statement as the truth, the whole truth and nothing but the truth, that I have always looked upon you as the greatest shortstop and most dangerous man at bat the game has ever known.
>
> I only hope that nature will preserve you for the game for another 15 years at least. You have been the one most brilliant star, in my opinion, and my only regret is that I, being in another league, am unable to meet you and see you perform, scooping 'em up with that big mitt and hitting 'em where they ain't.
>
> Yours very truly,
> Joe Tinker,
> Manager, Chicago Federals[223]

Having delivered his tribute to the Flying Dutchman, Joe turned to the business at hand. On March 19, he prepared a press release and had it issued out of the ChiFeds spring training camp in Shreveport, Louisiana. It confirmed the idea that Tinker had every intention of winning the pennant in 1915.

Joe knew what to do. Frank Chance had been his teacher and Tinker had learned his lessons well. He announced the acquisition of infield prospects, a promising pitcher and the use of a double set of outfielders. The latter idea was what the Miracle Braves had done the year before in becoming world champions. Tinker figured his team would be 25 percent stronger this year because of the reserve strength carried by the club. He claimed he was greatly handicapped the previous year by not having a good utility man, but it would be different this season.[224]

When the curtain rose on the playing season, the Federal League had already filed an antitrust suit against organized baseball in the U.S. District Court in Chicago. The presiding judge was Kenesaw M. Landis. Litigation continued through the spring and summer as the baseball wars resumed both on the field and on the dotted line.

Two plums were plucked for the Feds when star hurlers, Eddie Plank and Chief Bender, were induced to leave Connie Mack's Athletics. Other stars also jumped to the "outlaw" league.

As the season moved forward, Tinker complained of pain in his side. It was severe and he couldn't play most of the time, but Tinker was able to manage the team from the bench. Finally, he agreed to see a doctor.

On May 9, *The Chicago Tribune* reported: "Tinker, manager of the Chicago team of the Federal League, has suffered a rupture in his right side and will be out of the game as a player for a month, if not longer.

"Before he left Chicago, Tinker was warned to rest, owing to pains in his side, and his physicians told him the penalty for disobedience would be an operation."

On May 29, a press release reported: "A simple course of treatment is expected to restore Joe Tinker, of the Chicago Federals, to his normal health, according to physicians who examined him yesterday to ascertain the cause of severe pains in his side, which have kept him out of the game much of the time this season. It was decided a surgical operation would not be necessary."[225]

Joe Tinker returned to the team. On some days he played but he preferred to let Jimmy Smith cover short. A close race took shape with Chicago, St. Louis and Pittsburgh racing head-to-head down the stretch. The Chicago Whales received offensive firepower from Dutch Zwilling and Max Flack, and Joe Tinker uncovered a pair of surprise pitching aces in thirty-seven-year-old George McConnell and thirty-eight-year-old "Three Finger" Brown.

The prospects for winning the pennant looked good. As the team forged ahead, Federal League officials put together a $1,000,000 war chest to fight organized baseball as they prepared for the 1916 season.[226]

Going into the final day of the 1915 season, a single game separated the three contenders. After a double-header split between Chicago and Pittsburgh and a St. Louis victory, the smoke cleared on a .001 pennant-winning margin for Chicago over St. Louis. The finish marked the second straight exciting and breath-taking race by the Feds.

Although jubilant over winning the pennant, Joe was troubled. He was still in pain. He was finally hospitalized, and on December 15 the press reported: "Joe Tinker, manager of the Chicago Whales, and prospective leader of the Cubs in the event the proposed baseball peace plans go through, was successfully operated upon today at the Henroitin Hospital by Dr. L.M. Harris for kidney trouble. Dr. Harris predicted that the patient would be home before New Year's, but not before Christmas."[227]

While Joe Tinker lay in the hospital, the legal battle between the major leagues and the "outlaw" league continued. Judge Landis whose partiality in the case eventually led to him becoming organized baseball's first commissioner, urged the parties before the bench to discuss an amicable settlement. Finally, due to mounting losses and the possible U.S. entry into World War I, the Feds were forced to sue for peace. The treaty was signed on December 21 with several key arrangements.

Part of the peace settlement allowed Charles Weeghman, the owner of the Chicago Feds, to buy the Chicago Cubs from the Taft family, who had backed Charles Murphy. Weeghman then made it known that the 1916 manager for the Chicago Cubs was to be Joe Tinker.

Joe couldn't have been happier. He had been handed two Christmas presents that made him jump high and click his heels in spite of his operation. He would manage his old team and he had a new son, born on December 22. His wife named him William (Billy). He now had a family of four and the whole gang would soon be watching him manage the Chicago team at the new Cubs ballpark.

When asked if he would also play at short, Joe said he would "retire from the playing end of baseball." He decided the time had come.

> When a man plays baseball, he should think of nothing else but the game before him. He should have his mind riveted on what he himself is to do. Nothing should distract him. But there is a lot of distraction when that player is trying to manage his club at the same time.
>
> I found that out when I managed Cincinnati in 1913 and again last year when I managed the Chicago Federals. Instead of paying attention to my job at shortstop—and paying attention to that alone—I had to pay attention to what the other eight men were doing.
>
> I think a ball club should be managed by a bench manager to insure its success. A manager on the bench has it all over a playing manager when it comes to directing the team. A bench manager sees everything, and sees it from the viewpoint of a spectator. A playing manager doesn't see everything because he is occupied to a certain extent with his own playing job.[228]

In 1916, Joe Tinker became a bench manager for the Cubs.

Johnny Evers, 1915

Johnny Evers and his wife were hit hard by the death of their daughter in August 1914, as reported in an October 2001 interview with John Evers, a great-grandnephew. Helen had pointed an accusatory finger at her husband and angrily said, "Where were you? You are never around!"

This altercation was one of many. The two of them had similar personalities: aggressive, stubborn, never admitting wrong. Butting heads had become a common occurrence in their relationship.

The death of the three-year-old resulted in Helen packing her things, taking their son, John, Jr., and walking out, never to return. This permanent separation was not followed by a divorce because they were Roman Catholic. A divorce was out of the question. Nevertheless, Helen Evers wanted to guarantee her future. She had a son to raise and there would be expenses. So she went to court, obtained a legal separation and an order from the judge for alimony.[229]

The great-grand nephew reported, "Johnny Evers now lived alone, hung around the Elks club, played cards, drank, but was not an alcoholic."

In February, friends began to worry about Johnny Evers because it looked as if he was having another nervous breakdown. He was encouraged to live up in the mountains in the northern part of New York and reports circulated that he was not recovering. The press wondered if Evers would be able to start the season with the world champions, but it was soon announced that he "was now in better shape than ever before."

Evers was quoted as saying: "The main reason for the breakdown was too much business worry and life indoors in winter. A winter in the woods is the best doctor."[230]

So it was. In 1915, Johnny Evers headed out for spring training in Macon, Georgia. Baseball was the one thing that still had meaning for him. He suited up and began to play the game he loved.

At the opening game of the season in Boston, he fractured his ankle and was not able to play for many weeks. There were times when his depression turned to agitation and his hot temper prevented him from using reasonable judgement.

His ankle finally healed and he could once again take to the infield. Nevertheless, it didn't take much to get him fired up. On August 10, he had a stormy encounter with Fred Clarke of the Pittsburgh Pirates. Fisticuffs were the weapons of choice.

Since Evers was always good copy, the newspapers made much of it. Some of the critics were for immediately burning Johnny at the stake, others thought life imprisonment would be about right. President Tener gave Evers a three-day suspension. He announced he would look into the case further and if deemed warranted, additional punishment would be handed out.[231]

Evers had another problem in addition to emotional flare-ups. His ability to play heads-up baseball was not as it used to be. There were times when he just didn't have his mind on what was happening.

The August 21 *Boston Herald* reported on a game between the Braves and the Cards. "Troy John pulled his boner in the fifth," it said. " Troy John was on first with only one out. Connolly, who replaced Compton for the day, wafted a soft fly to right field. Just as though the ball was soaring into the bleachers, Troy John went tearing around the bases. Consequently, a double play was a very simple matter after Chief Wilson had grabbed the ball. Thereafter, John rapped his head at frequent intervals and made more fun of himself than the crowd made of him. It furnished a lot of amusement and added to the gaiety of a rather tame occasion, the Braves blanking the Cards, 1–0."

This was not the Johnny Evers who had been embraced by Jim Gaffney, owner of the Boston club in 1914. The Jim Gaffney who walked up behind the Trojan in the Polo Grounds, slipped an arm around his shoulder and spoke to reporters so eloquently about the Braves' captain, that Evers was seen to blush. The Jim Gaffney who, pinching Evers on the cheek said, "This is the best investment I ever made. He came high but he's paid wonderful dividends. He has made the team what it is. On the field, he employs the brains and the baseball talent, and he has been worth every cent he cost the Boston club. No championship team ever existed without a pair of fine players hovering around second base. Evers and Maranville have been the keystone kings for the Braves. Such fielding as they did yesterday makes pitchers great."[232]

There were times when Johnny Evers perked up and again became great. He helped the Braves win a ball game on September 13. He executed a spectacular play in the seventh inning at the most critical stage of the game. It was against the Chicago Cubs, who like the Braves, were still contenders in another heated National League pennant fight. The Braves led by one run, 5–4, and the Cubs had three men on the bases and two out. Bob Fisher was at bat. A hit meant the ball game. Fisher hit a low, spiral, short fly to center field. Bash Compton, the Braves center fielder, came in at top speed, but he never could have caught the ball. Evers started back the minute the ball was hit at a breakneck pace. He stretched out his gloved hand to the limit and speared the ball.

Evers was going so fast that he finished with a big wide circle way out in left center, all the time holding out his hand with the precious ball.

Johnny Evers (third from right), captain of the Braves, and the team at spring training in Macon Georgia, in 1914 (W.W. Somers).

Two runs at least would have counted if he hadn't caught the ball, and two runs at that time would have meant a victory for Chicago. How Evers ever managed to get the ball and still avoid a collision with Compton was a matter for conjecture. Johnny felt so elated it looked as if he wanted to throw his cap in the air and give three cheers but he just kept right on running, semi-circled around, doffed his cap and, with affected nonchalance, returned to the bench. Those that saw it were talking about it thirty-four years later, the greatest catch they ever saw.[233]

If that catch was a gloating maneuver, you could hardly blame the little Trojan. He had been the toast of Chicago as the middleman on the immortal Tinker-to-Evers-to Chance double play combination for the Cubs' halcyon days.[234] He was finally given his chance to manage the Cubs in 1913, then was unceremoniously sent away after he finished "only" third in his one managerial season. That catch and his circling the field could have been his way of rubbing it in on the Cubs organization and reminding the fans of how good he used to be and still was.

He may have continued to feel that way because the Boston club did fairly well during the 1915 season, finishing second with an 83–69 record; Philadelphia won the pennant at 90–62. A number of reasons can be given for the second-place finish but it can be said, without hesitation, that Johnny Evers was not the player he had been in 1914. Instead of playing in 139 games, he played in 83. His power at the plate was significantly diminished: his BA dropping from .279 to .263, doubles went from 20 to 4, triples from 3 to 1, homers remained at 1. Stolen bases also suffered, going from 12 to 7 and his base on balls plummeting from a whopping 87 to 50. A review of seven issues of *The Chicago Daily News* over twenty-two months clearly demonstrated that Troy John had gone down hill.[235]

Little Johnny Evers was no longer the slim little fellow who had eyes that snapped with vitality, a firebrand on the attack, putting every ounce of energy: mental, physical and vocal into playing, giving everything in order to win. He could no longer inspire the team because he no longer had the kind of inspiration that had fired him up in the past.

Johnny Evers talking baseball to his son John, Jr. (University Libraries of Notre Dame).

Johnny Evers teaching his son to slide (University Libraries of Notre Dame).

He was depressed. His hanging around the Elks club, playing cards and drinking were indications of the loneliness he must have felt after his wife left him. He wanted her back. He still loved her. He wanted his son back. He missed going outside and teaching John, Jr., how to play baseball. He had a soft spot in his heart for both of them. Yet, he still had that big stubborn jaw that would not allow him to attempt a reconciliation.[236]

Frank Chance, 1915

While Joe Tinker played ball with the ChiFeds, and Johnny Evers with the Braves, Frank Chance was growing oranges in Glendora, California. He tended to his orange groves with loving care and they in turn rewarded him handsomely. They allowed him to gather 12,000 boxes a season and he sold them for $1 a box.[237]

Frank handled his money carefully. In addition to his investment in

Frank Chance (left) and friend Jack Buss in orange groves at Glendora, California (courtesy Gloria Tinker).

orange groves, he invested in mines and oil wells that were beginning to pay him profits with a promise to pay better.[238] Investing in stocks of solid business corporations that paid good returns were not overlooked. He grew up knowing about the investments his father had made and followed his example by buying Sinclair Oil.[239]

After tending to his investments, Frank would relax at home with friends. There was always a great amount of time for swapping stories and jawing baseball. When a neighbor stopped by, he soon learned that Frank had as many superstitions as he had friends. Frank liked to play cards with his ball players at a quarter limit, but he would not play unless real money, and not poker chips were on the table. When his team lost a game after he had eaten fish for lunch, fish was passed up for a month. If he had smoked a cigar on the way to the ballpark and the Cubs were beaten, he devoted himself to cigarettes until he forgot the reason for the defeat.[240]

One of Frank's neighbors was I.N. Hockett and he too had orange groves. He would stop over and talk about the days when he was living in Cincinnati rooting for the Reds. He claimed he knew Charley Mur-

Tinker (left) visits Manager Chance of the Red Sox, 1923 (courtesy Gloria Tinker).

phy when C. Webb Murphy was a drug clerk at Wilmington. He talked about his visits to the Sunfish Mountains, less than 100 miles from Cincinnati in the picturesque Adams County. Hockett had a bucket of information that just flowed out endlessly and he talked with everybody.

Hockett often told how he had seen Frank Chance go 20 rounds in a lively glove fight. When asked, Frank admitted to its veracity. It soon became widely known that Gentleman Jim Corbett considered Chance the best amateur fighter in the world. Chance remembered the day he had a real slugfest with Gentleman Jim in Corbett's Broadway cafe and had to be pulled off the champ to stop the fight.[241] John L. Sullivan, the one-time heavyweight champion, called Frank Chance "the greatest amateur brawler in the world."[242] An amateur? He was more than an amateur.

Although life at his *Cub Ranch* was pleasant and restful, Frank Chance missed baseball. He wanted to get back in the game and was trying to find a way to do just that.

CHAPTER **10**

Trying to Hang On

Frank Chance, 1916–1923

The glory years were over. The "Trio of Bear Cubs" would never again race around the bases. Never again bring cheering fans to their feet after stabbing the ball or sliding home under the throw. For each of them, there was still hope that in some way they could hold on and be part of the game.

Frank Chance let it be known that he was fit as a fiddle. After all, he had that letter from Dr. W.G. Frolich, the New York specialist who removed the blood clot from his brain. The doctor had said: "I will stake my reputation in asserting that Frank Chance is in good health. The operation I performed, completely cured him of a nervous condition, which had caused frequent headaches and compelled him to give up playing ball. This ailment was caused by being hit on the head by pitched balls. He has a rugged constitution and a remarkable will power and recovered from the operation rapidly. He is the same robust man who led the Cubs to victory in four pennant races and two world's championship series."[243]

To prove his fitness, Frank joined the Los Angeles Athletic Club. He also took on additional responsibilities. Frank became vice president of the Glendora Heights Orange-Lemon Company and owner of the Frank Chance Building at Glendora. He wasn't about to sit still and not make things happen. When John Powers, president of the Angel City Baseball Association approached him, Frank bought a one-third interest in the Los Angeles (Pacific Coast League) team in 1916–1917. He became a vice president and manager of the Angels.[244]

There were times when he must have smiled as he watched his Angels slug it out with the Cubs. This occurred in Pasadena on March 1, 1917, in the second of two exhibition games. His boys had taken the first game on the previous day and the Chicago team was trying to even the series, but the game ended in a 4–4 tie. Frank knew that the Cubbies had not done well since Murphy fired him. The club dropped to fourth in 1914 and '15, then slid to fifth in 1916. After watching the Cubs play his Los Angeles team, he could not have predicted any great improvement. The Angels played excellent ball and Frank managed the club to a pennant. He began making plans for the following year when poor health again attacked him and he was forced to quit.

Feeling somewhat better in 1923, he returned to the majors to manage the Red Sox. He tried to rebuild the team decimated by the sale of stars (including Babe Ruth) to the Yankees. When asked by a writer what his chances were, he replied, "This bunch will unquestionably finish last." He was dead right. The one bright spot in managing the team was the sudden appearance of Joe Tinker who walked into the dugout before the start of a game. They loved seeing one another. The bond that had developed was always there and they truly enjoyed talking about the "good old days."[245]

Charles Comiskey offered Frank a contract to pilot the White Sox for the 1924 season. He could not refuse. He still had that indefinable urge to stay in the game that had been his life. He was looking forward to a season with the team that had once been his cross-town rival, the "Hitless Wonders," the team that had captured the world championship after beating his powerhouse 1906 Cubs.

Johnny Evers, 1916–1923

Just as the "Peerless Leader" tried to hold on to baseball, so did the little Trojan. It was the only thing he had. His wife and son had left him. With them no longer part of his life, he sold the house in Troy.

His life was empty except for baseball, so he returned to the Braves in 1916. His BA plummeted from .263 to .216. He only played in 71 games.

His extra base hits consisted of 4 doubles, 1 triple and no homers. Johnny only stole 5 bases and his base on balls went from 50 to 40.

Johnny was making errors in early 1917. By mid-year, after playing 24 games, Johnny's downward spiral showed a BA of .193 with no extra-base hits. He was sold to Philadelphia after Evers held a press conference assuring Manager Pat Moran, the Phillies pilot, he was in good health. Moran assumed Evers's contract for a salary of $10,000. In November, however, the Phillies released Johnny Evers unconditionally.

All winter long from his hotel room in Troy, he made no special plans for baseball. Throwing out a few lines that might lead him into a business other than baseball, he was suddenly contacted by Red Sox manager Ed Barrow. Johnny was asked to return to Boston as a coach with the chance of playing second base more or less regularly. The offer hit the little tyke in a vital spot. He grabbed it. He dashed off a letter saying, "I am glad to get back to Boston. Be sure, I am going to work as hard as I can."[246]

When the 1918 season started, Johnny Evers was again in uniform as coach to the raw recruits that had just signed on with the Red Sox. Johnny soon saw that Dave Shean was going to play second base full time instead of him. So he upped and quit.

The press reported: "There is more or less of a mystery attached to the passing of Johnny Evers as a Red Sox. President Frazee says he is still a member of the team and Manager Barrow says he is not. You can take your choice."[247] But both men knew why Johnny suddenly decided to walk out the door. Barrow had changed his mind about Johnny playing second base. And Troy John did not like it one bit.

He had to do something. His restless spirit was not satisfied with the Elks club, playing cards and drinking. On occasion, he did see his son but they traveled in different circles and they shared no common interests. Life for Johnny had no meaning. One morning he walked into a recruiting office and tried to enlist for the army. World War I was in full swing. He was told he was a little too old for duty (he was 36), but his name and reputation were well known to the military brass. So he agreed to serve as a Knights of Columbus Athletic Director for U.S. servicemen in Europe.[248]

The City of Troy celebrated their hero and held a game in his honor in which he played. It was the All-Troys against the Provisional Company, No. 1. When Troy John first came to bat, the Knights of Columbus presented him with a handsome wristwatch.

On June 17, the *Troy Times* carried the story: "More than 5,000 persons turned out to see Johnny Evers, former big league star, play his last

**Johnny Evers, Knights of Colum-
bus Athletic Director for U.S. servicemen in Europe (University
Libraries of Notre Dame).**

game in America before leaving for
France, where he will direct athletic
work for the Knights of Columbus
among the American troops. Evers
played third base for Provisional
Company No.1 of the Watervliet
Arsenal against the All-Troy team at
Center Island Park. The soldiers won
by a score of 4 to 3."[249]

On December 16, 1918, a week
before Christmas, Johnny was back.
The *Troy Times* reported, "Evers came
home on the steamer, Lorraine, which
docked in New York at 11 o'clock in
the morning. He was met by a *Troy
Times* representative as he disem-
barked from the steamer and gave the
Times man a cordial greeting. Questions were fired at Mr. Evers and were
just as quickly answered.

Times: What was the effect of athletics
   upon the fighting morale of the men?
Evers: It was most wonderful.
Times: What did the French soldiers
   think of baseball?
Evers: They were very enthusiastic over
   it.
Times: Are you considering any proposi-
   tions for the baseball season here?
Evers: Not any yet.
Times: Will baseball get into the
   Olympic games?
Evers: Hardly. Baseball is strictly an
   American game.[250]

As the reporter fired away, little
did he realize there were tantalizing
questions he could've asked about
people Johnny had been hobnobbing
with: royalty, Allied generals as well
as front line troops. Johnny had
become friends with General John

"Black Jack" Pershing and a score of French generals. Johnny even visited Pope Benedict XV in Rome.[251]

After the war, on January 29, 1919, *The Herald* reported, "Johnny Evers is on the stage, and you want to see his act as soon as you can. He is and always will be full of surprises, original and peppery, on and off the field of baseball. The leader of the orchestra better not start any arguments with Troy John."

On May 15, 1919, from Utica, New York, the *Herald* again reported, "John J. Evers was elected chairman of the Board of Directors of the new State Baseball League at a meeting of franchise holders here last night."[252]

The Trojan had to keep busy. He was still living alone and loneliness was something he could never adjust to. It was painful, and he did not need another nervous breakdown. Two were more than enough.

In 1920, Evers was coach for, of all people, Giants manager John McGraw, the same man whose team was beaten out by the Cubs for four pennants. After the season ended, while with the Giants in Cuba for an exhibition game, it was announced that Evers would succeed Fred Mitchell in 1921 as manager of the Chicago Nationals.

Johnny Evers again had communication problems with his players. They weren't very good anyway, according to Johnny. In August, the Trojan was fired after 98 games with the team in seventh place. As usual, the *Troy Record* gobbled up every bit of news about the town's hero. On August 21, 1921, it reported, "Johnny Evers Deposed As Manager at Chicago. Trojan Baseball Expert Officially Retired with Full Pay for Rest of Season; Bill Killefer His Successor; Veeck Makes Statement."

In 1923, Johnny took the job of a White Sox coach. At the end of the season he was pleasantly surprised when he was invited to a baseball meeting in Chicago and learned that his old sidekicks Tinker and Chance wanted to get together for a gab session. The reunion made him smile again as the trio talked about old times.[253]

Time passed quickly and he was soon back in Troy, still living alone. There was a moment of gaiety on February 5, 1924. He was honored at a farewell dinner prior to his departure to take up the reins as assistant to Frank Chance, leader of the White Sox.[254] He was again honored in New York on May 9, 1924, when the City of Troy held an "Evers Day." Members of the teams of the Yankees and White Sox were presented with a dozen shirt collars. The name of each player appeared on the collar and they were wrapped in special boxes and tied with purple ribbon, the color of the Lodge of Elks through whom they were presented.[255]

The moments of happiness did not occur too often and Johnny was again feeling the pain of despair. He finally decided to move. There was

Evers is flanked by John McGraw (left) and Frank Chance, 1923 (International Newsreel).

nothing for him in Troy except loneliness. He had an indefinable long-ing. He wanted something.

Nearby Albany bristled with people. It was more alive. He reflected on the shoe venture in which he had lost every penny. It wasn't his fault. He had a corrupt partner who ran the business into the ground; now it would be different. He himself could manage the store and everybody knew Johnny Evers. He knew baseball and had a good familiarity with other sports. Troy John decided to open up a sporting goods store in a busy section of Albany. He could see the sign now, high above the out-side window, "John Evers Sporting Goods."[256] He just knew he'd make good.

Joe Tinker, 1916–1923

When Joe Tinker jumped into the "outlaw" league, Charles Ebbets, president and part owner of the Dodgers, branded Tinker a traitor and swore he would never be allowed to play in organized baseball again. After the peace settlement with the Federal League, Tinker, with a raucous hoot in the direction of his enemies, returned to the National League as manager of the Cubs to open the 1916 season.

Charles Weeghman combined the cream of the Whale crop with Cubs from the West Side Grounds. The Cubs now played at Weeghman Park. Mordecai "Three- Finger" Brown, like Tinker, also returned to the Cubs from the Federal League. For both of them it was like old times. They were together again.

But Mordecai, and the team as a whole, didn't play like in the days of old. "Three-Finger" could only scratch out two wins for the entire sea-son and the team did poorly. The one game that Tinker and Brown both wanted to win was on September 4, when the Reds were in town. It was a gate attraction for the second match of a Labor Day double-header. Tinker didn't play. He chose the view from the bench as Christy Math-ewson, now pitching for Cincinnati, dueled his archrival, Mordecai Brown.

As Tinker watched, he held in his hand an article Matty had given him before the game. Tinker smiled as he read what the great fadeaway pitcher had recorded for posterity

> Joe Tinker, the clever little shortstop of the Chicago club, is a man with whom I have fought many battles of wits, and I am glad to acknowledge that he has come out of the fuss with flying colors on many occasions. There was a time when Tinker was putty in my hands. For two years he

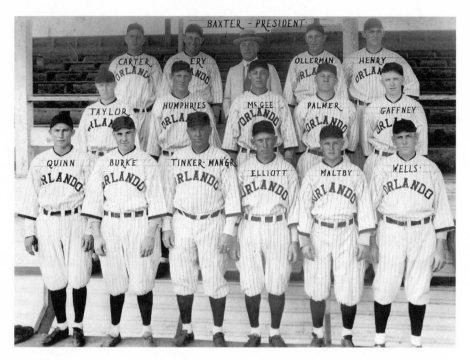

Manager Tinker (front row, third from left) and the Orlando Tigers in 1921
(courtesy Historical Society of Central Florida).

was the least dangerous man on the Chicago team. His weakness was a
low curve on the outside, and I fed him low curves so often that I had
him looking like an invalid every time he came to the plate. Then
Joseph went home one night and did a little deep thinking. He got a nice
long bat and took his stand at least a foot farther from the plate, and
then he had me. If I kept the ball on the inside edge of the plate he was
in a splendid position to meet it, and if I tried to keep my offerings on
the outside, he had plenty of time to step into 'em. From that day on,
Tinker became one of the most dangerous batters I have ever faced, not
because his natural hitting ability had increased, but because he didn't
propose to let the pitcher do all the out-guessing.[257]

Tinker was choked up by this compliment from one of the greatest
pitchers to take the mound. He felt like crying. He felt like an old man
watching the end of an era as Matty outlasted Mordecai, 10–8. It was the
last game either one of them ever pitched.

Appropriately, it was to be the last season for Tinker as well. Joe hung
up his spikes after his Cubs finished fifth with a 67–86 record, the Cubs'

worst mark since 1901. Nevertheless, Joe was never one to completely quit the game. He opened negotiations for a baseball franchise. On December 22, 1916, he and Thomas E. Wilson, the Chicago stockyard capitalist and sporting goods manufacturer, closed a deal for the purchase of the Columbus Senators of the American Association for $65,000.[258]

The March 1, 1917, *Chicago Tribune* told the rest of the story: "Chicago friends plan to give Joe Tinker a warm sendoff when his Columbus American Association club opens at home with Louisville on April 17. A committee of fifteen ardent admirers of Tinker met last night on the north side and arranged to

Joe Tinker, nattily-attired dapper man about town exuding confidence in the early days of the Florida land boom (courtesy Tom Tinker).

send a special train from Chicago for the opening. Over 200 fans have pledged themselves to make the trip. President Weeghman of the Cubs has promised to go, and President Comiskey of the White Sox also may make the trip."

Joe Tinker took over as captain, manager and team president. Having seated himself solidly in the big chair at the headquarters of the Columbus club, President Tinker's duties were to assemble a team and pick a camp down South where his team could get in shape for the season. A number of locations were considered, the most favored was Daytona, Florida.[259]

Although Joe had announced he would get in shape and play third, he played only briefly. He remembered his statement about being a full-

Joe Tinker's home as it looks today, 437 Ruth Lane in Orlando (photograph by the author).

time bench manager but the urge to take to the infield was always with him. He was modestly successful in his three years, keeping the Columbus Senators in contention for the first two seasons. Joe did a good job considering the loss of many key players to the Army.

The Columbus team was the hardest hit of any Association club by the World War I draft, but Joe Tinker took it in stride. In March 1918, he showed the baseball world his patriotic side. He announced he would use exclusively women employees in his ball park: ticket takers, change makers, ushers, peanut vendors, scorecard sellers, scoreboard operators, ground crew ... all women. "Women and girls will take the place formerly held by men and boys so that the man labor of Columbus may be spared to sterner work relative to winning the war."[260]

During his tenure as manager, Tinker became annoyed when his players couldn't hit Indianapolis's spitball pitchers (legal at that time). Being a fighter, he sent one of his own hurlers to the mound with a large file and the Columbus pitcher publicly hacked away at the ball, causing

Tinker, Evers and Chance in Chicago talking baseball in 1923 (University Libraries of Notre Dame).

much controversy, as intended. By the end of the season, the pitch was abolished in the American Association. The major leagues soon followed suit. Some corners credited Tinker with helping ban the spitball from the national game.[261]

While in Columbus, Tinker's wife continued to have medical problems like she had in Chicago. A sunny climate was recommended. So for the benefit of her health, Joe sold his interests in the team. In December 1920, he packed it all up and moved his family to Orlando, Florida.[262]

Once settled in his new surroundings, Joe looked around for new challenges and soon became owner-manager of the Orlando Tigers. The September 4, 1921, *Orlando Morning Sentinel* picks up the story:

> The curtain will drop upon the 1921 season of the Florida State League tomorrow, Labor Day, bringing to a close the most successful of the three seasons of play, and with the Orlando Tigers in first place and in undisputed possession of the pennant.
> Since the first of the season, Joe Tinker has kept his Tigers in first

place and they have never been ousted. He has injected into his players his personality and brilliance and the result has been a hard-hitting, fast fielding, aggressive club which has maintained a satisfactory and comfortable lead throughout the season.

In winning the state championship, Joe Tinker brought home the Temple Cup, formerly owned by the Tampa Smokers.[263] A grateful city began building a small baseball field in Joe's honor and announced it would be called Tinker Field.

Joe had another vision as the Florida land boom began heating up. He wanted to be an entrepreneur, dreamed of making a fortune, not knowing that he was about to enter a realm fraught with danger and heartaches. Joe formed a partnership and opened an office in the 45 Watkins Building in Orlando. It was the Tinker-McCracken Realty Company (Inc). Roy McCracken was president, Jay F. Pitts, vice president, and Jos. B. Tinker, secretary and treasurer. In addition to real estate, the firm dealt in stocks, bonds, and insurance. Tinker had his new business listed in the 1922 *City Directory*. He soon came to be seen as a nattily-attired, dapper man about town, who exuded self-confidence in the early days of the Florida land boom.

He was now a real estate developer, and one of the first things he did was buy a home for his family at 437 Ruth St. The literature claims he named the street after Babe Ruth. Not true. Orlando City Hall records, Platbook F, page 26, shows Ruth St. (now called Ruth Lane) to be so named on February 27, 1912.

Plans were in the works for the development of large subdivisions. Although Joe busied himself with real estate matters, his heart would not let go of baseball. On October 2, 1922, he penned a letter to a friend, Karl Finke, who was with the Cincinnati Reds' organization. Joe asked for a position "as a scout, some place in the South, the Florida State League, South Atlantic and Southern Colleges." Joe ended his letter by saying, "If you can help me out on this, would appreciate it very much."[264]

Joe also wrote Garry Hermann, owner of the Reds, selling him on the advantages of holding spring training at a new baseball stadium soon to be completed in Orlando.[265]

Six months later, On April 19, 1923, Tinker Field was dedicated. The Orlando Tigers met the Highlanders of Lakeland. Gates opened at 2:45 P.M., with Mayor Duckworth giving the dedicatory address. All business houses closed for the occasion, and more than 1,700 fans were on hand to see the Tigers beat Lakeland, 3–1.[266]

The name Tinker became well known throughout Orlando as Joe and his partners began buying up vacant land on which they planned to build large housing developments, commercial buildings and recreational sites. The future indeed looked bright for the entrepreneur. He was still involved with baseball; he had a realty firm that looked promising; two of his sons, Joe Jr. and Roland (Rollie), worked alongside him; the new house was first class and he had a beautiful wife he simply adored. What more could he ask for?

In the midst of all this, Joe Tinker suddenly suffered a devastating blow. In early December 1923, Ruby Tinker again became ill and was under the care of a physician. On Christmas Day, she went into a bedroom and killed herself with a shot to her head from a revolver.[267]

CHAPTER 11

Goodbye to the Game

Joe Tinker, 1924

The news reports about Ruby Tinker's death differ from what a grandson reported during an interview. *The Chicago Daily News* claimed: "Mrs. Tinker had been under the care of physicians as a result of a shock sustained when the Tampa special on which she and her husband were returning from Chicago was wrecked at Altamonte Springs. She had accompanied Mr. Tinker to Chicago where he attended the recent baseball meeting.

"Members of the family said Mrs. Tinker took an active part with her husband and children in the celebration around the Christmas tree. About noon, Mrs. Tinker was said to have left a party of friends in the living room and gone to her bedroom, where she shot herself with a small revolver. She died soon afterward."[268]

Tom Tinker, a grandson, claimed, "The newspaper reports were wrong. My father Rollie told me, my grandmother Ruby was in a hospital and my grandfather Joe wanted her home for Christmas. He told his sons, Rollie and Joe, Jr., to bring her home. So they did. On Christmas Day, everyone tried to get Ruby to go with them to deliver Christmas presents to friends. She declined, saying she was tired and would stay with the housekeeper. When they returned, they found she had shot herself. Ruby had long-standing mental health problems, one of her symptoms being depression.

"I had the impression that Joe blamed himself for his wife's death. It was he and he alone that decided to bring her home. Joe also blamed himself for going out and leaving her alone with the maid. Joe had always been madly in love with Ruby and her death hit him hard.

"Joe was never quite the same after her death. He paid less and less attention to his children, which put more responsibility on daddy (Rollie) to raise his younger brother and sister, Billy and Ruby. I don't know where Joe, the oldest son, was at this time, but he had already left home and never returned to help my father with the siblings."

When questioned about reports that Joe Tinker had at one time provided his own blood for a transfusion to his wife, the grandson had no explanation for that, since his father didn't like to talk about the past.

Following her death, Joe Tinker threw himself into his real estate business as a way of trying to dull the agony and pain and guilt that had taken hold of him. The land boom had finally taken off. Joe was determined to make good. Times were propitious for an entrepreneur who wanted to make good.

Joe Tinker had arrived in Orlando after victory had been achieved in World War I. Flush with optimism and money, people climbed into their cars and puttered down the open roads toward America's near tropics, away from congested cities with their foul air, general filth and cold weather. The "boom" was a collective national lust for land, an orgy of town building and construction. Florida possessed whatever a person sought: a healing climate, year-round recreation and abundant fertile ground.[269]

Joe jumped into the frenzy with both feet and his usual aggressive spirit. He began a second career, buying and selling land in Orange and Seminole counties with plans for building housing subdivisions and other developments. He had a vision of expanding the borders of Orlando into areas where nothing but forested land had existed before. Financially, Joe Tinker soon began to prosper.[270]

Johnny Evers, 1924

Johnny Evers now lived in Albany. His wife Helen and John Jr. were already there because she found a job in an upscale furniture store. His

ROY C. McCRACKEN
PRESIDENT

JOE B. TINKER
SEC. & TREAS.

TINKER-McCRACKEN REALTY CO.

STOCKS   BONDS

INSURANCE

REAL ESTATE

ROOM 45 WATKINS BLOCK

P. O. BOX 101

ORLANDO, FLORIDA, **Oct. 2, 1922.**

Mr. Carl B. Firke,
c/o Cincinnati Reds,
Cincinnati, Ohio.

Dear Carl:

Glad to hear you arrived home safe and sober. You should have ridden back with us. It rained all the way but we enjoyed it nevertheless.

Don't believe you will have to worry as to things being in first class chape when the team arrives next season as these men are all alive and very anxious to have everything as you may wish it.

Note you have written the Washington and Cleveland Clubs and I believe those games will draw very well.

I was sure pleased this morning to read that you made a "Garrison finish" and landed second. That means more money for the Boys. If there is anything that you want me to do why justlet me know.

You might do me a favor Carl, if you will. Tell Pat I would like to secure a position as scout some place inthe South, The Florida State League, South Atlantic and Southern Colleges. If you can help me out on this, would appreciate it very much.

Kindly remember me to Mrs. Finke and best of luck to you.

Yours very truly,

Joe B. Tinker
Rm

Joe Tinker asking for job as a baseball scout (courtesy Tom Timker).

youngest brother Joseph also moved to Albany.[271] Johnny must have known that his wife and son had moved. Could this have been the reason for Johnny to also head that way? Did he want to run into her, say "hello," and perhaps talk things over? His motives remain mere speculation but husband and wife never worked out their differences.

Johnny's first residence was in the Berkshire Hotel at 140 State Street. Below was an empty store. It was along a fine street, bustling with traffic and people. There were all kinds of fine shops along the avenue. Right next door to where he lived was the Elks club, the one place he could go when feeling low. Johnny liked the location and had no problem in renting the store. He firmed up plans for going into the sporting goods business, and his brother Joe agreed to help.[272]

The store opened for the 1923 Christmas rush. Business was brisk. Johnny was now the proprietor of something he was familiar with, something he had feelings for. When customers came in, they recognized him even though he was portly—the skinny ball player now weighed 180 pounds. They wanted to shake his hand. At times, it seemed as if all of Albany had crowded into his store. This helped relieve the loneliness he felt when he trudged upstairs to his one-room flat. He never stayed there long. Next door was a game of cards, a chance to reminisce about old times and a drink with friends.

On February 17, 1924, Johnny received a call. He learned that Frank Chance had agreed to manage the White Sox but had suddenly become ill. Chance was ordered by his physician to return to California and Johnny was asked to take over as acting manager for the entire season. Should the "Peerless Leader" return, Johnny agreed to be his assistant.[273]

The team wasn't doing well even though Johnny had steady Earl Sheely at first and nonparalleled batsman Eddie Collins at second. In May, as the team headed into Boston, Johnny could not carry on as manager. He became ill, was confined to his hotel and Big Ed Walsh took over as pilot of the club.

On May 19, the *Troy Record* reported:

> On the advice of physicians in Boston, Johnny was rushed to Troy Saturday where his case was diagnosed as acute appendicitis. He was ordered to the Troy Hospital, and at two o'clock yesterday afternoon, was operated upon by Dr. Walter T. Diver, and assisted by Dr. James W. Fitzgerald. Late last night, the patient was reported to be resting very comfortably.
>
> When Evers arrived in Troy, it was decided to operate at once, and the wisdom of this plan was well borne out when the appendix had been removed. It was in a dangerous stage of the disease.
>
> The Chicago American League team has been obsessed with a jinx this year. Originally, Manager Frank Chance was scheduled to take the team on the road. When it came time for reporting, he was unable to do so because of an aggravated asthmatic condition. When this trouble had cleared away somewhat, he announced he would join the team for the opening game of the season. However, he has not been able to report.[274]

On May 20, the *Troy Record* reported that the operation had gone well and that Evers was doing well. It concluded its report by saying, "Unless complications set in, the patient will soon recover."[275]

Johnny was soon back managing the White Sox, but the team was a bust and ended the season in last place. Johnny was ready to head back home until he learned that plans were in place for the White Sox and Giants to visit London as part of a world tour. The teams were to play an exhibition game for King George V, who was to be a spectator. John McGraw was to give the King a running commentary of the game.[276]

How this all came about was a mystery to Troy John. After all, his team was at the bottom. Why would anyone want to see a last-place team? But since he was invited and his boss arranged everything, he was delighted to go. He knew he would be home well before the Christmas rush.

Frank Chance, 1924

Frank Chance never had a real opportunity of taking charge of the White Sox. He came to Chicago to join the club after it completed its spring training. Johnny Evers had been performing his duties as acting manager and Frank was pleased. Illness however, forced Chance to return to his California home.[277]

Owner Charles Comiskey offered Frank a leave of absence so he could return to the coast for a rest before taking on his managerial responsibilities. Shortly thereafter, the "Peerless Leader" returned in time for the initial game between Chicago and the Yankees. Illness again overtook him, and in a few weeks he was back in Southern California fighting against overwhelming odds.[278]

Frank Chance must have sensed that his time had come. He put in a call to Johnny Evers's sporting goods store and told the Trojan he was in poor physical condition and wanted to have a night in his room with the old famous combination. He said if John would come, Joe Tinker said he would come. John said he would be there and jotted down the address of Frank's home in Los Angeles, 653 South Burlington Avenue.[279]

When John got to Chance's home, Tinker was already there. It was an emotional occasion and they put in several days together shedding some tears for the way it used to be. When John and Joe left, they knew the end was near for their "Peerless Leader." They had agreed to keep the meeting quiet so as to keep away the newsmen who knew that Chance was seriously ill. A final meeting of the three of them would have been a gem of a story.[280]

Evers and his team in Bridge, England, November 15, 1924, for an exhibition game with the Giants before King George V, part of a world tour (International Newsreel; photograph mislabeled "King Edward").

Johnny Evers in his sporting goods store (National Baseball Hall of Fame Library).

At times, however, Frank seemed to be recovering from the combination of bronchial asthma and heart trouble that clung to him after he developed influenza in the fall of 1923. He and his family quietly celebrated his forty-seventh birthday on September 9, 1924. Six days later, September 15, Frank Chance took a turn for the worse. He was seized by recurrent asthmatic spasms that refused to abate. In the late afternoon the spasms became more severe. At 6:30 P.M., Mrs. Chance called an ambulance and rode with Frank to the Good Samaritan Hospital in Los Angeles. They arrived at 6:45 P.M. and half an hour later, the man who had piloted the national pastime into new horizons, faded quietly into unconsciousness and died.

Reportedly, Chance's last remarks about baseball concerned the White Sox, who were being managed by Johnny Evers. Chance said: "Johnny's having a hard row to hoe, but he's doing everything possible. He got more out of some of those White Sox fellows then they knew they had in them." Chance then told how overjoyed he would be to lean forward in the dugout and take the reins himself again next season.

Death certificate cites reason for Chance's demise (Los Angeles County Clerk).

News of Chance's death did not become known for hours. Then old friends, such as Barney Oldfield, Jim Jeffries and Abe Lyman vied in their condolences with bank presidents, newsboys, bootleggers, actors, jurists, reporters and trainmen.[281]

John McGraw, an old foe, joined in an expression of regret at Frank's death. He said: "I am losing an old and bitter battler but a warm friend. Chance was a great baseball man because he could fight desperately on the field and then forget his enmities afterward. He was a great player— I think one of the best first basemen ever in the game—but in addition he was a great leader because he asked no man to take any chance that he would not take."[282]

Under a pall of California lilies and roses, Frank Chance was interred at the Rosedale Cemetery in Los Angeles, Section N, Lot 109, Grave 2 NE. Surrounded by dozens of his friends, including several members of the organization he led four times to league championships, the former manager was buried in a cemetery shaded with cypress trees not far from Washington Baseball Park. Hundreds stood in a silent tribute to the "Peerless Leader."

Huge trucks were required to carry floral tributes to the graveside from men in the world of sport the country over, which included wreaths from the Chicago Cubs, White Sox, Boston Nationals, New York Yankees and other teams. Leaders in practically every other profession were also represented.

The pall bearers were: Barney Oldfield, famous automobile racer; Orvie Overall, who pitched ball for Manager Chance; John Powers, baseball magnate for whom Chance directed a Los Angeles team; Arthur Braley, Rodney Webster and John Kipper, all close friends of the famous first baseman.[283]

While Earl Houck, blind baseball fan and close friend of Chance, sang "Lead, Kindly Light," the gray casket was lowered away.

In Washington Park, the game between the San Francisco and Vernon clubs of the Pacific Coast League was halted, and players and fans bowed their heads for two minutes.

On the day after his death, newspapers across the country paid tribute to Chance's brilliant major league career. John J. Peri, of the *Stockton Daily Evening Record*, also told of the "Peerless Leader's" glorious early days, playing for Stockton, Fresno and San Jose in the Old State League.

Chance's death certificate listed Pulmonary Edema and Acute Glomerular Nephritis as the cause of death with Bronchial Asthma as a contributory cause. Since Frank had no children, his Last Will And Testament bequeathed all of his property, both personal and real, to his wife, Edythe.

CHAPTER 12

Hectic Years

Joe Tinker, 1925–1930

Joe Tinker and his associates formed the "Tinker-Joe-Land Co." and the "Orlando Florida Land Co." and stormed onto a vast acreage of scrubby land throughout the Orlando area, transforming it into a Florida paradise.

The Tinker Building at 18 West Pine Street that housed Joe's real estate business was completed in 1925. The colorful facade was a combination of buff bricks, cut limestone, glazed ceramic tile, stained glass and wood. A beautiful sight. Emblazoned across the top of the building was the landlord's name: Tinker.[284]

When the building was completed, Joe severed his relationship with McCracken and went into equal partnership with Jay Pitts and his wife Maude. They began the construction of JAMAJO, a subdivision near Lake Susannah. The name JAMAJO was taken from the first two letters of Jay's, Maude's and Joe's names.[285]

Dr. Pitts was a practicing dentist and physician at 64 West Randolph in downtown Chicago.[286] The two families became best of friends when Joe was playing at the West Side Grounds in the early 1900s. After

Joe went into the real estate business, Jay and Maude bought half the stock (250 shares) in the JAMAJO subdivision for $25,000. They were listed as officers and members of the Board of Directors in the realty business even though they lived in Chicago.[287]

Business took off and continued to climb. By December 31, 1925, accounts receivable were $144,885.92.[288] Joe took his son, Joe, Jr., into the business and started planning for other projects. He began two other subdivisions, Tinker Heights and Lawson Park, and invested in commercial buildings, buying the landmark Longwood Hotel in 1926. Joe then teamed up with Edward Henck and built the Henck-Tinker Building. It housed the Longwood State Bank, the first bank in town. The rest of the building was leased to MacReynolds Drug Store, Jackson's Grocery and a barbershop. Joe was instrumental in inducing the City of Orlando to purchase the fair grounds. It became a city park of some 40 acres.[289]

Tinker was said to have been worth a cool $1 million, according to Florida friends quoted in Orlando newspapers. He once said he had $400,000 in the bank.[290]

Busy as Joe was, he still had time for baseball. His friendship with Gary Herrmann, owner of the Cincinnati Reds, enabled Joe to sell him on the idea of using Tinker Field for spring training. He took personal charge of letting the Cincinnati club know what was needed to keep the ballpark in tiptop shape.

In a letter to Herrmann, dated June 27, 1925, Joe said:

Dear Gary:

Wish to let you know that we have used up all of the funds in taking care of Tinker Field. So I wish you would mail me some money to take care of the ground keeper and also pay to run the mower, as we have to keep the grass cut once a week in order to keep the weeds down. The field looks fine and in great shape.

We have allowed a little amateur here on Thursdays, of which I received $50.00 and will receive $50 more the middle of July, which will show in the bank statement. I also had to take care of some insurance on the stands.

Glad to see that the Club has had a nice home stay and I hope they will continue the winning streak on their next trip.

Florida is sure booming. There is as much business here now at this time in the winter. The people are coming down here faster than they are going north.

That 1,200 acres that I spoke to you about was sold a while back for $75 and will eventually go to $100 per acre. You missed a great chance to pick up some nice easy money.

With best wishes to everyone, I remain,
Yours very truly,
By Joe Tinker[291]

Joe was adept at shifting from one activity to another and he soon became a boosting force behind building the Sanford-Orlando Kennel Club and the Seminole Race Track in Longwood. He was instrumental in locating the site for the track. It was unique in its time by its design, encircling a lake.[292]

Joe also had time for romance. On April 15, 1926, while in Cincinnati, he married Mary Edington at the Hamilton County Courthouse. Jack Hendricks, manager of the Reds, and Mrs. Hendricks were best man and matron of honor.[293]

Mary was born and reared in Orlando as a member of the Rock family and had been married to Eddie Ross Edington, one of the greatest black-faced comedians on the vaudeville stage. His stage name was Ross. In 1925 he was listed in the *Orlando City Directory* as an actor. Mary was listed as his wife. They had one son, Jerry. One can speculate that Joe met the couple as they toured the vaudeville circuit and that Eddie died, for he was not in the *City Directory* in 1926.

After the marriage, Joe moved into his wife's home at 809 Lucerne Terrace while the rest of the Tinker clan continued to live at 437 Ruth Lane. Amidst the gaiety of his marriage and the satisfaction Joe must have had as to the wealth he had been accumulating, Tinker was suddenly hit with a summons, filed February 3, 1927. He was ordered to appear before the Circuit Court in Orange County to answer a Bill of Complaint filed against him by Jay F. Pitts, his real estate partner. The complainant proved he was an equal partner in the JAMAJO subdivision and gave numerous instances where money had been used without being voted upon by the Board of Directors. Pitts claimed that he had not been given his fair share of the profits.

On February 26, 1927, Frank A. Smith, Judge of the Circuit Court, ruled in favor of the Complainant, giving the JAMAJO contracts and all monies to be received to Jay Pitts.[294]

Other calamities followed. On October 27, 1928, the local newspaper reported:

> Joe Tinker arrested by Orlando police. Nine other persons were arrested with Tinker. They were charged with operating a Bolita gambling house.
> Bolita—Spanish for "little ball"—is a game played by tossing a sack of numbered balls among the participants. The winning ball is selected by grasping it from the outside of the sack. The payoff is 60 to 1.

Sheriff Karel, who led the raid on the establishment, said Tinker had his
hand on some bolita tickets resting on a table when the raiders
entered.[295]

Tinker was released on $300 bail. It was no big deal, pretty much
like the cops raiding a private poker party, which they sometimes did. It
never came to court.

Shortly after the Bolita incident, Joe appeared in court to answer
charges by Christeen Evans and her husband, residents of Orange County
owed money by Tinker. They in turn received a promissory note that
guaranteed 8 percent per annum and a mortgage deed on property that
secured payment on the note. They filed suit on December 5, 1928, claiming thousands of dollars in back payments. Judge Frank A. Smith again
ruled in favor of the Plaintiff, thus allowing the complainants to foreclose
on the property Joe had deeded to them.[296]

The court rulings were severe blows, but even before the Judge had
handed down his decisions, the Florida land boom had started to collapse.
A pullback in stock prices in March 1926 forced some investors to take
their money out of Florida land to cover losses in the stock market. Even
more devastating was a September 1926 hurricane that ravaged Miami and
much of South Florida, killing almost 400 people. An investigation by
the National Better Business Bureau into fraudulent real estate promo-
tions also tempered buyers' enthusiasm for Florida land. The boom turned
into a bust and with the '29 crash, real estate developers were wiped out.
Tinker was no exception. For him, it was even worse because of the court
rulings that had been adjudicated against him. His savings were gone.[297]

Joe's hard driving will to win and his fiery spirit put him back into
solvency. He and Johnny Evers signed a contract for a ten-week theatri-
cal tour to the leading cities of the country doing a baseball skit.[298]
Performing in front of a crowd was old hat for Joe Tinker. He had experience on the vaudeville stage. He was well received, having gotten rave
reviews from *Variety*, the *Chicago Journal* and the *New York Telegraph*.[299]

Having completed the vaudeville tour and with money in his pocket,
Joe Tinker continued on with his realty business. He still owned the Tinker Building, and selling lots and homes for clients was something he had
learned to do. He was hopeful that the realty market would improve.

His life with Mary, his second wife, was a happy one. She adored
him and told stories about her famous husband to friends and neighbors.
When quoted by the local press, the readers learned: "Joe attends the
World Series every year, and laments the fact that baseball is not the two-
fisted sport it was in the days of Tinker-to-Evers-to-Chance. He thinks

Upper Longwood Hotel, a Tinker commercial investment in 1929 (photograph by the author).

modern ballplayers 'can't stand the gaff' and regards Babe Ruth as the greatest figure the game has produced. Although he won fame with the Chicago Cubs, he likes the American League teams better and thinks the New York Yankees are the last word in baseball teams."

Mary Tinker described her husband as "a home-loving man who has three sons and a daughter by a previous marriage. Joe doesn't think any of his boys will become baseball players, but he is trying to develop my ten-year old son by my first marriage into a star. The youngster told me the other day that he is undecided whether he wants to become a ball player or motorcycle policeman."[300]

Nothing was said about Roy Tinker who had just moved in with Joe, Jr., and Rollie Tinker at 437 Ruth Lane. It was the first time the name Roy had appeared in any of the research documents related to Joe Tinker. Roy was listed as working for Fariss & Fariss. As a salesman, he sold automobiles, trucks, tractors and farm implements. Joe, Jr. and Rollie Tinker were both listed as salesmen working for Joe Tinker's Realty Co.

In interviews with the Tinker families today, not one had ever heard of Roy Tinker. Tom Tinker, Joe's grandson, speculated that this may have

Henck-Tinker building built during land boom, as viewed today (photograph by the author).

been Joe Tinker's twin brother, but whoever he was, Roy disappeared from the *City Directory* as quickly as he had appeared, never to be heard from again. This is a real mystery about a Tinker who suddenly appeared and just as suddenly disappeared.

Meanwhile, the life of Joe Tinker was a busy one. In addition to his realty business, Joe was soon back in baseball, his old love. In 1929, he scouted the Philadelphia Athletics for the Chicago Cubs. The two teams were about to start World Series play and Joe said, "If we can stop Simmons and Foxx, the Series is ours. They are the only men we are afraid of. The Athletics have a good ball team but the kid on first and the big boy in the outfield are the only ones we'll worry about."[301]

The Cubs could not stop the two sluggers—or Jimmy Dykes, who batted .421 in the five games, or Mickey Cochrane (.400) or Bing Miller (.368)—and Chicago lost the World Series.

While in Chicago, Joe sold a floral store he owned and headed back to Orlando. On the way back he decided to stop at Chattanooga to see old friends. After visiting with them, he hopped on a train carrying President Frank Offerman and Manager Bill Clymer of the Buffalo Bisons. Joe met them in the observation car. When the Buffalo pair asked Tinker what he was up to, he told them he hoped to land a job as coach or

Joe Tinker and his second wife, Mary (courtesy Historical Society of Central Florida).

Joe Tinker (center), Buffalo Bisons coach in 1929 (courtesy Gloria Tinker).

business manager to some Class AA team. Offerman took the tip and with Manager Clymer adjourned to their stateroom, leaving Tinker alone in the car. After a short conference, Manager Clymer left the stateroom. Approaching Tinker, he said: "Say, if you are not kidding, we have a post for you. It's all a question of salary. The boss wants to see you up in car II." Tinker accepted the first offer from the Bisons.[302]

Tinker was a big help to the Bisons. He was a chatterbox on the coaching lines and demanded hustle from his mates. But in mid-season 1930, Clymer resigned and Tinker quit with him. Joe was quickly snatched up by the Jersey City International League Club. He replaced Nick Allen as manager and finished the season.[303]

The appointment of Tinker was taken to mean a stronger interest in the Jersey club on the part of the Yankees office. This evaluation came about after Ed Barrow had offered Tinker a job as official mascot for the Yankees. Tinker watched the Yankees beat the Browns on June 10, 1929. He had been going to Yankees games for three seasons and when asked, Joe said, "I have yet to see them beaten. In so far as I have been able to see, nobody's got a chance with them. But of course, I haven't been a regular attendant at the Stadium."[304]

Joe Tinker (standing, third from right) and the Buffalo Bisons team (courtesy Tom Tinker).

Baseball is a strange business. Superstitions reign supreme. Ed Barrow may have wanted Joe in the stadium because as Joe said, he had yet to see them lose. The once great shortstop was seen as a good luck omen.

Good luck omen or not, Joe Tinker wasn't about to sit around and be a "mascot." He was soon back in Orlando. He learned that after seven seasons at Tinker Field, Cincinnati was going elsewhere for spring training. Joe arranged for the Brooklyn Dodgers to take over.[305]

In the midst of finalizing this arrangement, he received a call from Jacksonville. It was his son Rollie. Joe learned that a thief had broken into his son's home in Jacksonville at 310 East Church Street and had stolen his World Series medal. This was the gold, ruby and diamond medal Joe had received as a member of the 1908 Cubs championship team. He had given it to Rollie four years earlier. His son prized it highly, not for its monetary worth but for its sentimental value.

The stolen medal was one of two that Joe Tinker received from the Chicago Cubs. Each of them was engraved with the head of a bear. For eyes, the bear had two blazing rubies and in the mouth was a huge diamond. The Jacksonville police investigated the crime, but the medal was never found.[306]

As Joe fretted over the lost medal, he thought about the loss of the

Joe Tinker wearing his 1908 World Series medal (courtesy Tom and Gloria Tinker).

wealth he had accumulated. He knew that in spite of lack of demand for real estate, Florida had a wonderful climate that would be attractive to people living up north. So he decided to try something new in an effort to regain his fortune.

Johnny Evers, 1925–1930

When Johnny Evers returned from the Giants-White Sox European exhibition, the 1924 Yuletide season was well underway in Albany. His brother was doing a hefty business selling sports equipment. There was quite a hum in the store when Johnny walked in, and he went right to work. He was once again a celebrity. While working, he would revert to his old self and talk baseball. By the end of the day he had nothing more to look forward to except the lonely climb to the second floor of the Berkshire hotel.

His Elks brothers encouraged him to join the Albany Democratic Party and he became quite active in politics. The locals soon learned that Johnny was quite a story- teller. He became a popular speaker at political smokers. This clearly cheered him up.[307]

A favorite story was about umpire Cy Rigler. He was behind the plate in a very important game, with the Cubs battling it out with John McGraw's Giants. Trouble started brewing late in the game. With the bases full, Rigler called the batter out on what the fans believed was a low ball. The bleachers went wild. Several players also yelled at the umpire, among them Evers.

In the ninth inning, Rigler called a ball on one of the visiting players that Evers thought high enough to be a strike. When the fans had grown tired of voicing their opinions, and everything had grown nice and quiet, Evers decided it was time for him to assert himself. In a voice plainly audible to the crowd he yelled, "No wonder he misses the low ones, he can't see over his chest."

The crowd howled in laughter, but Evers paid the penalty by "retiring" from the game. Later, he was requested to rest up for three days by the league president for his public display of humor.

Another little story concerned umpire Bill Klem. Evers enjoyed telling how this famous umpire pulled a fast one on him. Chicago was playing in Philadelphia and as was customary, quite a few of the players planned to spend the Sunday off day in Atlantic City. Umpire Klem also intended to make the trip. Several times during the Saturday game, Klem beseeched Evers not to go but failed to give any reason. Finally, when curiosity got the better of Evers, he asked: "Say, Klem, why shouldn't I go to Atlantic City tomorrow?"

"Well," replied Klem, "I intend taking a dip in the surf myself and if you're there it will be mighty uncomfortable, as all the crabs in the sea will flock around to see you."

"Umpires," admitted Evers, "were sometimes also crabs."[308]

When Johnny told these stories it was obvious to everyone that the once fiery Trojan had mellowed considerably with age. He became the *piece de resistance* on the banquet circuit. His 23 years in the big show had given Johnny an inexhaustible reservoir of mirth provoking stories. Anyone interested in such stories could listen to him for hours without becoming bored. In fact, it became a common occurrence for friends to pass the time enjoyably by sitting down with a bowl full of pretzels and some drinks to listen to Evers. He had held just about every important post on a ball team. He knew the game from A to Z and knew the angles. Although age was creeping up on him, he was still as active as ever.[309]

During the 1925 season, Evers organized and managed the Evers All-Stars, a semi-professional organization that played at Saratoga during the racing season. Suddenly out of the blue, John McGraw called. The lure of the diamond was strong and Evers became a scout for the New York Giants in 1926 and '27.

In 1928, when Judge Emile Fuchs, president and managing director of the Boston Braves, began his ill-fated venture as manager, he called Johnny back to Boston as assistant manager and coach. In his new post, Johnny was expected to provide the inspiration needed to bring about a winning team.

In a press release to the *Troy Evening Record*, Johnny said: "My return to baseball will not result in any change in my plans as far as my residence and my business in Albany. I am more than glad to get back into the game and I am particularly glad to return to Boston."[310]

The club did poorly, finishing seventh. Johnny demonstrated that he didn't like defeats any more now than he did when he was one of the mainsprings of Frank Chance's Cubs. After a losing game, he walked off the field with Ben Cantwell, a Braves pitcher, who had been tagged for New York's winning run. Johnny's jaws were going up and down, his face was crimson red. He didn't enjoy losing a game in which 14 members of his team were left on base.[311]

The 1929 Braves came in last. On the field, Johnny was no different than before. His age didn't change the way he reacted to decisions made by umpires. He was still the same old Johnny. On May 23, 1929, he was suspended for three days by National League President John Heydler for trouble with the umpires in the New York series. In 1930, in addition to being coach and assistant manager to Emile Fuchs, Johnny was asked to be a scout for the Braves. He now had the additional responsibility of finding new players for this down and out club. It was quite a challenge and one he had not faced before.

CHAPTER 13

Difficulty in
Staying Afloat

Johnny Evers, 1931–1936

In spite of difficult financial times in 1931, Johnny Evers headed out for Los Angeles. Years had passed since Frank Chance had died, and Johnny wanted to put a wreath on his gravesite. Although people saw the Trojan, when he was crossed, as an insolent, snarling, aggressive grouch with a tongue that knew neither fear nor control, he also had a very sensitive side that was not often recognized. His trip from Albany to Los Angeles for the purpose of laying down a wreath clearly demonstrates Johnny's warm, close, tender feelings for the man that had been his boss for so many years. He had a need to again be close to his friend, to tell him in his own quiet way that he had always admired and still missed him.

Upon Johnny's return to Albany, he found it hard to stay afloat financially. The Depression had made it difficult if not impossible for people to live normal lives. Money was now needed for rent and food and a pair of shoes, not bats and balls. Johnny Evers, however, was able to remain

Johnny Evers lays a wreath on the Frank Chance gravesite in 1931 (Associated Press).

in business. When he was away earning a salary coaching, managing or scouting for the Braves, his brother Joe continued to manage the store. Even so, Johnny found it difficult to pay his wife the alimony ordered at the time of their separation.

He decided to go to court. He wanted a reduction in the yearly payments. The lower courts ruled in favor of his wife but Johnny was a fighter and aggressively took the matter to a higher court.

On March 8, 1934, *The Sporting News* reported: "Johnny Evers, former second baseman of the Chicago Cubs, lost a decision in the Supreme Court in Troy, N.Y. last week. Evers, who has been separated from his wife, petitioned for a reduction in his alimony payments to $1,200 a year. Justice Pierce J. Russell denied the petition. Mrs. Evers claimed he was in arrears on the alimony while Johnny asserted he had no source of income."

Johnny was with the Braves through 1934. He then became general manager of the Albany Senators in the International League club for the

1935 season. He was once again thrust into the national limelight when he signed Edwin "Alabama" Pitts, a paroled convict-turned-ball player, to a contract. President W.G. Bramham of the National Association declared Pitts ineligible.

Evers disagreed with the ruling. Even in the twilight of his career, he carried on like in the old days. Johnny spoke his mind straight out, no ifs, ands, or buts. Once said, he would not back down. He continued to surprise the baseball world. He fought for the right to have Pitts play for Albany despite the National Association's protests. He went head to head with baseball Commissioner Judge Kenesaw Mountain Landis and won! Landis finally overruled President Bramham.[312]

The townspeople of Troy loved to see their boy win a battle and never tired of inviting Johnny to local events. The *Troy Times* reported every bit of news about their hero.

On February 19, 1935, Evers addressed a meeting of the American Legion where he told veterans what he did in France during the war. Johnny recounted a ball game he once arranged at Verdun, while the roar of the cannon could be heard three miles away. He was umpiring a game between artillery and infantry teams and made a decision on a close play. When the squawking became hot, he ordered the military band to play "The Star Spangled Banner." Everyone stood up and Johnny seized the moment to walk off the field.[313]

The American Legion boys then listened to an umpire story, the one topic Johnny loved to talk about and the one topic everyone loved to listen to. The veterans were no exception. They listened to the time when the Trojan was actually kind to an umpire and his kindness was wasted.

Years earlier, when Evers was in his prime as a player, and an exponent of argumentative words, he ran into a tangle with umpire Bob Emslie over a decision. Like all other such players, Evers came out second best and was shooed from the game by "Uncle Bob." Before departing however, Evers exploded some of his choicest vocabulary. He called Emslie about everything that was in the book and invented a few new pet names for good measure.

"You ought to be ashamed of yourself for such language directed at me," said Emslie. "I am a respectable man that has raised a family and I have two darling daughters."

Evers remembered the incident after the season was over and felt bad about having spoken so to the veteran arbiter. By way of atonement, he purchased two large dolls about three feet high, all dressed in the latest fashions and sent them to Emslie for his darling daughters.

Next season, when Emslie and Evers first crossed trails, the umpire sought out Johnny to thank him for the nice Christmas presents. "And do you know," said Emslie, "that one of my babies is 32 years old and the other is 28."[314]

Such generosity from the man who had been called "Crab" was indeed a rarity, but shows another side of Johnny Evers. He was a player who fought for every inch to win a game. Off the field, he could reflect on his behavior and words, and could recognize his impropriety. He would then try to make amends. It did not happen too often but the capability was there.

As the 1935 season moved forward, Johnny took on the responsibility of general manager to the Albany Senators. On September 9, however, he handed in his resignation. He claimed his authority had been restricted and that he was hampered in his efforts to build up a winning team.

It started at an International League meeting in winter. Owner Joe Cambria voted for Evers for president of the circuit. In the spring, an "Evers Day" was arranged in Toronto. That was when the issue of the uniform came to the fore. Johnny wanted to appear on the coaching lines in the toggery of his championship playing days. President Charles Knapp refused. Admirers of Johnny took this action as a backhanded slap at one of the game's outstanding figures.

In June, there was interference with his plans and Evers tried to quit. Because of his popularity, Cambria wouldn't let him withdraw. Friends of Johnny then expected the club owner to visit Albany and to settle the question of countermanded orders. But he failed to appear.

It was late in the schedule when Cambria and Evers finally got together in New York. It was thought that plans for the next season had been gone over and that Evers would have more authority. Johnny however, immediately wrote to Cambria, giving him five days notice for his departure. Apparently, the Trojan was not at all satisfied.[315]

In April 1936, Johnny was again on the warpath, fighting for a gold lifetime pass to any and all ball parks. He knew he qualified for such a pass. He wrote Ford Frick, president of the National League. He listed his years as an active member of league teams and concluded his letter by saying, "I am surely entitled to a gold pass and I feel sure you will give this your prompt attention."[316]

There was then an exchange of letters where Johnny's time as an active player was being checked up on. He was soon given his gold pass. Once again, the Trojan knew he was correct and was willing to fight for what he believed to be a just cause.[317]

By May 1936, Johnny had his lifetime pass, but he no longer had a job. He no longer had money. He had insurmountable debts and was unable to pay a whopping $10,499. He filled out a voluntary petition and filed for bankruptcy in the United States Court.[318]

His health began to fail and his brother Joe took over the store full time. Johnny's plight became known to the baseball world, and an effort was made to find him a job. On May 20, a letter testified to this effort:

> Dear Bill:
>
> The enclosed is just a suggestion—but don't you think it would be a nice gesture for the National League to do something for Johnny Evers in the hour of his need? There certainly ought to be a place in baseball for one who was as smart a player as he was.
>
> Very truly yours,
> Edgar Forest Wolfe
> Linden Apts.
> Lansdowne, Pa.[319]

It's not known whether anything positive came about as a result of this letter. What is known, is that people in Troy and Albany were not going to let their hero go down swinging in his time of need.

Joe Tinker, 1931–1936

Joe Tinker was determined to regain his fortune. Although he was no longer a young man, his relentless fighting spirit was still there. So was his enthusiasm. All he needed was a strategy, a new approach to selling real estate.

The idea came to him when he explored the ways in which he could reach people who might want a place of their own in the Orlando area. Even people who might want to rent before buying, to see how it felt, to see if they would be happy living in a sunny climate.

Joe took flying lessons, and with his experience in the execution of dashing and daring plays on the field, he soon executed one off the field. He dropped leaflets from the sky, offering a variety of real estate holdings by people who wanted to sell. Joe was now working for a commission on everything he sold.[320]

Although he reached a lot of people and had dreams of possibly making it big in real estate once again, he still had that itch to get back into baseball. He put the word out that he was interested in becoming an umpire in the Pacific Coast League. Joe even had Connie Mack recommend him to Harry Williams, president of the League. But the word soon came back that "the umpiring for 1931 is complete."[321]

Joe then had another idea. On June 4, 1931, he sent a letter to Honorable R.A. Gray, Secretary of State, Tallahassee, Florida. It said, "I am enclosing herewith, Certificate of Incorporation of Joe Tinker Billiard Company, Inc., which please kindly file in your office." Joe had gone into the business of "...buying, selling and dealing in pool and billiard tables and all equipment appertaining thereto and used in connection therewith; to own, operate and maintain pool or billiard parlors anywhere in the State of Florida or in the United States of America...." The corporation issued 100 shares of stock at $100 per share. The Board of Directors were Joe Tinker (50 shares), Mary Tinker, Joe's wife, (49 shares), and Charles Rock, Jr., Mary's brother (1 share).[322]

A billiards and pool parlor was opened at 6 West Church Street. On April 14, 1932, James Isaminger, a sportswriter, wrote a piece on Joe Tinker. He said:

> Chubby Joe Tinker, he is 52 years old now and is happy and contented in Orlando, Fla., where he operates the most successful billiard room in this gem of the orange belt. During the last few weeks of the spring training season, if you visited this establishment, you would have found such players as Walberg, Haas, Miller, Boley, DeShong, Cain, Carter and Heving of the Athletics, Maranville, Spohrer and Berger of the Braves, and Babe Herman, Durocher, Lombardi and Lucas of the Reds, trying to land the eight ball in the side pocket.[323]

By 1933, Joe had expanded his billiard parlor to include Tinker's Lunch Room. He hired Harry A. Stone to be his manager while he busied himself with the realty office. Harry was an old friend who Joe first met at the West Side Grounds in Chicago. On December 5, 1933, prohibition was repealed. Joe immediately made plans to open one of the city's first bars, Tinker's Tavern.[324]

As soon as the bar opened, Joe Tinker was laid low when his wife became ill and was hospitalized. She had an operation, but was believed to be on the way to recovery when complications suddenly set in. She died on February 28. She was buried at the Greenwood cemetery amongst members of the Rock family. Mary Rock Tinker's headstone lay not more than 20 paces away from Ruby Tinker, Joe's first wife.[325]

Mary's will bequeathed her personal property to her sisters and brother. The remainder of her estate was left to her son. In listing her personal property, she had itemized four secure notes, #254, #256, #354 and #356. These notes were for $1,000 each from the Joe B. Tinker Bil-

Left to right, Rollie, Ruby and William Tinker at Tinker Field (National Base-ball Hall of Fame library).

liard Company. Mary had helped her husband form the Tinker-Joe-Bil-liard Company, Inc.[326]

When Mary's home at 809 Lucerne Terrace was sold, Joe had to move. He could not return to the home at 437 Ruth Lane, which he had purchased after he first arrived in Orlando. It too, had been sold. His children had last lived there in 1928 and were out of there in 1929. That was during the time Joe had been dragged into court by a number of suits. It's possible that he had to sell his home out of necessity. Orlando *City Directories* do not show where Joe lived after Mary died.

On March 29, 1934, a month after Mary's death, sportswriter, Rud Rennie, walked up a flight of stone steps beside a garage on Wall Street and entered Tinker's Tavern. The legendary infielder seemed content:

> He is stout now. His once black hair is turning gray. He will be fifty-four in July. His face and hands are browned by the sun. He has the look of a sturdy man who has lost neither his courage nor daring. At a table in the bare-walled back room Tinker sat and talked.
>
> "We were good," he said, talking about the old Tinker-Evers-Chance combination, "because we had confidence and were not afraid to try

things. Infielders nowadays make me tired. Few of them are ever in position to go through with difficult plays. They may get the ball but they can't rifle it because they are all out of position.

"(Travis) Jackson is one of the few who can throw the ball. And (Rabbit) Maranville stands out even yet because he was always in position to make a play. He got the ball away fast. He is the only one who did the things I am talking about and he is an old-timer."[327]

Whether in baseball or business, Joe always did things in a big way. One saloon was not enough. A clipping from a Miami paper said: "Joe Tinker, a visitor here, has become a permanent resident and business man. Joe, the same Joe of the Evers and Chance days, is now a partner in the Wonder Bar at 23 N.E. First Avenue, and if Joe runs true to form, it's another notable sports gathering point for this sector."[328]

Joe may have allowed his name to be used at the Wonder Bar in exchange for remuneration. It is difficult to envision him in Miami at the Wonder Bar, at Tinker's Tavern in Orlando and at the Tinker Building handling realty properties, while a few blocks away, Fred Stone managed the former shortstop's billiard and pool parlor as well as a lunch room.

In the midst of all this activity, Joe Tinker suddenly disappeared. Orlando City records do not show where he lived in 1935 and 1936. Two of his children were still around, living in Orlando. Rollie was chief clerk at a hotel and Ruby was a nurse in training. On occasion, their brother William, a dancer, would come to visit and they went to Tinker Field and horsed around with bats and balls.[329]

In checking other records, it was learned that on September 16, 1936, the Tinker-Joe-Billiard Company, Inc. was "Dissolved by Proclamation" by the Florida Department of State, Division of Corporations. On the same day, the Tinker-Joe-Land Company and the Orlando Florida Land Company suffered the same fate. The Florida Division of Corporations said that when Tinker's corporations failed to file a business report with the state for that year, the corporations were automatically erased from the state's files.[330] The only corporation left standing was the Tinker-Joe-Realty Company. With all this going on, and with two of his kids living in town, where was Joe?

Red Newton, a sports columnist, explained Tinker's whereabouts in his column, "The Morning After." He showed what Joe was doing in 1935 and most of 1936.

> A ghost out of baseball's colorful past strode into our office yesterday afternoon, a gray-haired, semi-portly ghost 54 years old, yet with a sparkle in his eyes.

"What are you doing in Tampa?" I asked. "I thought you had moved from Orlando to Miami."

"I did," said Mr. Joe Tinker, of the Tinker-to-Evers-to-Chance double play fame of 25 years ago, who spent the spring of 1916 at Plant field here as manager of the Chicago Cubs. "But I've taken a new job. I'm the good will ambassador for a big beer company. My territory is Florida and my duties consist in keeping our dealers in a good humor. But I'm tired of talking beer, so I came up to talk baseball."

After talking about the current pennant race, Red asked:

"What's the difference between the game as played today and the baseball of your day?"

"Huh!" said Mr. Tinker, "If I tell you, why you'll put it down as nothing but the ravings of a washed-up old-timer."

"No, I won't."

"All right," said Mr. Tinker, "I'll tell you. They don't play baseball today."

"What do they play?"

"They play hitting home runs," said Mr. Tinker. "They talk about Babe Ruth saving baseball after the 1919 Black Sox scandal. Why Ruth is the one who ruined baseball."

"You mean old Babe Ruth, the big fellow who has collected more than a million bucks from baseball?"

"Yep! I mean old Babe. When he came along and started popping the ball over the fence, everybody quit playing baseball and went to straining their backs trying to knock home runs. And they don't try in baseball today as they did back in my day."

"They don't try?"

"That's right. I've watched a hundred of these big league infielders training in Florida during the last seven or eight springs, and they let many a base hit get by them simply because they don't or won't go after it. Baseball players today are lazy. And for some strange reason the managers don't even try to pep 'em up."

"I don't quite understand your argument."

"I'll explain it," said Mr. Tinker. "When a batter today bangs the ball to the right of an infielder, what does the infielder do? Why he reaches across his body with his gloved left hand, wastes both time and motion, and if he does retrieve the ball, he's in no position to make the throw. He then loses more seconds by having to stop and turn around to make the throw. That's why so many of these sure-fire outs go for scratch singles these days. Either that or these modern infielders are afraid they'll get a little dirt on their uniforms by diving after the ball."

"How did you fellows twenty-five years ago field the grounders hit to your right?"

"Hell. We caught 'em with our bare right hand. Therefore, we were in a position to throw without losing a second simply by coming through with our right hand."

"Well, what has Ruth to do with this particular default of modern infielders?"

"He's to blame for this, too. Most modern ball players defend Ruth because his $80,000 a year salary was responsible for their bigger and better paychecks. There you have the trouble. Most of these high-priced stars are getting too much money. They've become plutocrats, not base-ball players. When they're out there on the field, they're thinking of how they're going to invest their $10,000 or $20,000, not how to cut off an enemy run by making an impossible stop. I tell you, they let too many outs go for singles. But tell me something. What is the matter with your fight game?"

"You've already explained that, too. My fighters, like your baseball players, have gone plutocrats. You give any young fellow a lot of money and right then he quits trying."

"Well," said Mr. Tinker. "What is your cure for the boxing depression?"

"Why I would make that bozo Max Baer defend his title once a month in a 15-round fight. Then I would fire his new valet, Skettles by name. Can you imagine a pugilistic plutocrat too damned lazy to put on his own shirt?"

"You said it," said Mr. Tinker.[331]

After that discussion, Joe Tinker must have traveled many miles and must have jawed away with many a beer dealer throughout Florida over the next year and a half or so. Somewhere along his route, something dramatically happened.

CHAPTER 14

Still Plugging Away

Joe Tinker, 1937–1940

In 1937, Joe Tinker was back. He had a new wife, his third wife, Helen. They were living at 45 Bonnie Loch Court in Orlando.

Where he met her and where she came from is anybody's guess. What she was like, God only knows. One thing is for certain, they were not married in Orlando for the city had no record of a marriage certificate. They had to have been married between March 1934 (after Mary's death) and August 25, 1936 (the date in the *City Directory* showing they were married).

Once back in Orlando, Joe Tinker returned to the realty business. His only corporation not dissolved was The Joe Tinker Realty Co. It listed Joe as president, Jas. E. Harper as vice president and Arth. E. Harper as secretary. The office was no longer in the Tinker Building. It was at 29 W. Central Ave.

There was no more flying, no more leaflets floating down from the sky. Instead, Joe placed ads in local newspapers. His business was selling parcels of land and homes, selling and renting anything his clients wanted to dispose of. Even a gas water heater was offered, the ad saying, "sell cheap

213

for cash." A buck here, a buck there, generated income, and income was what Joe desperately needed.[332]

Illness overtook him in 1937 and he was laid low by influenza, kidney problems and heart complications.[333] Joe bounced back however, and was soon out of the hospital, still in need of income. Even so, the mere mention of anything baseball, veered him off in that direction.

He soon found himself at Wrigley Field to honor his former teammate and one time boss, Frank Chance. The news report said:

> Chicago, June 23, 1937—Batteries for Today! For Chicago, Three Fingered Brown pitchin'; Jimmy Archer catchin'.
>
> That was the set-up in Wrigley Field today when former teammates of the late Frank Chance, manager of the great Cubs from 1906 to 1912, honored the "Peerless Leader," celebrating Frank Chance Day in an exhibition game before the Cubs and Giants took the field.
>
> At the keystone sack capered Joe Tinker and Johnny Evers, baseball's most famous double-play combination. Old Jack McCarthy patrolled left field, Ginger Beaumont, center and Ward Miller, right. Manager Grimm and Coach Corridon of the present Cubs filled in at first and third. A bronze plaque, to be mounted at Wrigley Field, was dedicated in memory of Chance, Tinker and Evers making the presentation and Charley Grimm accepting it.[334]
>
> Before their appearance at Wrigley Field, the famous athletes of days gone by, were guests of honor at a luncheon. The old-timers paid a stirring tribute to "The Peerless Leader." Tinker, who was near death last winter, declared he saw Chance when his life almost ebbed away.[335]

After returning to Orlando, Joe Tinker took on an additional responsibility. The press reported that he had been "appointed manager of the Orlando Gulls of the Florida State League." His job was to begin immediately. "And it was going to be a real task," the newspaper said, "for the Gulls are in the league cellar with a record of only seven wins in thirty games."[336]

Joe never got started. An Associated Press release on July 24 said, "Joe Tinker resigned today as manager of the Orlando club in the Florida State League. The former big leaguer said the club was unable to pay him."[337]

When Class AA minor league teams came to play at Tinker Field, Joe was seen to hurry out of his realty office and head that way, going there as often as he could. He loved to sit at the end of the left field bleachers and always had plenty of company. Friends and strangers crowded around Joe, who loved to tell stories.

Tinker said he once came close to being killed, or at least seriously

Tinker and Evers dedicate Chance plaque at Wrigley Field 1937 (Associated Press).

wounded as an aftermath of a game. The Cubs had been beaten and they stormed into the clubhouse snarling. Joe hopped on the player whom he blamed for the loss of the game.

"The trainer's shears were on top of a trunk," Joe said, "and he grabbed them and started for me. I was really scared because I knew he was a wild man and would have stabbed me sure, and I ran."

"And what happened?"

"Oh," he said, "four or five of the other fellows jumped on him from behind and took the shears away from him."[338]

Although Tinker didn't tell the next story, he sure must have remembered it well. The second baseman, Dick Egan of Cincinnati, got furious at Joe when he executed a vicious slide into second. The two men had words and Egan challenged Tinker to a fight, telling him that as "soon as this game's over, I'm gonna knock your blankety-blank-blank head off!"

Tinker accepted the challenge. Though hot-tempered, the Cubs shortstop cooled off rapidly and by the time the game ended he had forgotten about the dispute. Not so Egan. The furious Red waited outside the dressing room and then went inside, only to find that Tinker had just departed.

"He's yellow!" cried Egan. "He's run out on me."

Frank Chance spoke up, "Joe Tinker never ran away from a fight in his life. I'll get him for you."

Chance ran out onto the field and saw Tinker just passing second base, heading for the exit. "Hey, Joe," yelled Chance, and Joe turned around just in time to see the bellicose Egan racing toward him, fists clenched.

According to writers Ira and H. Allen Smith, Tinker calmly removed his coat, and in a moment the battle had begun inside a circle of ballplayers. It lasted perhaps five minutes. Witnesses said few men ever took such a beating in that length of time as Egan got from Tinker. When it was over, Tinker's hair wasn't even ruffled, though "unbiased witnesses" said he did have to straighten his tie a little.[339]

The afternoons at Tinker Field kept Joe in touch with old acquaintances. At times, he was offered different kinds of baseball jobs. In 1936, after the Washington Senators began training at Tinker Field, Joe signed on as a scout.

The next year he tried managing in the minors but had to give it up. His illness and its possible consequences made him give considerable thought to taking on a major responsibility. Yet, he still had that yen to keep in touch with the one thing he always loved, baseball.

Later in the year, Joe was offered a baseball opportunity he couldn't say no to. It was September 28, 1938, and the Chicago Cubs had just won the pennant on a ninth-inning home run by Gabby Hartnett, the famous "homer in the gloaming."

Johnny Evers told the story: "One night in Chicago, when the Cubs had won the pennant in 1938, we were asked to go on radio together and accepted. I guess we each figured we could get on and talk together, just as we had played together for a couple of years, without giving each other a tumble when the broadcast was over. But when we met in the studio, it was all off. Neither one had to say the first word. We just rushed together and put our arms around each other and damn near cried."[340]

In 1938, Joe and Helen were still married and had moved to 1115 West Central Avenue. Joe continued on in the real estate business with Harper & Harper several blocks away at 29 West Central Avenue.

Happy times for Joe were interspersed with a number of down days. One of those down days was in 1939 when Joe moved his residence to 409 West Central Avenue. That address was the Lamar Hotel.[341] Helen was no longer listed in Orlando's *City Directory* as his wife. Interviews with Joe Tinker's two grandsons and a granddaughter failed to uncover any further information about Joe's third wife, Helen.

Joe was no longer in the real estate business in 1940. In that year, Joe returned to the one activity he looked forward to, the one that gave him joy, the teaching of the game to hundreds of youngsters at Joe Stripp's School of Baseball. Joe T. and Joe S. became close friends. The extent of this friendship really showed itself when Joe Tinker became financially destitute and in need of help.[342]

Johnny Evers, 1937–1940

It seems as if everybody in Troy and in Albany knew that Johnny Evers was in dire financial straits. Word had quickly gotten around. He was a member of the Troy Council, Knights of Columbus Fourth Degree and the Troy Lodge of Elks. His name continued to be a household word. So Dan O'Connell, the Democratic County Chairman, had no problem in pulling a few strings, thereby giving the Trojan the job of Superintendent of Bleecker Stadium.[343]

Bleecker Stadium was one of the most outstanding municipal sports fields in the country. More than 150,000 people had viewed sports and civic events there over the past year. The well-groomed stadium, whose diamond would put many a minor league park in the shadows, was a beehive of activity from early April until the middle of November. And Johnny Evers was in charge of it all. He was the Director of Recreation for the City of Albany. He was the overseer of the town's athletics.

During the offseason, when the stadium was empty, its stands deserted, one man would walk carefully over the diamond to observe the progress of the field's early winter resodding. Somehow, you knew instinctively, even from a distance, that the lone figure was Johnny Evers, a man whose name was synonymous with many of the national game's most dramatic moments.

When interviewed one day in his Bleecker Stadium office, Johnny said: "When I was taken sick in 1936, my good friends in Albany obtained this position for me, thinking it would help my health to be outdoors. It has been great to work in Bleecker Stadium, watching these youngsters engaging in sports. I love to see them thrive in a safe place to play, their health-building activities developing them physically and mentally, making them good citizens."[344]

When a youngster with a baseball bat came along with friends, cor-

Johnny Evers in his office at Bleecker Stadium (*The Sporting News*).

ralling Evers into a clear space on the field, Johnny showed them how to stand at bat, how to hold the bat, and how to go for a ground ball. The kids loved it. It was evident that Johnny enjoyed it as well.

During the offseason, Johnny would wander into the sporting goods store and help his brother Joe. He would also go next door to the Elks club and visit with some of his buddies. He never tired of planting himself at a table in a dimly lit corner to talk baseball. There was always something new to talk about.

"Do you remember the last game you played?" a friend asked.

"Sure do," Johnny replied: "1922, the White Sox against Cleveland. Eddie Collins bobbed up with a bad wrist. I was coach for the Sox and volunteered to step in at second.

"I batted against Guy Morton, famous as a fastball pitcher. The first time I came up to bat it got down to three and two, and then I got my base.

I also walked in the next two times up, but after that I thought I'd like to hit one, and tried. The result was two outfield flies in my last two times up.

"I am not likely to forget that game. The White Sox got six runs in the first inning, getting off to an early lead of 6 to 0. It looked like one of those games in which I could just loaf along. Instead, the Indians tied us and the game ended in a 6–6 extra-inning tie. There was a lot of action, especially around second base.

"The next morning, I couldn't have put on a uniform if I tried. Every joint and muscle ached like a toothache. I couldn't have stood up at second base, and Eddie Collins, with his injured wrist, had to get back into harness. That was the last game of ball that I have played.

"Billy Evans umpired behind the bat in my last game and he treated me like a regular fellow," continued Johnny, reminiscing the past. "Some people may be surprised to know that an umpire gave me a break.

"Billy knew it was the first time I had faced a pitcher in five years. I was forty-five years old then. Evans really was rooting for me as much as an umpire could. He told me that Morton hadn't any more than he used to and indicated my best bet was to wait him out. That's how I got those three walks. Now, I won't say that I wasn't entitled to them, but I remember there were several pretty close ones in there. And that day I couldn't complain about not getting the close ones."[345]

Perhaps that is why Johnny went on telling everybody that the war between him and the umpire world was over and would not be resumed.

Another old-timer went on to ask about the differences in the game between the 1902–1915 era and the period after World War I.

Johnny replied: "Present day players will never suffer by comparison with the past. There are so many improvements in every way—parks, hotels, traveling. Bear in mind, there is a different ball and nine more men on a squad. In 1906, the Cubs had sixteen men, now they all have twenty-five. Everyone admits the principal change, other than the ball, is due to the number of pitchers in the present game."[346]

In 1940, Johnny's routine consisted of having a drink with his friends at the Elks Club, reminiscing about baseball, playing cards, tending to the Bleecker Stadium and helping his brother Joe. Overall, however, he was sad and lonely. He was also mellow and mild; no longer high spirited, feisty and ready for a brawl at the slightest provocation.

One might think it would have been easy for him to walk into a high-class furniture store in Albany where his wife was working, say hello and invite her out for a cup of coffee. Apparently, this was not an easy thing for Johnny to do. According to family members, there was never any communication between them.

As far as his son, family members described the relationship as "distant." The boy spent his time with his mother and her side of the family. Johnny knew he had gone to Georgetown University in Washington, D.C. as an undergraduate, then law school, then into the Navy during World War II. After discharge, he remained in Washington and practiced law. One must wonder why a son made little if any contact with his father for so many years, and vice versa. Family members had no answer.[347]

CHAPTER 15

Together Again

Johnny Evers, 1941–1948

Johnny Evers's routine continued to be pretty much the same. Then one day in August 1942, Johnny suffered a stroke from which he did not fully recover.[348] Nevertheless, when released from the hospital, he continued with his responsibilities at Bleecker Stadium, worked in the store and jawed with his friends. Overall, Johnny had always insisted on being independent, caring for himself. He was no different now. He moved from the hotel to an apartment near the Capitol at 256 State Street.

To the end, the old "Crab" retained a lively interest in baseball. Each year he watched the voting for the National Baseball Hall of Fame in Cooperstown, New York, which had opened in 1939. He longed to hear his name selected. In 1942, he wired *The Sporting News*, expressing his thanks to those baseball writers who had supported him in the poll. Johnny failed to gain election that year.

While waiting for the new selections to the Hall in 1944, Johnny had another stroke, physically crippling him for the rest of his life. At first, he agreed to live with his sister, Anna Evers Kennedy and her family in Troy, because he was confined to bed by paralysis of his right arm

221

and leg. His voice was also affected. The fighting Trojan rallied however, and once again was able to talk with his cronies from Elks Lodge 49.[349] Johnny talked about the good old days when he was one of the nation's most publicized ball players. He enjoyed having visitors, except of course, Mrs. Spoor, the visiting nurse who bullied him.[350]

The Trojan soon insisted on being independent. He moved back to his apartment in Albany after agreeing to allow Mrs. Spoor to look in on, and care for him on a daily basis. However, he would not tolerate tomfoolery. He was determined to do as much as he could by himself.

An anecdote told by John T. Evers of Albany, a great-grand nephew of Johnny Evers, demonstrated this attitude: "A family member helped Johnny to the voting place. He insisted on voting because of his loyalty to the Democratic Party. After being helped into the booth, the relative was fooling around and lifted Johnny's hand to the spot where he could then vote Republican. Johnny was aware of the proper place to cast a vote and even though he knew his relative was goofing around, he did not find humor in this and gave the man a hard poke with his elbow. That was Johnny Evers, rough and tough unto death."

On April 24, 1946, a special six-man committee selected eleven deserving old-timers for immortality in the baseball shrine.[351] They elected Tinker, Evers and Chance as a unit, to be enshrined in the Hall of Fame. Nothing like that had ever happened before or since.[352] Although confined to his bed, John Joseph Evers rejoiced. "I'm glad we made it all together," said Evers. "Chance should have been elected long ago. I wish he were alive to feel as happy about it as I do. I'm glad for Tinker too."[353]

When Joe Tinker received the news, he was in Atlanta looking over prospective big leaguers in his position as scout for the Boston Braves. O.B. Keeler, a sportswriter, went up to his room in the Piedmont Hotel. He found Joe holding a photo of Johnny that illustrated the second baseman's joy when he heard the news that the trio had been named to the Hall of Fame.

"I'm especially glad about good old Johnny Evers," said Tinker, looking at a photo of his friend, as he lay bedridden because of the stroke. Joe was more than pleased that all three of them had been elected to the Hall of Fame.[354]

That brief moment of glory went by quickly. On March 25, 1947, Johnny Evers suffered a cerebral hemorrhage. He was almost totally paralyzed and lingered only three days. He died at St. Peter's Hospital in Albany on March 28 at the age of sixty-five. Funeral services were held at St. Mary's Roman Catholic Church in Albany on March 31. Thou-

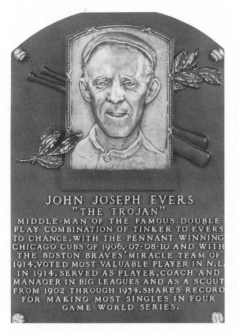

JOHN JOSEPH EVERS
"THE TROJAN"
MIDDLE-MAN OF THE FAMOUS DOUBLE
PLAY COMBINATION OF TINKER TO EVERS
TO CHANCE. WITH THE PENNANT WINNING
CHICAGO CUBS OF 1906-07-08-10 AND WITH
THE BOSTON BRAVES' MIRACLE TEAM OF
1914. VOTED MOST VALUABLE PLAYER IN N.L.
IN 1914. SERVED AS PLAYER, COACH AND
MANAGER IN BIG LEAGUES AND AS A SCOUT
FROM 1902 THROUGH 1934. SHARES RECORD
FOR MAKING MOST SINGLES IN FOUR
GAME WORLD SERIES.

JOSEPH B. TINKER
FAMOUS AS A MEMBER OF ONE OF BASEBALL'S
GREATEST DOUBLE PLAY COMBINATIONS-FROM
TINKER TO EVERS TO CHANCE. A BIG LEAGUER
FROM 1902 THROUGH 1916 WITH THE CHICAGO
CUBS AND CINCINNATI REDS AND THE
CHICAGO FEDS. MANAGER CINCINNATI
1913 AND CHICAGO N.L. 1916. SHORTSTOP
ON CUBS' TEAM THAT WON PENNANTS
IN 1906,'07 '08 AND 1910.

Hall of Fame plaques for the famous double play trio (National Baseball Hall of Fame Library).

sands passed by the bier to pay a final tribute to Evers. All those in the world of baseball who knew him sent messages. After a solemn requiem high mass, he was buried at Saint Mary's Cemetery in Troy, Section B, Lot 237, alongside his three-year-old daughter who died after coming down with scarlet fever.

Thomas E. Dewey, Governor of New York, said: "The untimely passing of Johnny Evers will sadden every American who loves competitive sports. As a member of the immortal Tinker-to-Evers-to-Chance combination, he was one of the greatest infielders of all time. More than a generation of Americans will join in mourning his loss."[355]

FRANK LEROY CHANCE
FAMOUS LEADER OF CHICAGO CUBS. WON
PENNANT WITH CUBS IN FIRST FULL SEASON
AS MANAGER IN 1906-THAT TEAM COMPILED
116 VICTORIES UNEQUALLED IN MAJOR
LEAGUE HISTORY-ALSO WON PENNANTS
IN 1907, 08 AND 1910 AND WORLD SERIES
WINNER IN 07 AND 08. STARTED WITH
CHICAGO IN 1898. ALSO MANAGER
NEW YORK A.L. AND BOSTON A.L.

A final tribute from the *Herald Tribune* was among the most endearing testimonials for the great second baseman.

> When Johnny Evers left Troy to join the Chicago Cubs he was a scout-discovered Irish kid not yet old enough to vote. He was five feet seven inches tall and weighed only about a hundred pounds, but at least ninety-five of this was the spunk and quick-wittedness which were to mark his many years in big league ball and make him one of the game's immortals.
>
> Baseball was a rougher sport forty years ago than in today's era of disciplined dugouts. Johnny Evers played the game aggressively and shrewdly, and he fought his way on infield dirt through many exchanges of tough adjectives, hard fists and sharp spikes. "My favorite umpire," he is recorded as saying, "is a dead one." And his fiery tongue proved it.[356]
>
> *The Trojan, the Human Splinter, the Crab*—as he was variously and quite accurately called—was the Cubs' second baseman for eleven years before he went to the Boston Braves. And they were years that saw some of the best-remembered baseball in major league history. Through these spectacular seasons Evers was one of the accomplished double-play trio that helped win four pennants for the Cubs, brought particular grief to the Giants and gave Franklin P. Adams his famous, never forgotten line, "Tinker to Evers to Chance."
>
> Evers was an invalid in Albany until his death this week. The old cheers are now but faint echoes. But when "batter up" sounds next month and stands fill, there will be stories swapped by old-timers who remember when Johnny Evers made his snappy throws and a "trio of bear cubs and fleet as birds" won headlines on sport pages.[357]

Ernest J. Lanigan, Director of the National Baseball Museum and Hall of Fame, announced that the plaque honoring Johnny Evers in baseball's Hall of Fame "will be placed on a special easel and draped in black for a 30-day period in mourning."[358]

Spidery little Johnny Evers with the pugnacious jaw and the flaming spirit, made his place in baseball history secure long before he departed. The chroniclers of our national game will never forget Evers. He was a bellicose chap who imparted most of the fight and fire to the Chicago Cubs of years ago. This spirit of the man outweighed his mechanical assets. He was deft enough on the field of course, and a fair-to-middling hitter, but it was his spirit that lifted the "Human Crab" to greatness.

The Albany County Court House had no record showing that Johnny Evers had left a will. His baseball memorabilia and photographs were donated to the University Libraries of Notre Dame by his son, who had moved to Albany and became a prominent attorney and Executive Vice President of the New York Automobile Dealers, Inc.[359]

Johnny left behind his only son, John, Jr., Marian, a daughter-in-law, and his wife Helen. There were no grandchildren.

Joe Tinker, 1941–1948

Joe Tinker was out of business and financially destitute. Since he had failed to file the annual report that was required by the State of Florida, the Tinker-Joe-Realty Company, Inc. was "Dissolved by Proclamation" on September 2, 1941.[360]

As destitute as Joe may have been, he still found time for romance. He took out a marriage license in Orlando, and on April 14, 1942, he and Suzanna Margaret Russell Chabot were declared man and wife. Available records show that Suzanna had been married to Earl R. Chabot until 1934. He was a building contractor in Orlando.

In an interview with Jon Jay Tinker, Joe's grandson, he said: "She's the one I met. They were living in abject poverty. I can remember a gravel road in front of the house, old beat-up furniture, screens were woven together to keep the flies out. Joe was hurtin' financially. My mother kept calling her 'that poor woman.'"[361]

Joe and his bride were not doing well financially even though Suzanna had been working as a saleswoman at various Orlando shops. Joe had some income because of his continued involvement with Joe Stripp's Baseball School but it was seasonal. His scouting activities of the southern schools and colleges for the Boston Braves may have been ongoing, but this too would have been seasonal. The marriage did not last long. Suzanna was soon out of Orlando, heading for New Jersey.

Joe Tinker's misfortunes continued to plague him. On February 1, 1944, the press reported: "Ex-Big Leaguer Under Oxygen Tent in Florida Hospital." It went on to say: "Joe Tinker was reported in a serious condition tonight in Orange General Hospital. Attendants said his condition was 'poor' and that he had been placed under an oxygen tent.

"Tinker entered the hospital last Wednesday suffering from influenza. A heart condition, Bright's disease and diabetes caused his condition to take a turn for the worse. Attending physicians said he had only a few days to live."[362]

Tinker's baseball pals came to his rescue. Joe Stripp was one of them. He told Tinker he had a job for him at his baseball school when he recovered. That was good medicine, better than anything the physicians could prescribe.[363]

The next press release said: "Dr. Spencer A. Folsom reported that

Tinker was slightly improved and out of the oxygen tent at intervals, but he is still a very sick man and a long way from being safely out of the woods."[364]

Tinker did get well. Before long, there was a picture in the local paper showing Tinker at Stripp's school. Standing beside him was long-time major leaguer Van Mungo, another of Stripp's instructors. Tinker appeared healthy. It would have been hard to believe that not so long ago Joe was near death.

Stripp was proud of his part in putting Joe back on his feet. "I was only paying up an old debt," he said. "Tinker taught me the ropes in the minors. He showed me how to deal with the big league owners." Since Stripp was one of the most business-minded of ball players, Tinker's advice must have been sound.[365]

During World War II, Joe was employed at the Army Air Force Tactical Center (AAFTC) in Orlando.[366] He was named civilian storekeeper of athletic equipment and supplies for the Physical Training Section at the AAFTC. He was photographed handing out bats to Cpl. Roy Spencer. Joe was quoted as saying, "It's a great thrill dishing out athletic equipment to these youngsters. Who knows but that some of these kids may be future diamond greats and take their place among the finest in the game."[367]

On December 20, 1944, Joe suffered a series of nasal hemorrhages and was admitted to the Orange General Hospital. Dr. Frank Gray, his physician, reported that Joe's condition had been caused by high blood pressure and that he was out of danger.[368]

He may have been out of danger physically but his financial plight continued. Although Joe Tinker had three sons and a daughter, they could not contribute much to the support of their father. Joe was able to continue working for the AAFTC even after the war. This brought him some income, but his friends knew that his physical problems would not enable him to work much longer.

Joe, however, kept plugging away. When a southern area baseball tournament got underway for the Army Air Force nines with competing teams playing at Tinker Field, Joe again found himself in uniform as coach of the Orlando AAF.

He traveled with the team, including a stop in Witchita where he was photographed with skipper Art Bramhall, a major league shortstop before entering service.

On April 24, 1946, Joe Tinker was elected to the Hall of Fame. As joyous as this may have been, he was unable to attend the induction ceremony in 1947. Sadly, none of the three Cubs greats made it to Cooperstown for the ceremony; Joe, at least was alive, but he was in trouble.

On January 14, 1947, an Orlando newspaper carried the story: "Joe Tinker will have his left leg amputated here tomorrow at Orange Hospital because of spreading infection. The erstwhile shortstop entered the hospital yesterday. He has been troubled with an infected foot since mid-October, and the middle toe of his left foot was amputated about five weeks ago. His leg will be amputated just above the knee."[369]

The hospital reported the difficult news on January 16:

> Joe Tinker today lost the left leg which helped make him one of baseball's greatest shortstops.
>
> The leg was removed just above the knee in an operation to arrest a gangrenous condition which set in last October. His surgeon, Dr. Duncan T. McEwan said, the former Chicago Cub star was doing "very nicely tonight."
>
> A tiny blister between his toes was the cause of the trouble and forced Tinker to leave St. Louis last fall where he had gone for the World Series. A month ago one of his toes was amputated, but the infection continued.
>
> Barring complications, the Tinker-to-Evers-to-Chance star should be out of the hospital in ten days or so, physicians said. He will convalesce at the home of his son, Rollie F. Tinker, in Orlando.[370]

While recuperating from the amputation, Joe reportedly said, "Guess I won't be able to pitch for a couple of weeks."[371] His attempt to josh around indicates a need to have the world see him as someone who could tough it out while hurting on the inside. Joe found it difficult to express his true feelings and made every effort to cover them up.

His feelings toward his granddaughter, however, were open and loving. Clancy Tinker Mundy (nickname Jaque) remembers her grandfather when he stayed at their home after his leg amputation. She can still see him sitting on the couch. He waved her over and said, "I'm going to teach you how to wink and curtsy." She remembers saying, "okay." She also remembered, "Grandpa pulling a five dollar bill out of his pocket and saying to someone, 'get her a nice Christmas present.'" That Christmas, she found a box with a holiday season wrapping. Inside was a blue plastic rain scarf with a card saying, "Love, Grandpa."[372]

Sometime after January 31, 1947, possibly while at his son's home, Joe wrote a letter to Johnny Evers. Although the letter was not dated, an approximate date can be established from the content. Evers was still alive, so it had to be before March 28, 1947. Johnny Kling died on January 31, 1947, so Joe's letter was written after that date. The letter was therefore written between the end of January and March 28, 1947.

Joe Tinker in a hospital bed after his leg amputation (courtesy Tom Tinker).

Dear John

Your friend Bill Bolte is here and I want to say hello old pal, and forget John we have had a lots of tough luck but look back at all the good times we have had. We have had our day just think of Sheckard & Kling they are signed up with Chance allready. Well, John lots of good luck and thank the good God we are still here. I hope I can see you some day.

Your old side Kick
Joe Tinker[373]

The letter is sad in that it shows Joe having some difficulty in clearly putting down his thoughts. And although Joe's signature is easy to read, it is not as sharply defined when compared to his signature on earlier letters.

Joe may have remembered his trip to California after Chance had called and asked to see both Tinker and Evers one more time. When Joe wrote, "Sheckard & Kling they are signed up with Chance already," he probably figured it would not be long until he would once again be play-ing for the "Peerless Leader."

Joe Tinker's friends knew how badly he needed a lift. Joe Stripp teamed up with John Ganzel who was the business manager of the Orlando Senators and formed a committee. It included Mayor William Beardall, President Walton McJordan of the Greater Orlando Chamber of Commerce, President George C. Johnston of Orlando Broadcasting Co. (WDBO) and Martin Anderson, publisher of the Orlando Daily Newspapers, Inc. The city and civic officials called for a Testimonial Night on May 16, 1947.

The committee forwarded ninety letters to major and minor league baseball clubs, inviting them to participate in honoring the famous Chicago Cub and Florida's only living member of Baseball's Hall of Fame. A Joe Tinker Testimonial Fund was established in an Orlando Florida Bank and teller Madeline Augenblick was put in charge of handling and recording all testimonial tokens received at a special window, appropri-ately marked.

A.B. (Happy) Chandler, Commissioner of Baseball, heartily endorsed the committee's plans. President Clark Griffith of the Washington Sen-ators, who served as an advisor to the committee, promised a sizeable cash gift as a gesture of his personal esteem for Tinker and his contributions to baseball.[374]

In the meantime, just twelve days after his leg was amputated, Joe Tinker put in an appearance at Tinker Field to watch Joe Stripp's School of Baseball undergo a workout. Joe, cigar clenched in his teeth, simply fought the idea of calling himself out.

Without any hesitation, Joe accepted an invitation from Rollins Col-lege in Winter Park, Florida, to speak at their Founder's Week event. On February 23, still using crutches, he was accompanied to the podium by his son, Rollie.[375]

Seated before the mike, Joe started his speech by telling the crowd how Tinker, Evers and Chance first started out on the Chicago team, how Frank Selee moved them around to different positions, and of how "Johnny Evers, Frank Chance and myself—sort of moved into the dou-ble play team by accident." After a little more history of the team's accom-plishments, Joe dived right into the sizzling hot pennant race of 1908.[376]

Not long after that, on April 26, Joe was fitted with an artificial limb. He wasn't about to attend his testimonial on crutches. "At my age now," quipped Joe, "I have to learn to walk all over again. But I'm mighty glad to know I can throw away my crutches in a few days."[377]

The testimonial came and went. Two months later, Tinker's physicians ordered Joe transferred from the Lamar Hotel to a private nursing home. His diabetes was not in control and a closer supervision of his diet had to be maintained.[378]

Joe's financial resources continued to be slim. When released from the nursing home, he returned to Joe Stripp's Baseball School even though he was in a wheelchair. On January 5, 1948, an over-capacity turnout of 140 youngsters answered the opening bell of a six-week session at Tinker Field. Joe was one of eleven former professional players making up the staff who were called upon to put the diamond aspirants through their paces. Joe truly enjoyed the activity.[379]

He also enjoyed going to Tinker Field to watch a game. Although he had an artificial leg, he preferred to use his wheelchair and sit with his friends at his usual place in the left field stands. Joe Stripp said he knew that although Tinker was in pain, he loved to be at the games. "Going to the ball park was the only time he was happy, the only damn time," Stripp said.[380]

In 1948, Joe's financial situation worsened. Richard M. Stewart III, a friend, allowed Joe to associate with his Orlando realty firm, thereby giving him an opportunity for added income.[381]

Nothing came of it, and in his last year, Joe Tinker was broke but not bitter. "I know better than anyone else that my time is near," he told a friend. "I've had a good life, and you don't stop and complain at this stage of the game. I've made some mistakes, and I'd like to stay around a little longer and overcome them, but there isn't time. I'll miss baseball. That I know."[382]

Joe financial plight was widely known. Before his death, Bob Hayes, Sports Editor of the *Sentinel Star*, wrote a letter to the Commissioner of Baseball:

Mr. A.B. Chandler:
Commissioner of Baseball
Carrow Tower
Cincinnati, Ohio
Dear Commissioner:

Joe Tinker, as you probably have read, was admitted to a local hospital over a week ago. His death now is but a matter of time—a relatively short time. His health has failed so much since his leg was amputated about 18 months ago that it is pathetic. He had been in a wheel chair since Spring. Chances are, so his physicians tell me, he will not be able to use his wheel chair again.

We raised $1,900 for him last year, with Clark Griffith's aid. We are now trying to raise some more money for him, with John Ganzel doing the work. But we will be lucky to get him $500 this time.

The money we raised last year, which was spread thin and administered by Ganzel and Joe Stripp, is gone. His family isn't able to help much financially, if at all.

Baseball—Major League baseball—has not been unkind to Joe. There are too, those still in baseball who haven't forgotten Joe's jumping to the old Federal League.

But no matter what his personal or professional shortcomings may have been, it just doesn't seem right that one of the game's old-time greats should pass out as a public ward or an object of charity. That's about the picture right now.

That one of baseball's Hall of Fame immortals should face such a fate now when the game is enjoying its best years, does not seem congruous to me.

There may be a half-dozen good reasons, technical reasons, why baseball should not do something for Tinker now. But I feel there's something of a moral obligation involved. Isn't there something that your office could do, or instigate, with some measure of dispatch, which might ease a pathetic situation which, in the final analysis, comes close to resting in baseball's lap? As much as $150 or $200 a month for a few short months would probably bridge the financial gap.

Respectfully,
Bob Hayes
Sports Editor[383]

On the day of Joe's death, his son Roland petitioned the Honorable Victor Hutchins, County Judge. The petitioner told the Judge that Joe Tinker had been on public aid and had been receiving $38 a month; that the petitioner was responsible for paying the hospital bills that had accrued; that the petitioner was asking for help. The petitioner then asked the court to "enter an order designating your petitioner as the proper person to receive the warrant from the State of Florida in the amount of such assistance as had accrued to the said Roland Tinker."[384]

Joe Tinker died on his sixty-eighth birthday, July 27, 1948. The report was understandably sad: "Ten days ago the last surviving member of the Chicago Cubs' Tinker-to-Evers-to-Chance double play combination was taken to Orange Memorial Hospital for treatment for his indisposition and to have his diet straightened out.

"A brief while before his death the hospital issued a bulletin saying 'Mr. Tinker's condition today is better than it has been at any time since he entered the hospital. He ate a hearty breakfast and appeared in excellent spirits.'"[385]

Tom Tinker (Joe's grandson) and Clancy Tinker Mundy, nicknamed Jaque (Joe's granddaughter), were at the hospital after their grandfather died. Tom remembers talking to Joe's roommate. He clearly remembered Joe saying: "'This is my birthday and this would be a good day to die.' Joe then turned over and died."

Jaque remembered Tinker's final scene almost exactly the same. She said the roommate told her: "Joe turned to me and asked, 'What day is this?'

"'It's July 27.'

"Joe then said, 'Today is my birthday. It's a good day to go.' And Joe then turned over and died."[386]

On November 28, 1999, the *Orlando Sentinel* interviewed Joe's great-grandson, Randy Tinker of Monticello, Florida. Randy had a different memory of Joe's death. Randy said: "The way the family lore has it, my great-granddaddy died with a cigar in his mouth, one hand on a shot of whiskey and the other hand reaching for his nurse."

Jersey Joe Stripp, former major league infielder, whose school was the granddaddy of all baseball schools, broke down and wept unashamedly when he learned of the death of his friend.[387]

Mayor William Beardall paid tribute to Tinker, "Orlando has lost a great friend and one of its most ardent supporters in all things, especially better baseball and other sports. In the baseball world, he was an ambassador of good will for his adopted city."[388]

On July 28, the day after Joe's death, a Western Union telegram arrived at Rollie Tinker's home in Orlando. It was from Atlantic City, New Jersey. It said: "I am greatly shocked at the sad news the family has my deepest sympathey regret I cannot be with you love : Suzanna R Chabot"[389]

Joe Tinker was buried at the Greenwood Cemetery in Orlando, Section L, Lot 21, next to his wife Ruby. A very short distance away, at another burial site, was his second wife Mary.

Joe left behind three sons and one daughter: Joe Jr. of Tallahassee, Florida, Roland (Rollie) of Orlando, Florida, William (Billy) of Baltimore, Maryland, and Mrs. Charles Clapp (Ruby) of Boulder, Colorado.

Jacque, Joe's granddaughter, has a story, a very special story that she wanted to share with everyone: "The family used to visit granddad in the hospital after church on Sunday. I can remember mother, on several occasions, talking with him about accepting Jesus Christ as his Savior. Grandad did not seem very interested at the time but always enjoyed arguing with mother.

"One Sunday, mother brought a pamphlet she had picked up at church that dealt with the subject. She didn't discuss it with him, she just left it laying on his bedside table. The next Sunday, as we were getting ready to leave, Joe said, 'Chloe, you might be interested to know that I now pray in Jesus Christ's name.' Joe died afterwards.

"About a month later, our housemaid Rosa came to work and told us she had a dream the night before about Joe. She said she was looking up a stairway crowded with angels, and near the top, standing in their midst was Joe, smiling down on her as if to say, 'Look where I am.'"[390]

If there is a heaven, and if there is baseball there, the "Trio of Bear Cubs" will once again be joined together. Come spring, they will don their uniforms in the clubhouse, go onto the field, talk it up with former teammates and wait for the umpire to holler, "Play ball!"

Conclusion

Before deciding that essential question as to whether or not Joe Tinker, Johnny Evers and Frank Chance deserve to be in the Hall of Fame, one must ask, what is great?

For the years 1903–1911, when they played together, the Chicago National team established amazing records. In 1906, the Cubs had a win-loss mark of 116–36 (.763), a record that still stands. The best Detroit could do, with Ty Cobb and Sam Crawford in 1909, was 98–54 (.645). Brooklyn, with Jackie Robinson, Pee Wee Reese and Duke Snider, pumped out their best with a 105–49 (.682). The 1927 Yankees gave it their best shot with Babe Ruth and Lou Gehrig for 110–44 (.714); the 1939 version with Joe DiMaggio, Gehrig and Bill Dickey finished at 106–45 (.702); and Mickey Mantle, Yogie Berra and Johnny Mize led the Yankees to 103–51 (.668); but the Indians of Larry Doby and Bob Feller took the flag at 111–43 (.721). The 1998 Yankees went 114–48 (.704) and the 2001 Seattle Mariners cranked up a remarkable 116–46 (.716). But the Chicago Cubs still hold the record for highest winning percentage in a season.

In 1906–1907, the Cubs went on to win a consecutive two-year record of 223 games. It still stands. The years 1906, '07 and '08 saw the Cubs win 322 games. Another record! The consecutive four-year total, from

'06–'09 saw another record of 426 wins. The five-year, 1906–1910 was no different. It chalked up 530 wins. The six-year, 1905–1910 was 622, the seven year, '05–'11 was 714 and the eight-year record, 1904–1911 was 807. After 91 years and despite the addition of more games to the schedule, the Cubs still hold all those records.

And they did it without a "Sultan of Swat," without a "Jolting Joe" and without a 565-foot blast from a Mickey Mantle bat. Based on this, it seems fair to say that the Cubs of 1903–1911 had one of the most outstanding teams in baseball history. And Tinker and Evers and Chance were the heart and soul of that team.

Why then did it become a common practice to badmouth the selection of Tinker, Evers and Chance to the Hall of Fame, claiming it was cronyism, claiming it was the Adams's poem that put them there? If the three did not have much to do in setting those fantastic records, who did?

The other Cubs? The Chicago offense was based on hustle rather than brawn. Tinker, Evers and Chance made the team function. The rest were all good ball players, yet none of them had the stats of a Ty Cobb or Honus Wagner. In fact, Frank Chance, with a career BA of .297 was the only member of the team close to .300. For those who say the Trio did not deserve Hall of Fame status, how do they explain all those wins? It seems reasonable to expect some answers before giving Tinker, Evers and Chance a thumbs down.

Could it have been the pitching? A careful examination of pitching records before and after joining the Cubs revealed interesting information. Nineteen pitchers pitched 150 or more innings for the Cubs between 1904–1913. Seventeen of those pitchers posted ERAs below 3.00, including Orval Overall and Buttons Briggs.

Before Orval joined the team, he was with Cincinnati. In 1905, he posted a 17–23 mark. Part way through '06, he was 3–5. Then he joined the Cubs. Orval immediately perked up and finished the season with 12–3. In '07, he dominated at 23–8. He continued on winning many more than he lost. Bob Wicker was with St. Louis in 1901, '02 and '03. His best year as a Cardinal was 5–12. He joined the Cubs in early '03 and finished the year at 20–9. Three Finger Brown, the only other Hall of Famer from the great Chance teams, was nearly unbeatable after joining the Cubs in 1904. But in 1903, his rookie year with St. Louis, he finished the season at 9–13.

Jack Pfiester was with Pittsburgh in 1903 and finished with 0–3. In '04 he went 1–1. Jack came to the Cubs in 1906 and finished the year with 20–8. He continued winning many more games than he lost, but in 1910, dipped to 6–3 and in 1911, his last year in the major leagues, he went 1–4.

It must be noted that in 1910, Chance missed close to half the season. In 1911, the Peerless Leader played in only 33 games and the Crab was out for most of the season because of a nervous breakdown. When Jack Pfiester pitched in '10 and '11, he did not have the backup of Tinker, Evers and Chance.

It seems fair to say that there was a dramatic change in pitchers after they joined the Cubs. Their ERAs dropped. Their win totals increased. They became stars. It also seems fair to say that Johnny Kling was an excellent catcher who knew how to handle pitchers, and that the pitching staff had the right stuff on the ball. But when you take a close look at the infield and consider their teamwork and infield play, Tinker, Evers and Chance were at the core of a Cubs machine that generated wins at an unprecedented pace. Their defensive plays saved many a game for the pitching staff by shutting down traffic on the base paths. Their harmony and united effort in fielding and brains were decisive factors to the winning of ball games.

The detractors of the three should be satisfied with the foregoing information, but they may insist on more facts and more numbers before they concede the trio deserves their place in the Hall of Fame.

Joe Tinker's BA was .264, among the lowest of any hitter in the Hall of Fame. Yet he helped the Cubs win ball games with his ability as a clutch hitter. In fact, he became famous for his clutch hitting. The legendary 1908 pennant race saw him beat the Giants repeatedly. On May 25, he drove in the winning run in the tenth, beating the Giants 8–7. July 17 witnessed his home run for a 1–0 victory. On July 18, Joe drove in the winning run in the ninth, beating New York, 5–4. August 11 was a 4–0 Cubs victory with Joe Tinker driving in two of the Cub runs. August 30 saw him score the winning run in a 2–1 victory over the Giants. On September 23, in the fabled Merkle game, Joe hit a home run, the Cubs' only run, in a controversial 1–1 tie. Two weeks later, October 8, in the do-or-die makeup of the tie game with the Giants, he led the winning attack with a third-inning triple. The Cubs won the game, 4–2, thus taking the pennant. His ability to hit in the clutch (especially against Christy Mathewson), coupled with his nonparalleled play at shortstop, made Joe Tinker a great player.

As for Johnny Evers, he had a career BA of .270, but he was considered to be the brainiest guy in baseball. He literally took the pennant away from John McGraw and his Giants in the 1908 Merkle game. It was he who called for the ball and touched second for the third out, thereby negating the winning run. And because of that play, the Cubs went on to win another World Series championship. Was Johnny's play first rate? Of course.

Of the three, Frank Chance had the best numbers. As player-manager, his career was highlighted by four pennants and two World Series championships. Many members of the Baseball Writers Association of America tried to vote him into the Hall. In 1945, he received 179 votes, but that was insufficient to gain entry into Cooperstown.

Although Chance's Cubs may not have led the league in double plays, the Trio's twin killings played havoc for opponents on the base paths. In August 1908, William Kirk, a writer for the *New York American*, said, "those double plays have done much to our boys here in Chicago." Tinker, Evers and Chance had become known for their uncanny ability for making a double play at crucial moments in a game. And their reputation for doing this was made two years before Adams's poem was penned.

Having said all of this, and with available records showing the impact the three had on the team's success, one need not wonder why Tinker, Evers and Chance entered the Hall. It was not cronyism. When they were selected in 1946, two members of that Committee were Connie Mack and Yankees general manager Ed Barrow, both of whom were astute judges of talent. They were serious baseball men whose observations went back to the turn of the century. They clearly felt that the three were extremely noteworthy players and deserved the honor.

This opinion is shared by a former detractor of Tinker, Evers and Chance. In his 2001 book, *The New Bill James Historical Abstract*, James did a complete turnaround. In his 1994 book, *Whatever Happened to the Hall of Fame*, he gave the Trio a thumbs down. James now admits they should be in the Hall of Fame. James defines a great ball player as one who helps his team win a lot of games. As such, Tinker, Evers and Chance qualify as three of the greatest baseball players to play the game, deserving of a place in the hallowed Hall.

When it comes down to it, baseball as once defined, is not about "three durn fools hittin' a ball and three other durn fools chasin' it." It is about winning and losing. It is about coming down to the wire and taking home the flag. It is about fighting it out for the number one spot. It is about winning the world championship. Tinker, Evers and Chance helped the Cubs do that. If that ain't great, what is?

If many Tinker, Evers and Chance bashers remain, it is comforting to know that Chicago fans and others, continue to honor the legendary Trio.

September 10, 2002, the Chicago Cubs took the field against the Montreal Expos at Wrigley Field. The stadium was packed with 30,000 fans. Sitting back in their seats, chatting and getting to know one another, were members of the Tinker, Evers and Chance families. The reunion of the families was in celebration of the 100th anniversary of the first double play from Tinker to Evers to Chance. Although the first twin killing occurred on September 14, 1902, the Cubs were scheduled to be in Cincinnati that day, so the celebration was held a few days earlier.

Joe Rios, Cubs Coordinator of Special Events and Entertainment, had a photo taken on the field of Tom Tinker, grandson of Joe Tinker, John Evers, great-grandnephew of Johnny Evers and Jeri Chance Moore, first cousin (twice removed) of Frank Chance. They were the official representatives of the three families. At the seventh inning stretch, all three were in the broadcast booth singing "Take Me Out to the Ballgame." They were then interviewed on radio and TV and responded to questions about their legendary ancestors.

The reunion of the three families was communicated to the fans in a lighted message at the lower end of the scoreboard.

Fans young and old stood and cheered for the three families, and also for the Trio that thrilled the baseball world when the ball was quickly scooped out of the dirt and rapidly fired from Tinker to Evers to Chance. Side retired.

Notes

1. Clough, Charles W., *Fresno County: The 20th Century.* Vol. 2, p. 462.

2. Woodruff, Harvey, "Frank L. Chance, the Peerless Leader." *The Chicago Tribune* (Sept. 29, 1912).

3. McGroarty, John, *Los Angeles from the Mountains to the Sea.* Vol. 3. (Chicago: American Historical Society, 1921), p. 766.

4. California State Library Book Collection, *Memorial and Biographical History of the Counties of Fresno, Tulare, and Kern, CA.* (Chicago: Lewis, 1892), p. 385.

5. Fresno Historical Society, Scrapbook news item. "Death Summons Mary Chance: Early Fresnan." *Fresno Bee* (Nov. 12, 1937).

6. Fresno Historical Society, Scrapbook news item."Here's Frank Chance in His First Uniform," *The Chicago Tribune* (Oct. 19, 1888).

7. Chance, Albert, Scrapbook news item. Uncredited (undated). "Frank Chance Tops Game's Notables: History Colorful." By Burt Leiper.

8. "Some Battling Young Ball Players," *Fresno Expositor* (Nov. 27, 1889).

9. Chance, Albert, Scrapbook news article. Uncredited (undated). "Frank Chance Tops Game's Notables: History Colorful." By Burt Leiper.

10. "Here's Frank Chance in His First Uniform," *The Chicago Tribune* (Oct. 19, 1888).

11. "Catcher Chance to Wed a Fresno Girl," *Fresno Chronicle* (April 7, 1899).

12. Fresno Historical Society. *Fresno High School Centennial: 1889 to 1989.*

13. Website: Ancestry.com @ http://world connect.rootsweb.com.

14. 14 Watrous, Tom, Geneological records. Personal communication (April 10, 2002).

15. *The New York Evening World* (Sept. 16, 1924).

16. McGroarty. *Los Angeles from the Mountains to the Sea.* Vol. 3., p. 766.

17. Holmes, Philip, Archivist, Fremont, CA. Personal communication (March 1, 2002).

18. "Death Summons Mary Chance: Early Fresnan," *Fresno Bee* (Nov. 12, 1937).
19. Ryor, Fred, Letter to Philip Holmes (March 11, 1991).
20. Ortiz, Maria, Archivist, Fresno Historical Society. Personal communications.
21. Williams, Andrew, "Back, Back, Back, It's Gone: A short history of baseball and ballparks in Fresno." www.fresnogrizzlies.com/history.htm: p. 1.
22. *Sporting Life* (Nov. 3, 1906).
23. Woodruff, Harvey T., "Frank L. Chance, The Peerless Leader." *The Chicago Tribune* (Sept. 29, 1912). Also, *The Chicago Tribune* (Sept. 16, 1924).
24. Gilruth, James C. "Chance of the Chicago Champs." *Baseball Magazine* (Dec. 1908), p. 24.
25. Allen, Lee, and Tom Meany, *Kings of the Diamond*. (G.P. Putnam's Sons, 1965), p. 102.
26. Ritter, Lawrence, and Donald Honig. *The Image of Their Greatness*. (New York: Crown), 1984: p. 18.
27. Galbraith, Dan, "Not Your Ordinary Joe." *Holton Recorder* (Aug. 13, 2001).
28. *The Sporting News* (May 9, 1940).
29. Tinker, Tom, Personal communication (Oct. 22, 2001).
30. Tinker, Jon J., Interview (Jan. 1, 2002).
31. Tinker, Jon J., Letter (Feb. 6, 2002).
32. Johnson, Dan, "Chancing Upon Tinker." *The Kansas City Kansan* (Aug. 6, 2000), p. 3.
33. *The Manhattan Mercury* (Aug. 14, 1994).
34. Warneke, Kevin, "Tinker's Hometown Looks for Traces of Him." *Baseball America* (April 17–30, 1995).
35. Huntley, Terry, Personal communication (Jan. 1, 2002).
36. "Joseph Tinker the Shortstop Manager and His Remarkable Career." *Baseball Magazine* (July 1936), pp. 46–47.
37. Johnson, "Chancing upon Tinker," pp. 1–5.
38. Tinker, Joe, "How I Became a Ballplayer." *New York Evening Telegram* (Aug. 27, 1913).

39. Lane, F.C., "Joseph Tinker the Shortstop Manager and His Remarkable Career." *Baseball Magazine* (July 1936), p 48.
40. Evers, John J., and Roger Connor, "Johnny Evers 'The Crab.'" *Troy's Baseball Heritage* (1992), pp. 29–30.
41. Baseball Hall of Fame, Scrapbook news item. Uncredited (undated).
42. Connor, Roger, and John T. Evers, "Johnny Evers 'The Crab.'" *Troy's Baseball Heritage* (1992), pp. 29–30.
43. Baseball Hall of Fame, Scrapbook news item, "Here's the Giants' Nemesis. Who? Why, Little Johnny Evers of the Cubs." By Robert Ripley. *The Globe* (Undated).
44. *New York Herald Sunday Magazine* (Jan. 22, 1911).
45. Baseball Hall of Fame, Scrapbook news item. Uncredited (undated).
46. Connor, Roger, Reprinted from "Johnny Evers: The Find of the 1902 Season." *Troy's Baseball Heritage*, p. 35.
47. Keetz, Frank, "Johnny Evers: The Find of the 1902 Season." *Baseball Research Journal* XII (1983), pp. 132–136.
48. *Ibid.*
49. Evers and Connor, *Troy's Baseball Heritage*, p. 30.
50. Lieb, Frederick G. "As Chicago Recruit: He Scaled 115." *The Sporting News* (April 1 9, 1947).
51. Brown, Warren, "Heading for Greatness." *The Chicago Cubs*. (New York: Putnam, 1946), p. 19.
52. Gollenboch, Peter, *Wrigleyville: A Magical History Tour of the Chicago Cubs*. (New York: St. Martin's Griffin, 1999), p. 96.
53. Woodruff, Harvey T., "View of Frank Chance As a Recruit Player." *The Chicago Tribune* (Sept. 16, 1924).
54. Brown, Warren, *The Chicago Cubs*. (Putnam, 1946), p. 18.
55. *The Chicago Tribune* (April 29, 1898).
56. Chicago Historical Society, *Chicago History* Vol.1 No. 2, New Series. "Tinker to Evers to Chance." By Will Leonard. (Chicago: Publisher unknown, 1970) p. 74.

57. Baseball Hall of Fame, Scrapbook news item. Uncredited (undated). "Frank Leroy Chance," pp. 13–14.

58. "Forty Years Ago," *Fresno Bee* (Oct. 28, 1938).

59. Chance, Frank L., Scrapbook news item. "Catcher Chance to Wed a Fresno Girl." *The Chronicle* (April 7, 1899).

60. Chicago Historical Society, City of Chicago Directories. Players' address: home and business.

61. Fresno Historical Society, Scrapbook news item. Uncredited (undated). "Wedding Invitation."

62. "Homan-Chance: The Wedding of a Well Known Couple," *The Fresno Morning Republican* (Jan. 4, 1900).

63. Chance, Albert, Scrapbook new item. *Sport Magazine* (Undated); p. 38.

64. McBride, Joseph, "*High & Inside: Baseball Nicknames*." (Warner Books, 1980).

65. Baseball Hall of Fame, Scrapbook news item. *New York Evening World* (Feb. 16, 1924).

66. *Ibid.*

67. Baseball Hall of Fame, Scrapbook news item. Uncredited (undated): pp. 46–48.

68. Baseball Hall of Fame, Scrapbook news item. Uncredited (undated): "Frank Leroy Chance," pp. 13–14.

69. Stang, Mark, *Cubs Collection—100 Years of Chicago Cubs Images*. (Orange Frazer Press, 2001), p. 8.

70. Golenbock, *Wrigleyville*. pp. 95–98.

71. Smith, Ira L., *Baseball's Famous First Basemen*. New York: A. S. Barnes, 1956: pp. 64–65.

72. Golenbock, *Wrigleyville*, pp. 96–100.

73. "Breaking Into the Base Ball Game," *Sporting Life* (May 26, 1917), p. 3.

74. *Ibid.*

75. Smith, Robert, "The Toy Trojan." *Heroes of Baseball.*" (World, 1953), p. 186.

76. Graham, Frank, "One for the Book." *Sport Magazine* (June 1949), p. 37.

77. Golenbock, *Wrigleyville*, p. 117.

78. Pietrusza, David, Matthew Silverman, and Michael Gershman. *Baseball: The Biographical Encyclopedia*. (New York: Total Sports Publishing, 2000), p. 339.

79. Brown, Warren, *The Chicago Cubs.* (Putnam, 1946), p. 23.

80. *Sporting Life* (Oct. 31, 1903).

81. Advertisement, *The Metropolitan West Side Elevated Railroad*. Rand McNally, 1898.

82. Golenbock, *Wrigleyville*, p. 98.

83. Lane, Frank C., "The Gamest Player in Baseball." *Baseball Magazine* (Sept. 1913), pp. 51–61.

84. "Joseph Tinker: The Shortstop Manager," *Baseball Magazine* (Aug. 1914), pp. 44–45.

85. University of Notre Dame Libraries, Scrapbook news item. Uncredited (undated). "Tinker to Evers to Chance." By Frank Graham.

86. Brown, *The Chicago Cubs*, p. 26.

87. The Baseball Online Library, "Frank Chance." http://cbs.sportsline.com

88. Smith, Robert, *Heroes of Baseball*, p. 186.

89. Brown, *The Chicago Cubs*, p. 26.

90. Evers, John J., and Hugh Fullerton, *Touching Second*. (Reilly and Britton, 1910), p. 65.

91. Pope, Edwin, *Baseball's Greatest Managers*. (New York: Doubleday, 19600, pp. 25–33.

92. Baseball Hall of Fame, Scrapbook news item. Uncredited (undated), pp. 46–48.

93. *New York Evening World* (Feb. 16, 1924).

94. "Joe Tinker," *The Chicago Daily News* (July 27, 1948).

95. Williams, Joe, *The World Telegram* (Dec. 9, 1938).

96. Shatzkin, Mike, and Jim Charlton, *The Ballplayers*. (New York: Arbor House/William Morrow, 1990), pp. 1091–1092.

97. "Joseph Tinker: The Shortstop Manager," *Baseball Magazine* (August 1914), pp. 44–45.

98. Farris, Bruce, "Chance Was Greatest Fresno Contribution to Baseball." *Fresno Bee* (Oct. 27, 1960).

99. Golenbock, *Wrigleyville*, p. 103.

100. Galbraith, Dan, "Not Your Ordinary Joe." *Holton Recorder* (Aug. 13, 2001).

101. Rice, Grantland, "Tinker to Evers to Chance." *Collier's* (Nov. 29, 1930), p. 11.

102. Pietrusza, *Baseball: The Biographical Encyclopedia*. p. 39.

103. *Greensboro Daily News* (Feb. 9, 1926).

104. Baseball Hall of Fame, Scrapbook news item. Uncredited (April 16, 1906). "Joe Tinker and Frank Chance Get Into a Row with Spectators at Cincinnati and Are Roughly Handled."

105. "President Murphy Returns from Redville and Talks of Change," *The Chicago Tribune* (April 16, 1906).

106. *The Chicago Daily News* (April 29, 1906).

107. *Ibid.*, (June 8, 1906).

108. Pope, *Baseball's Greatest Managers* pp. 25–33.

109. Chance, Albert, Scrapbook news item. Uncredited (Sept. 29, 1906). "A Game Unfinished."

110. Wallace, Joseph, *Baseball: 100 Classic Moments in the History of the Game.* (Dorling Kindersley, 2000), pp. 26–27.

111. Brown, *The Chicago Cubs*, p. 31–32.

112. Pope, *Baseball's Greatest Managers.* pp. 25–33.

113. Golenbock, *Wrigleyville*, p. 104.

114. Thorn, John, *Treasures of The Baseball Hall of Fame.* (Villard, 1998), p. 46.

115. Chance, Frank L., "Chance and Tinker Evolved New Play." *New York Times* (March 28, 1915).

116. Golenbock, *Wrigleyville*, p. 108.

117. Dryden, Charles, "Leader of Cubs Nearly Mobbed." *The Chicago Tribune* (July 9, 1907).

118. Dryden, Charles, "Cubs Defeat the Superbas 7 to 1." *The Chicago Tribune* (July 10, 1907).

119. *The Chicago Tribune* (July 10 and 11, 1907).

120. *The Chicago Daily News* (July 11, 1907).

121. Dryden, Charles, "Chance Can Play Again Tomorrow." *The Chicago Tribune* (July 15, 1907).

122. *The Chicago Daily News* (Oct. 2, 1907).

123. *Ibid.* (Oct. 10, 1907).

124. *Ibid.* (Oct. 12, 1907).

125. Baseball Hall of Fame, Scrapbook news item. Uncredited (Dec. 26, 1936). "Johnny Evers Speaks."

126. *The Chicago Daily News* (Oct. 5, 1907).

127. Baseball Hall of Fame, Scrapbook news item. Uncredited (Dec. 26, 1936). "Johnny Evers Speaks."

128. Golenbock, *Wrigleyville*, p. 107.

129. *Ibid.*, pp. 128–129.

130. "Joyous Fan Falls 50 Feet As Tinker Bats Home Run," *The Chicago Tribune* (July 18, 1908). Also, "Tries to See Game: Is Killed." *The Chicago Daily News* (July 18, 1908).

131. Pope, *Baseball's Greatest Managers*, pp. 25–33.

132. Holtzman, Jerome, "How Poem Helped Elect Infield Trio to Hall of Fame." *Baseball Digest* (March 1933), p. 72.

133. Golenbock, *Wrigleyville*, p. 142.

134. Baseball Hall of Fame. Scrapbook news item. (undated). "One for the Book." *Sport Magazine.*

135. Golenbock, *Wrigleyville*, p. 144.

136. Ritter, Lawrence S, *The Glory of Their Times*, p. 100.

137. Mix, Sheldon, *The Cubs Reader.* Edited by David Fulk and Dan Riley. (Houghton Mifflin, 1991), pp. 12–27. Also, *The Chicago Tribune* (Oct. 9, 1908).

138. Golenbock, *Wrigleyville*, p. 149.

139. *Ibid.*, pp. 149–150.

140. *The Chicago Tribune* (Oct. 9, 1908).

141. Wallace, Joseph, *The Baseball Anthology.* (New York: Abradale Press, Harry N. Abrams Inc.), pp. 108–109.

142. Golenbock, *Wrigleyville*, p. 151.

143. *The Chicago Tribune* (Oct. 12, 1908).

144. "Tinker Sued: Magnates Hit." *The Chicago Tribune* (Oct. 14, 1908).

145. *The Sporting News* (Jan. 14, 1909).

146. Evers, John T., Interview (Oct. 19, 2001).

147. Tinker, Tom, Scrapbook news item. Uncredited (Aug. 27, 1953). "Joe Tinker's Greatest Play, in One Act: A Prize Story." By Charles S. Adelman.

148. Library of Congress Jefferson

Bldg. Microfilm Reading Room (Film No. 03722).

149. Ghio, Joanne, "James Reveals Feud with Evers." *Baseball Digest* (Oct.–Nov. 1964), pp. 15–16.

150. Lardner, Richard W., "Frank Leroy Chance." *Baseball Magazine* Vol. 7 No. 6 (Oct. 1911), p. 9.

151. Baseball Hall of Fame, "Frank L. Chance: The Peerless Leader." By Harvey T. Woodruff. *The Chicago Tribune* (undated).

152. Lynch, T.J. and August Herrmann. "No. 597. In re Application of Player John G. Kling for Reinstatement." *Seventh Annual Report of the National Commission* (1911): pp. 37–38.

153. Website: http://cbs.sportsline.com

154. Lardner, *Baseball Magazine* Vol 7 No 6 (Oct. 1911), pp. 10–12.

155. Rice, Grantland. "Tinker to Evers to Chance." *Colliers* (Nov. 29, 1930).

156. Chance, Frank L. Personal communication (April 25, 2002).

157. Lane, *Baseball Magazine* (Sept. 1913), pp. 51–61.

158. Adams, Franklin P., "Baseball's Sad Lexicon." *New York Evening Mail* (July 18, 1910).

159. "Frank Chance Is Dead: Gave City 4 Ball Pennants." *The Chicago Tribune* (Sept. 16, 1924).

160. "The Greatest of All Second Basemen." *Baseball Magazine* (Dec. 1912), pp. 43–44.

161. Lane, *Baseball Magazine* (Sept. 1913), pp. 51–61.

162. *Ibid.*

163. "When I 'Murdered Matty': Joe Tinker's Biggest Day." *Baseball Digest* (Sept. 1945), pp. 10–12.

164. *The Cincinnati Commercial Tribune* (Jan. 13, 1912).

165. Weller, Sam, "Chance's Career As Cub Manager Ends This Year." *The Chicago Tribune* (Sept. 12, 1912).

166. Tinker, Tom, Scrapbook news item. Uncredited (Sept. 2, 1912). "Chafing Cubs: Acting Manager Tinker's Authority Resented by Infielder Evers to the Point of Fisticuffs on the Bench During a Ball Game."

167. *The Chicago Daily News* (Sept. 27, 1912).

168. Chance, Albert, Scrapbook news item. Uncredited (undated)."Frank Gives Vain-Glorious Charlie Murphy Fine 'Panning' and Charlie Will Take It Like a Good Little Boy." By Carl W. Ross. Also, *The Chicago Daily News* (Sept. 28, 1912).

169. *The Chicago Daily News* (Sept. 27, 1912).

170. Chance, Albert, Scrapbook news item. Uncredited (undated). "Frank Gives Vain-Glorious Charlie Murphy Fine 'Panning' and Charlie Will Take It Like a Good Little Boy." By Carl W. Ross. Also, *The Chicago Daily News* (Sept. 27, 1912).

171. *Ibid.* (Sept. 12, 1912).

172. Golenbock, *Wrigleyville.* pp. 160–161.

173. Stack, C.P., "Loyal John Evers." *Baseball Magazine* (April 1914): pp. 39–42.

174. Brown, *The Chicago Cubs,* p. 47.

175. Golenbock, *Wrigleyville,* p. 161.

176. "Done with Chicago."*Sporting Life* (Dec. 7, 1912).

177. Chicago Historical Society, "Tinker to Evers to Chance." By Will Leonard. *Chicago History* Vol. I, No 2. New Series. Chicago: Publisher unknown, 1970, p. 79.

178. University of Notre Dame Libraries, Scrapbook news item. Uncredited (undated). "Tinker to Evers to Chance." By Frank Graham.

179. Baseball Hall of Fame, Scrapbook news item. Uncredited (Dec. 21, 1912). "Evers Task As Manager of the Decadent Cubs By No Means an Easy One."

180. Baseball Hall of Fame, Scrapbook news item. Uncredited (undated).

181. Baseball Hall of Fame, Scrapbook news item. Uncredited (undated). "Johnny Evers Is a Very Sensitive Player."

182. Pietrusza, et al. *Baseball: The Biographical Encyclopedia,* p. 339.

183. Stack, C.P., "Evers and the Umpires." *Baseball Magazine* (January 1914), pp. 71–72.

184. *The Troy Times* (May 8, 1913).

185. "Trojan Fans to Invade New York." *The Troy Times* (May 10, 1913).

186. Baseball Hall of Fame, Scrapbook

news item. Uncredited (undated). "McGraw May Sign An Evers."

187. "Comment of New Yorkers," *The Troy Times* (May 12, 1913).

188. Website *http://memory.loc.gov*. Johnny Evers.

189. Keetz, *Baseball Research Journal* XII (1983), p. 135.

190. Lane, *Baseball Magazine* (Sept. 1913), pp. 51–61.

191. Baseball Hall of Fame, Scrapbook news item. Uncredited (undated).

192. Baseball Hall of Fame, Scrapbook news item. "The Firing of Evers." *The Literary Digest* (Feb. 28, 1914).

193. Lane, F.C., "The Sensational Evers Deal." *Baseball Magazine* (August 1914): pp. 27–32.

194. Golenbock, *Wrigleyville*, p. 163.

195. Brown, *The Chicago Cubs*, p. 50.

196. Evers, John J., *Troy's Baseball Heritage*. (undated): p. 32.

197. Lane, *Baseball Magazine* (August 1914), p. 112.

198. "Tinker's Blood for Wife." *New York Times* (July 15, 1913).

199. Graham, Frank, "They Warred Over Tinker." *Baseball Digest* (Sept. 1948), pp. 60–61.

200. *The Sporting News* (Jan. 8, 1914): p 5.

201. Lane, F.C., "Joseph Tinker the Shortstop Manager and His Remarkable Career." *Baseball Magazine* (July 1936): p 54.

202. "Federal Leaguers Talk War." *The Chicago Tribune* (Oct. 15, 1913).

203. Kush, Raymond Collection. Application Department of Buildings, City of Chicago (March 5, 1914).

204. Baseball Hall of Fame, Scrapbook news item. Uncredited (Dec. 25, 1912). "Chance Right Says the Surgeon Who Operated on Him." By Joseph Vila.

205. "Chance Signs at Immense Salary," *New York Morning Telegraph* (Jan. 9, 1913).

206. *The Chicago Tribune* (Sept. 16, 1913).

207. Woodruff, Harvey T., "Chance Loses Zeider Claim." *The Chicago Tribune* (July 25, 1913).

208. Chance, Frank L., Personal communication (April 25, 2002).

209. Peschel, Stan, Personal communication (June 11, 2002).

210. Rosencranz, Robert, Phone interview (June 12, 2002).

211. Ghio, *Baseball Digest* (Oct.–Nov. 1964), pp. 15–16.

212. Evers, John J. "Johnny Evers." *Troy's Baseball Heritage* (undated): p. 23.

213. "Troy's Tribute to Johnny Evers," *The Troy Record* (Oct. 20, 1914).

214. Evers, Helen, Medical Certificate of Death, No. 953. Troy, NY.

215. Weller, Sam. "Tinker Fires Broadside." *The Chicago Tribune* (April 2, 1914).

216. *Ibid.*

217. Sam Wellerisms. *The Chicago Tribune* (April 17, 1914).

218. "Chicago Welcomes Feds: Who Triumph Over Packers, 9–1." *The Chicago Tribune* (April 24, 1914).

219. *The Chicago Tribune* (April 27, 1914).

220. Golenbock, *Wrigleyville*, pp. 165–166.

221. Tinker, Jon J., Interview (Jan. 1, 2002).

222. Hartel, William, *A Day at the Park: In Celebration of Wrigley Field.* (Champaign, IL: Sagamore, 1994) p. 6. Courtesy of Chicago Historical Society.

223. Baseball Hall of Fame, Scrapbook news item. Uncredited (March 14, 1915). "Tinker's Tribute: The Chicago Fed Manager Honors Hans Wagner on His Birthday."

224. Tinker, Gloria, Scrapbook news item. Uncredited (March 15, 1919). "Joe Tinker's Plans." By Philip Morgan.

225. Tinker, Tom, Scrapbook news item. Uncredited (May 29, 1915).

226. *The Chicago Tribune* (July 16, 1915).

227. Tinker, Gloria, Scrapbook news item. Uncredited (Dec. 15, 1915).

228. "You Can't Do Two Things at Once, Says Tinker, Who Plans to Become a Bench Boss." *Philadelphia Public Ledger* (May 9, 1915).

229. Evers, John T., Interview (Oct. 19, 2001).

230. Baseball Hall of Fame, Scrapbook news item. Uncredited (Feb. 20, 1915). "Evers Not in Poor Health."

231. Baseball Hall of Fame, Scrapbook News item. Uncredited (Aug. 12. 1915). "What Critics Say When Evers Fights."

232. Baseball Hall of Fame, Scrapbook news item. Uncredited (undated).

233. Glaser, David, "When Evers Circled the Field." *Baseball Digest* (October 1949): pp. 41–42.

234. *The Chicago Daily News* (March 28, 1947).

235. *Ibid.*, (July 1, 1915; July 1, 1916, July 18, 1916, July 20, 1916, Sept. 8, 1916, May 16–17, 1917). Comparing seven of the *Chicago Daily News* to demonstrate Johnny Evers's increasing ineffectiveness in the field.

236. Ever, John T., Interview (Oct. 19, 2001).

237. Woodruff, Harvey T., "Frank L. Chance, the Peerless Leader." *The Chicago Tribune* (Sept. 12, 1912).

238. Lardner, *Baseball Magazine* Vol 7 No 6 (Oct.1911), p. 102.

239. Chance, Edythe. Last Will and Testament listing husband's stock holdings.

240. Lardner, *Baseball Magazine* Vol 7 No 6 (Oct.1911), p. 102.

241. 242 Baseball Hall of Fame, Scrapbook news item. Uncredited (Sept. 4, 1915). "VACATION PICK UPS."

242. Ward, Geoffrey C., and Ken Burns, *Baseball: An Illustrated History.* (New York: Alfred A. Knopf, 1994), p. 80.

243. Baseball Hall of Fame, Scrapbook news item. Uncredited (Dec. 25, 1912). "Chance Right Says the Surgeon Who Operated on Him." By Joseph Vila.

244. McGroarty, *Los Angeles from the Mountains to the Sea.* Vol. 3, p. 766.

245. Pietrusza, et. al., *Baseball: The Biographical Encyclopedia*, p. 192.

246. *The Troy Times* (March 3, 1918).

247. Evers, John T., Scrapbook news item. Uncredited (April 16, 1918).

248. Evers and Connor, *Troy's Baseball Heritage*, p. 32.

249. "5,000 Fans Pay Tribute to Trojan Johnnie Evers." *The Troy Times* (June 17, 1918).

250. "Evers Is Home, He Landed Today on American Soil." *The Troy Times* (Dec. 16, 1918).

251. Evers and Connor, *Troy's Baseball Heritage*, p. 32.

252. Baseball Hall of Fame, Scrapbook news item. Uncredited (undated).

253. *The Chicago Tribune* (Sept. 16, 1924).

254. *The Troy Times* (Feb. 1, 1924).

255. *Ibid.* (May 9, 1924).

256. Evers and Connor, *Troy's Baseball Heritage.* Uncredited (undated): p. 25.

257. Ahrens, Arthur R., "Tinker vs Matty: A Study In Rivalry." *Baseball Research Journal* III (1974), pp. 14–15.

258. *The Chicago Tribune* (Dec. 24, 1916).

259. Tinker, Tom, Scrapbook news item. Uncredited (undated). "Tinker Seeks Training Camp."

260. Tinker, Gloria, Scrapbook news item. Uncredited (undated).

261. Tinker, Tom, "Joe Tinker Is Dead: A Baseball Great." Scrapbook news item. Uncredited (July 28, 1948).

262. James, Bill, *Whatever Happened to the Hall of Fame.* (New York: Simon & Schuster, 1994), p. 212.

263. Orlando Historical Society, Scrapbook news item. Uncredited (undated). "High Spirits and the Calico Kid."

264. Baseball Hall of Fame, Tinker letter to Karl Finke (Oct. 2, 1922).

265. Baseball Hall of Fame, Tinker letter to Garry Hermann (Dec. 21, 1922).

266. Bacon, Eve, *Orlando: A Centennial History* Vol. 2. (The Mickler House, 1977).

267. *The Chicago Daily News* (Dec. 26, 1923): p 23.

268. Baseball Hall of Fame, Scrapbook news item. Uncredited (Dec. 12, 1923). "Mrs. Joe Tinker Ends Her Own Life While Ill."

269. Derr, Mark, *Some Kind of Paradise.* (New York: William Morrow, 1989), p. 181.

270. Andrews, Mark. "Tinker's fortunes vanished quickly: Flashback." *The Orlando Sentinel* (Nov. 28, 1999), p. K-2.

271. Evers, John T. Personal communication (May 14, 2002).

272. Evers, John T. Interview (Oct. 19, 2001).

273. *Baseball Magazine* (June 1924).

274. *The Troy Times* (May 19, 1924).

275. *The Troy Times* (May 20, 1924).

276. University of Notre Dame Libraries, "Evers and White Sox in England before King George V." Uncredited. (Nov. 15, 1924).

277. *Fresno Morning Republican* (Sept. 16, 1024).

278. "Frank Chance Dies on Pacific Coast," *The Chicago Daily News* (Sept. 16, 1924).

279. Chance, Frank L. Home address. *Los Angeles Times* (Sept. 16, 1924).

280. Baseball Hall of Fame, Scrapbook news item. Uncredited (undated). "Front 'n' Center." By Ray Joyce.

281. *The Chicago Tribune* (Sept. 16, 1924).

282. "McGraw and Robinson, Old Time Foemen, Join in Expression of Regret at Death." *New York World* (Sept. 17, 1924).

283. "Frank Chance Laid to Rest by Old Pals." *San Francisco Chronicle* (Sept. 18, 1924).

284. Orlando Historic Preservation Board, *Orlando History In Architecture*. (City of Orlando: Best Litho, 1984.)

285. Schooping, Elaine, "Tinker to Evers to Chance to Orlando." *Florida Vertical File: Baseball* (undated): p. S-22.

286. Beuttler, Fred, Letter regarding Dr. Jay F. Pitts (Nov. 7, 2001).

287. Baseball Hall of Fame, Letter on JAMAJO stationary (Jan. 10, 1924).

288. Orange County Court, 17th Judicial Circuit. Documents: File #8633 filed (Feb. 26, 1927). Jay F. Pitts vs Jamajo Subdivision Company, et al.

289. City of Longwood, Florida. Historic brochure (2001).

290. *The Orlando Sentinel* (Nov. 28, 1999).

291. Baseball Hall of Fame, Tinker letter to Gary Hermann (June 27, 1925).

292. Schooping, Elaine, "Tinker to Evers to Chance to Orlando." *Florida Vertical File: Baseball* (undated), p. S-21.

293. "Tinker, Noted Shortstop, Weds," *Herald Tribune* (May 12, 1926).

294. Orange County Court, 17th Judicial Circuit. Documents.

295. Tinker, Tom, Scrapbook news item. Uncredited (Oct 8, 1930). "Tinker-to-Bolita-to Bail."

296. Orange County Court, 17th Judicial Circuit. Documents. Book 006, p. 546.

297. Andrews, Mark, "Tinker's fortunes vanished quickly: Flashback." *The Orlando Sentinel* (Nov. 28, 1999): p. K-2.

298. Bacon, Eve, *Orlando: A Centennial History* Vol. 2. (The Mickler House, 1977), p. 42.

299. Schooping, Elaine, "Tinker to Evers to Chance to Orlando." *Florida Vertical File: Baseball* (undated), p. S-21.

300. Tinker, Gloria, Scrapbook news item. Uncredited (undated). "Rabid Fan, Joe Sees Every World Series and Wife of Old Cub Here Tells All About Him."

301. Tinker, Tom, Scrapbook news item. "Cubs Must Stop Simmons and Foxx, Says Tinker." *Herald Tribune* (Sept. 14, 1929).

302. Tinker, Gloria, Scrapbook news item. *Buffalo Evening News* (1929). By Bob Stedler.

303. "Joe Tinker Is Named Jersey City Manager," *The Times* (Aug. 12, 1930).

304. Tinker, Gloria, Scrapbook news item: "Joe Tinker, New York Mascot." *Telegram* (June 11, 1929).

305. Andrews, Mark, "For 75 years, Tinker Field linked city with pro baseball." *The Orlando Sentinel* (Nov. 21, 1999), p. K-2.

306. Tinker, Tom, Scrapbook news item. Uncredited (June 26, 1930).

307. Evers, John T., Interview (Oct. 19, 2001).

308. *The Troy Times* (Aug. 21, 1921).

309. Duval, Daniel J., "Memories by John J. Evers." *Schenectady Union Star* (Dec. 7, 1933).

310. Evers, John T., Scrapbook news item. Uncredited (undated).

311. Baseball Hall of Fame, Scrapbook news item. Uncredited (March 20, 1931). "Cutting the Plate." By Fred Lieb.

312. Evers and Connor, *Troy's Baseball Heritage*, p. 32.

313. *The Troy Times* (Feb. 20, 1935).

314. Baseball Hall of Fame, Scrapbook news item. Uncredited (undated). "Evers Kindness Wasted."

315. Baseball Hall of Fame, Scrapbook news item. Uncredited (Sept. 19, 1935). "Evers Steps Out at Albany: Resignation Handed in Due to Restriction of Authority as General Manager."

316. Baseball Hall of Fame, Johnny Evers's letter to Ford Frick.

317. Baseball Hall of Fame, Series of letters by Johnny Evers and others (April 1936).

318. Baseball Hall of Fame, Scrapbook news item. AP news release (undated). "Evers Goes Bankrupt."

319. Baseball Hall of Fame, Scrapbook letter. From Edgar Wolfe (May 20, 1936).

320. Schooping, Elaine, "Tinker to Evers to Chance to Orlando." *Florida Vertical File: Baseball* (undated): p. S-22.

321. Tinker, Tom, Scrapbood news item. Uncredited (Feb. 13, 1931). "Joe Tinker Fails to Get Coast Post."

322. Florida Department of State documents, Joe Tinker Billiard Company Certificate of Incorporation.

323. Tinker, Gloria, Scrapbook news item. Uncredited (April 14, 1932). "Joe Tinker Beats His Way Back After Many Reverses to Prosperity in Florida." By James C. Isaminger.

324. *The Orlando Sentinel* (Nov. 28, 1999).

325. Tinker, Tom, Scrapbook news item. Uncredited (undated).

326. Tinker, Mary, Last Will and Testament. Filed in Court of County Judge, Orange County, Florida, March 5, 1934.

327. Tinker, Gloria, Scrapbook news item. Uncredited (March 29, 1934).

328. Tinker, Tom, Scrapbook news item. Uncredited (undated).

329. Tinker, William, Photograph of William, Ruby and Rollie Tinker playing ball at Tinker Field photo.

330. Department of State, Division of Corporations information.

331. Tinker, Tom, Scrapbook news item. Uncredited (undated). "The Morning After." By Red Newton.

332. Tinker, Joe, Newspaper ads.

333. *The Chicago Daily News* (July 27, 1948).

334. Baseball Hall of Fame, Scrapbook news item. Uncredited (June 27, 1937). "Chance Honored."

335. Baseball Hall of Fame, Scrapbook news item. Uncredited (undated). "Evers, Tinker Honor Chance at Cub Game."

336. "Joe Tinker Back In Game as Club Pilot," *The American* (May 23, 1937).

337. "Joe Tinker Quits Post As Manager of Orlando," *The World Telegram* (July 24, 1937).

338. Graham, Frank, "They Warred Over Tinker." *Baseball Digest* (Sept. 1948), p. 60–61.

339. Golenbock, *Wrigleyville* p. 106.

340. Evers, John T., Scrapbook news item. Uncredited (undated). "Tinker to Evers to Chance."

341. Porter, Tana, Archivist, Orlando Historical Society. Personal communication (Oct. 13, 2001).

342. "Archives and History: Biography N–Z, Register Additions." *Florida Vertical File* (undated).

343. Evers, John T., Interview (Oct. 19, 2001).

344. Evers, John T., Scrapbook news item. Uncredited (undated).

345. Baseball Hall of Fame, Scrapbook news item. Uncredited (undated). "Cutting the Plate." By Fred Lieb.

346. *Ibid.*

347. Evers, John T., Personal communication (Oct. 10, 2002).

348. *The Chicago Daily News* (March 28, 1947).

349. Lieb, Frederick G., "As Chicago Recruit, He Scaled 115." *The Sporting News* (April 9, 1947).

350. Evers, John T., Personal communication (June 10, 2002).

351. Danzig, Allison, "Sports of the Times." *New York Times* (April 25, 1946).

352. Holtzman, *Baseball Digest* Vol 52 No 13 (March 1993), pp. 70–73.

353. Baseball Hall of Fame, Scrapbook news item. Uncredited (undated). "Evers Thinks of Others as He Rejoices Over Baseball's Hall of Fame Selection."

354. Baseball Hall of Fame, Scrapbook news item. Uncredited (undated). "Tinker Rejoices Again Over 1908 Club's Victory." By O. B. Keeler.

355. Lieb, *The Sporting News* (April 9, 1947).

356. Keetz, *Baseball Research Journal* XII (1983), p. 135.

357. Baseball Hall of Fame, Scrapbook news item. "Johnny Evers." *Herald Tribune* (March 29, 1947).

358. AP news release (March 28, 1947).

359. Baseball Hall of Fame, Scrapbook Letter. From John J. Evers, Jr. to Lee Allen (Jan. 7, 1965).

360. Florida Department of State, Division of Corporations Report.

361. Tinker, Jon J., Interview (Jan. 1, 2002).

362. Tinker, Tom, Scrapbook news item. Uncredited (undated).

363. Tinker, Gloria, Scrapbook news item. Uncredited (undated).

364. Tinker, Tom, Scrapbook news item. Uncredited (undated). "Tinker Improves."

365. Tinker, Gloria, Scrapbook news item. Uncredited (undated).

366. *The Wichita Beacon* (Aug. 12, 1945).

367. "Tinker Gets Back Into Game and Discovers New Thrills," *Sporting News* (June 7, 1945).

368. Tinker, Tom, Scrapbook news item. Uncredited (Dec. 21, 1944). "Joe Tinker Out of Danger."

369. "Tinker to Have Leg Amputated," *The United Press* (Jan. 14, 1947).

370. Tinker, Gloria, Scrapbook news item. Uncredited (Jan. 16, 1947). "Tinker's Leg Amputated."

371. James, *Whatever Happened to the Hall of Fame,* p. 214.

372. Mundy, Clancy (Jaque) Tinker, Interview (Nov. 12, 2001).

373. University of Notre Dame Libraries. Letter from Joe Tinker to Johnny Evers (undated).

374. *The Orlando Star* (April 4, 1947).

375. Olin Library Archives, Rollins College. *The Rollins Animated Magazine* Vol. XX No. 1 (Feb. 23, 1947).

376. Olin Library Archives, Rollins College. Tinker's speech.

377. Tinker, Tom, Scrapbook news item. Uncredited (April 26, 1947).

378. "Former Cub Star Is Confined for Supervision of Diet." *New York Times* (July 16, 1947).

379. *The Orlando Sentinel* (Jan. 5, 1948).

380. *The Orlando Sentinel* (Nov. 28, 1999).

381. Orlando Historical Society, City of Orlando Directory (1948).

382. *The Orlando Sentinel* (July 28, 1948).

383. Tinker, Tom, Donated letter from Hayes to Chandler (July 27, 1948).

384. Petition Application No. 5355, filed with the County Judge (July 27, 1948).

385. *The Chicago Tribune* (July 28, 1948).

386. Tinker, Tom, and Clancy (Jaque) Tinker Mundy. Interview (Nov. 12, 2001).

387. "He'll Be Missed," *The Orlando Sentinel* (July 28, 1948).

388. *Ibid.*

389. Tinker, Tom, Donated Western Union telegram.

390. Mundy, Jaque T., Personal communication (Nov. 12, 2001).

Bibliography

Books

Alexander, Charles. *Our Game: An American Baseball History*. New York: Holt, 1991.

Allen, Lee, and Tom Meany. *Kings of the Diamond*. New York: G. P. Putnam's Sons, 1965.

Bacon, Eve. *Orlando: A Centennial History Vol. 2*. Chuluota, FL: Mickler House, 1977.

Brown, Warren. *The Chicago Cubs*. New York: G.P. Putnam's Sons, 1946.

Caren, Eric C. *Baseball Extra*. Edison, New Jersey: Castle Books, 2000.

Clough, Charles W. *Fresno County In The 20th Century: From 1900 to the 1980s, Vol 2*. Fresno, CA: Panorama West Books, 1986.

Cole, S.H., H.S. Dixon, Frank Buffey and J. E. Denney. *History of Central California: A Memorial and Biographical History of the Counties of Fresno, Tulare and Kern, California*. Chicago: Lewis Publishing Co., 1892.

Cox, Merlin G., and J.E. Dovell. *Florida: Secession to Spaceage*. St. Petersburg, FL: Great Outdoors Publishing Company, 1975.

Evers, John J., and Hugh S. Fullerton. *Touching Second*. Chicago: Reilly & Britton Co., 1910.

Fresno High School Centennial Committee. *Fresno High School Centennial, 1889–1989*. Fresno, CA: Fresno Historical Society, 1989.

Fulk, David, and Dan Riley. *The Cubs Reader*. Boston: Houghton Mifflin Co., 1991.

Golenbock, Peter. *Wrigleyville: A Magical History Tour of the Chicago Cubs*. New York: St. Martin's Griffin, 1999.

Hartel, William. *A Day at the Ballpark: In Celebration of Wrigley Field*. Champaign, IL: Sagamore Publishing, 1994.

Holtzman, Jerome, and George Vass. *Baseball, Chicago Style: A Tale of Two Teams, One City.* Chicago: Bonus Books, 2001.

_____. *The Chicago Cubs Encyclopedia.* Philadelphia: Temple University Press, 1997.

James, Bill. *What Happened to the Hall of Fame?* New York: Simon & Schuster, 1995.

_____. *Historical Baseball Abstract.* New York: The Free Press, 2001.

Koppett, Leonard. *Koppett's Concise History of Major League Baseball.* Philadelphia: Temple University Press, 1998.

LaBlanc, Michael L. *Hot Dogs, Heroes & Hooligans.* Detroit: Visible Ink Press, 1994.

McBride, Joseph. *High & Inside: The Complete Guide to Baseball Slang.* New York: Warner Books, 1980.

McGroarty, John. *Los Angeles from the Mountains to the Sea, Vol. 3.* Chicago: American Historical Society, 1921.

Neft, David S., and Richard M. Cohen. *The Sports Encyclopedia: Baseball.* New York: St. Martin's Press, 1994.

Okkonen, Marc. *The Federal League of 1914–1915: Baseball's Third Major League.* Garrett, Md.: Society for American Baseball Research, 1989.

Pietrusza, David, Matthew Silverman and Michael Gershman. *Baseball: The Biographical Encyclopedia.* Kingston, NY: Total Sports Illustrated.

Pope, Edwin. *Baseball's Greatest Managers.* New York: Doubleday, 1960.

Porter, David L. *Biographical Dictionary of American Sports—Baseball Volume.* Westport, CT: Greenwood Press, 1987.

Ritter, Lawrence. *The Glory of Their Times.* New York: The Macmillan Company, 1966.

_____, and Donald Honig. *The Image of Their Greatness: An Illustrated History of Baseball from 1900 to the Present.* New York: Crown Publishers, Inc., 1984.

Shatzkin, Mike, and Jim Charlton. *The Ballplayers.* New York: Arbor House/William Morrow, 1990.

Smith, Ira L. *Baseball's Famous First Basemen.* New York: A.S. Barnes, 1956.

Smith, Robert. *Heroes of Baseball.* Cleveland: World Publishing Company, 1953.

Stang, Mark. *Cubs Collection: 100 Years of Chicago Cubs Images.* Wilmington, Ohio: Orange Frazer Press, 2001.

Thorn, John. *Treasures of the Baseball Hall of Fame.* New York: Villard, 1998.

_____, Pete Palmer and Michael Gershman. *Total Baseball: The Official Encyclopedia of Major League Baseball, Seventh Edition.* Kingston, NY: Total Sports Publishing, 2001.

Turkin, Hy, and S.C. Thompson. *The Baseball Encyclopedia: the Complete and Official Record of Major League Baseball, Ninth Revised Edition.* New York: Dolphin Books, 1977.

Walker, Ben R. *The Fresno County Blue Book.* Fresno, CA.: A.H. Cawston, 1941.

Wallace, Joseph. *The Baseball Anthology: 125 Years of Stories, Poems, Articles, Photographs, Drawings, Interviews, Cartoons & Other Memorabilia.* New York: Abradale Press, Harry N. Abrams Inc., 1994.

_____, Neil Hamilton and Marty Appel. *Baseball: 100 Classic Moments in the History of the Game.* London, England: Dorling Kindersley, 2000.

Ward, Geoffrey C, and Ken Burns. *Baseball: An Illustrated History.* New York: Alfred A. Knopf, 1994.

City Directories

Chicago, IL   Orlando, FL   Troy, NY

Articles

Adams, Franklin P. "Baseball's Sad Lexicon." *New York Evening Mail* (July 18, 1910).

Ahrens, Arthur R. "Tinker vs. Matty: A Study in Rivalry." *Baseball Research Journal III* (1974).

Andrews, Mark. "For 75 Years, Tinker Field linked city with pro baseball." *The Orlando Sentinel* (Nov. 21, 1999).

_____. "Tinker's fortunes vanished quickly: Flashback." *The Orlando Sentinel* (Nov. 28, 1999).

Baseball Hall of Fame scrapbook articles (chronological order):

"Joe Tinker and Frank Chance Get Into a Row with Spectators at Cincinnati and are Roughly Handled." Uncredited (April 16, 1906).

_____. "Evers Task As Manager of the Decadent Cubs By No Means an Easy One." Uncredited (Dec. 21, 1912).

_____. "Johnny Evers Is a Very Sensitive Player." Uncredited (undated).

_____. "McGraw May Sign an Evers." Uncredited (undated).

_____. "The Firing of Evers." *The Literary Digest* (Feb. 28, 1914).

_____. "Tinker's Tribute: The Chicago Fed Manager Honors Hans Wagner on His Birthday." Uncredited (March 14, 1915).

_____. "Evers Not in Poor Health." Uncredited (Feb. 20, 1915).

_____. "What Critics Say When Evers Fights." Uncredited (Aug. 12, 1915).

_____. "Vacation Pick Ups." Uncredited (Sept. 4, 1915).

_____. "Mrs. Joe Tinker Ends Her Own Life While Ill." Uncredited (Dec. 25, 1923).

_____. "Evers Kindness Wasted." Uncredited (undated).

_____. "Evers Steps Out at Albany Resignation Handed in Due to Restriction of Authority as General Manager." Uncredited (Sept. 19, 1935).

_____. "Johnny Evers Speaks." Uncredited (Dec. 26, 1936).

_____. "Evers Goes Bankrupt." Associated Press (undated).

_____. "Chance Honored." Uncredited (June 27, 1937).

_____. "Evers, Tinker Honor Chance at Cub Game." Uncredited (undated).

_____. "Evers Thinks of Others as He Rejoices Over Baseball's Hall of Fame Selection." Uncredited (undated).

_____. "Johnny Evers." *Herald Tribune* (March 29, 1947).

Chance, Albert. Scrapbook article. "A Game Unfinished." Uncredited (undated).

Chance, Frank L. Scrapbook article. "Catcher Chance to Wed a Fresno Girl." *The Chronicle* (April 7, 1899).

_____. "Chance and Tinker Evolved New Play." *New York Times* (March 28, 1915).

"Chance Signs at Immense Salary." *New York Morning Telegraph* (Jan. 9, 1913).

"Chicago Welcomes Feds: Who Triumph Over Packers, 9–1." *Chicago Tribune* (April 24, 1914).

Danzig, Allison. "Sports of the Times." *New York Times* (April 25, 1946).

"Done with Chicago." *Sporting Life* (Dec. 7, 1912).

Dryden, Charles. "Chance Can Play Again Tomorrow." *The Chicago Tribune* (July 15, 1907).

_____. "Cubs Defeat the Superbas 7 to 1." *The Chicago Tribune* (July 10, 1907).

_____. "Leader of Cubs Nearly Mobbed." *The Chicago Tribune* (July 9, 1907).

"Evers Is Home, He Landed Today on American Soil." *Troy Times* (Dec. 16, 1918).

Evers, John T. "Johnny Evers." *Troy's Baseball Heritage* (undated)."

_____. "Johnny Evers 'The Crab.'" *Troy's Baseball Heritage* (1992).

Evers, John T. Scrapbook article. "Tinker to Evers to Chance." Uncredited (undated).

Farris, Bruce. "Chance Was Greatest Fresno Contribution to Baseball." *Fresno Bee* (Oct. 27, 1960).

"Federal Leaguers Talk War." *Chicago Tribune* (Oct. 15, 1913).

"5,000 Fans Pay Tribute to Trojan Johnny Evers." *Troy Times* (June 17, 1918).

"Former Cub Star Is Confined for Supervision of Diet." *New York Times* (July 16, 1947).

"Forty Years Ago." *Fresno Bee* (Oct. 28, 1938).

"Frank Chance Dies on Pacific Coast." *Chicago Daily News* (Sept. 16, 1924).

"Frank Chance Is Dead: Gave City 4 Ball Pennants." *Chicago Tribune* (Sept. 16, 1924).

"Frank Chance Laid to Rest By Old Pals." *San Francisco Chronicle* (Sept. 18, 1924).

Fresno Historical Society, Scrapbook article. "Death Summons Mary Chance: Early Fresnan." *Fresno Bee* (Nov. 12, 1937).

_____. "Here's Frank Chance in His First Uniform." *The Chicago Tribune* (Oct. 19, 1888).

Galbraith, Dan. "Not Your Ordinary Joe." *Holton Recorder* (Aug. 13, 2001).

Ghio, Joanne. "James Reveals Feud with Evers." Baseball Digest (Oct.–Nov. 1964).

Gilruth, James C. "Chance of the Chicago Champs." *Baseball Magazine* (Dec. 1908).

Glaser, David. "When Evers Circled the Field." Baseball Digest (Oct. 1949).

Graham, Frank. "One for the Book." *Sport Magazine* (June 1949).

_____. "They Warred Over Tinker." *Baseball Digest* (Sept. 1948).

_____. "Tinker to Evers to Chance." University of Notre Dame Libraries Scrapbook article (undated).

"The Greatest of All Second Basemen." *Baseball Magazine* (Dec. 1912).

"He'll Be Missed." *Orlando Sentinel* (July 28, 1948).

Holtzman, Jerome. "How Poem Helped Elect Infield Trio to Hall of Fame." *Baseball Digest* (March 1993).

Isaminger, James C. "Joe Tinker Beats His Way Back After Many Reverses to Prosperity in Florida." Gloria Tinker Scrapbook article uncredited (April 14, 1932).

"Joe Tinker Is Named Jersey City Manager." *New York Times* (Aug. 12, 1930).

"Joe Tinker Quits Post As Manager of Orlando." *New York World Telegram* (July 24, 1937).

Johnson, Dan. "Chancing Upon Tinker." *The Kansas City Kansan* (Aug. 6, 2000).

Joyce, Ray. "Front 'n' Center." Baseball Hall of Fame Scrapbook article (undated).

"Joyous Fan Falls 50 Feet As Tinker Bats Home Run." *Chicago Tribune* (July 18, 1908).

Keeler, O.B. "Tinker Rejoices Again Over 1908 Club's Victory." Baseball Hall of Fame Scrapbook article. Uncredited (undated).

Keetz, Frank. "Johnny Evers: The Find of the 1902 Season." *Baseball Research Journal XII* (1983).

Lane, Frank C. "The Gamest Player in Baseball." *Baseball Magazine* (Sept. 1913).

_____. "Joseph Tinker the Shortstop Manager and His Remarkable Career." *Baseball Magazine* (July 1936).

Lardner, Richard W. "Frank Leroy Chance." *Baseball Magazine* Vol. 7 No. 6 (Oct. 1911).

Leiper, Burt. "Frank Chance Tops Game's Notables: History Colorful." Albert Chance Scrapbook article (undated).

Lieb, Fred. "As Chicago Recruit: He Scaled 115." *The Sporting News* (April 19, 1947).

_____. "Cutting the Plate." Baseball Hall of Fame Scrapbook article uncredited (March 20, 1931).

"McGraw and Robinson, Old Time Foemen, Join in Expression of Regret at Death." *New York Evening World* (Sept. 17, 1924).

Morgan, Philip. "Joe Tinker's Plans." Gloria Tinker Scrapbook article uncredited (March 15, 1919).

Newton, Red. "The Morning After." Tom Tinker Scrapbook article uncredited (undated).

Orlando Historical Society. Scrapbook article. "High Spirits And The Calico Kid." Uncredited (undated).

"President Murphy Returns from Redville and Talks of Change." *Chicago Tribune* (April 16, 1906).

Rice, Grantland. "Tinker to Evers to Chance." *Collier's* (Nov. 29, 1930).

Ripley, Robert. "Here's the Giants' Nemesis. Who? Why, Little Johnny Evers of the Cubs." Baseball Hall of Fame Scrapbook article. *Atchison Daily Globe* (undated).

Ross, Carl W. "Frank Gives Vain-Glorious Murphy Fine 'Panning' and Charlie Will Take It Like a Good Little Boy." Albert Chance Scrapbook article (undated).

Schooping, Elaine. "Tinker to Evers to Chance to Orlando." *Florida Vertical File: Baseball* (undated).

"Some Battling Young Ball Players." *Fresno Expositor* (Nov. 27, 1889).

Stack, C.P. "Evers and the Umpires." *Baseball Magazine* (Jan. 1914).

_____. "Loyal John Evers." *Baseball Magazine* (April 1914).

Tinker, Gloria. "Joe Tinker, New York Mascot." *New York Evening Telegram* (June 11, 1929).

_____. Scrapbook article. "Rabid Fan, Joe Sees Every World Series and Wife of Old Cub Here Tells All About Him." Uncredited (undated).

_____. Scrapbook article. "Tinker's Leg Amputated." Uncredited (Jan. 16, 1947).

Tinker, Joe. "How I Became a Ballplayer." *New York Evening Telegram* (Aug. 27, 1913).

Tinker, Tom. Scrapbook article. "Cubs Must Stop Simmons and Foxx, Says Tinker." *Herald Tribune* (Sept. 14, 1929).

_____. "Joe Tinker Fails to Get Coast Post." Uncredited (Feb. 13, 1931).

_____. "Joe Tinker Is Dead: A Baseball Great." Uncredited (July 28, 1948).

_____. "Joe Tinker Out of Danger." Uncredited (Dec. 21, 1944).

_____. "Tinker Improves." Uncredited (undated).

_____. Scrapbook article. "Tinker Seeks Training Camp." Uncredited (undated).

_____. Scrapbook article. "Chafing Cubs: Acting Manager Tinker's Authority Resented By Infielder Evers to the Point of Fisticuffs on the Bench During a Ball Game." Uncredited (Sept. 2, 1912).

_____. "Tinker-to-Bolita-to Bail." Uncredited (Oct. 8, 1930).

"Tinker Gets Back Into Game and Discovers New Thrills." *Sporting News* (June 7, 1945).

"Tinker, Noted Shortstop, Weds." *Herald Tribune* (May 12, 1925).

"Tinker's Blood for Wife." *New York Times* (July 15, 1913).

"Trojan Fans to Invade New York." *Troy Times* (May 10, 1913).

"Troy's Tribute to Johnny Evers." *Troy Record* (Oct. 20, 1914).

Vila, Joseph. "Chance Right Says the Surgeon Who Operated on Him." Baseball Hall of Fame Scrapbook article (Dec. 25, 1912).

Warneke, Kevin. "Tinker's Hometown Looks for Traces of Him." *Baseball America* (Apr. 17–30, 1995).

Weller, Sam. "Chance's Career As Cub Manager Ends This Year." *Chicago Tribune* (Sept. 12, 1912).

_____. "Phil's Secretary Invades Fed Camp: Quest Futile One."

_____. "Tinker Fires Broadside." *Chicago Tribune* (April 2, 1914).

"When I 'Murdered Matty': Joe Tinker's Biggest Day." *Baseball Digest* (Sept. 1945).

Woodruff, Harvey. "Chance Loses Zeider Claim." *Chicago Tribune* (July 25, 1913).

_____. "Frank L. Chance, the Peerless Leader." *Chicago Tribune* (Sept. 29, 1912).

_____. "View of Frank Chance As a Recruit Player." *Chicago Tribune* (Sept. 16, 1924).

Newspapers and Periodicals

Atchison Daily Globe
Associated Press
Baseball Digest
Baseball Magazine
Baseball Research Journal
    XII
Buffalo Evening News
Chicago Daily News
Chicago Tribune
Cincinnati Commercial
    Tribune
Collier's
Fresno Bee
Fresno Chronicle
Fresno Expositor
Fresno Morning Republi-
    can
Greensboro Daily News

Irvington News
Kansas City Journal
Kansas City Kansan
Kansas Holton Recorder
Kansas Sports
Literary Digest
Manhatten Mercury
New York American
New York Evening Mail
New York Evening
    Telegram
New York Evening World
New York Herald Tribune
New York Morning Tele-
    graph
New York Times
New York Tribune
New York World Telegram

Orlando Journal
Orlando Sentinel
Orlando Star
Philadelphia Ledger
Richmond Times Dispatch
Rollins Animated Maga-
    zine
San Francisco Chronicle
Schenectady Union Star
Sporting Life
Sporting News
Stockton Daily Evening
    Record
Troy Record
Troy Times
United Press
Wichita Beacon
Winter Park (FL) Topics

Websites

Ancestry.com
baseballhallof fame.org/library
cbs.sportsline.com/u/baseball
fresnogrizzlies.com/history.htm
http://memory.loc.gov
sportingnews.com/archives/research
thebaseballpage.com

Index